(M)otherhood

ALSO BY PRAGYA AGARWAL

Sway: Unravelling Unconscious Bias
Wish We Knew What to Say: Talking With Children About Race

(M)otherhood

On the choices of being a woman

Pragya Agarwal

CANONGATE

First published in Great Britain in 2021
by Canongate Books Ltd, 14 High Street, Edinburgh EH1 1TE

canongate.co.uk

1

British Library Cataloguing-in-Publication Data
A catalogue record for this book is available on
request from the British Library

ISBN 978 1 83885 316 7

Typeset in Bembo Std by Palimpsest Book Production Ltd,
Falkirk, Stirlingshire

Printed and bound in Great Britain by Clays Ltd, Elcograf S.p.A.

'My vagina no longer needs a monologue. It demands a dialogue.'

Priya Malik

For Ma, and Papa
for loving me.

CONTENTS

INTRODUCTION

'I walk through my unbirth as in a tunnel
with bizarre perspectives.
Ten years before,
a hundred and fifty years before,
I walk, my steps thump,
a fantastic journey through epochs
in which there was no me.
How long is my minus life,
nonexistence so much resembles immortality.'

Anna Swir, 'Woman Unborn'[1]

AS YOU READ THIS BOOK, you might wonder if it is a memoir, a manifesto, auto-fiction, or a form of political writing. It is all of these, and none. Does it really have to sit in a box? Who is to say what labels we put on our stories? And does it really matter in the end? All that matters as a writer is that I hold your trust in my hands – as valuable to me as to you – and you hold my stories in your heart – as resonant to you as to me.

Even as I sit down to write what is – in part at least – the story of an aspect of my life, I wonder why anyone would write a memoir, especially when memories are not so infallible. As a very private person,

1

I used to wonder what would compel someone to rake up their personal lives. It sounded so courageous and audacious to me, to put yourself out there for all to see and know, to bare the bones of your life and relationships to people who don't know you. At the same time, writing a memoir always seemed so self-indulgent, turning the light inwards, while there is so much to intrigue and fascinate outside of us.

It is also easy to assume that our story is mundane, not of value or interest to anyone. 'Why would it be?' we wonder, because we live it every day. We muddle along in the most inconsequential manner sometimes. And sometimes lives only take meaning when we look at them from the outside. When we are inside them, they often just seem ordinary. Our struggles seem hackneyed, our wanderings so conservative and cautious, our triumphs so commonplace. Like many women, I used to think this too.

I used to wonder how someone can be a reliable narrator of their own life, when there is no one self, rather many pieces with jagged edges colliding and collapsing, overlapping and obfuscating, somehow making up a single person. One hopes that these pieces will come together miraculously into a coherent image, with their sharp edges fitting perfectly into a jigsaw. But so often there are pieces lost and missing, and these holes remind us of the selves we have misplaced along the way.

But stories matter. Individual stories project into universal experiences. And women's stories have long been hidden, ignored, sidelined. Stories about women's bodies are usually not heard, until and unless they are told from a man's perspective, a male gaze adoringly caressing a woman's body or dissecting it gratuitously. There are few testimonies available from women as to why they make certain life choices, without pontificating on their virtue and goodness. Women's bodies are messy, bleeding, swelling, leaking, with all their protrusions and cyclical phases, transmogrifying like the shifting shapes of the moon. We so rarely hear stories of bodies that do not fit the norm; the way they grow and shrink, their desires and lusts. When we do hear these stories, we don't feel as alone in the tangle of our lives. The icy peripheries of shame and stigma that hold some words back seem to melt away, leaving vast open expanses for these words and stories to roam freely in.

This book is about the relationship women have with their bodies, sometimes fractured, sometimes fractious, but so often not whole or entirely satisfactory. Women's bodies can be seen as a threat. They become a battleground, desired and lusted upon, but also considered a monstrosity, defiled regularly, stigmatised and not their own terrain to navigate. While being placed on a pedestal and worshipped as goddesses, they are also being monitored, patrolled, controlled and abused. The body, the shell we inhabit all our lives, seems alien to us, and we spend so much time in this scrimmage between our own selves, pulling and pushing against our own bodies, moulding and shaping them to surrogate selves.

•

Paradox: a seemingly absurd or contradictory statement or proposition which when investigated may prove to be well founded or true. [2]

I could have chosen anything. This was my only choice.

Ambivalence: the state of having mixed feelings or contradictory ideas about something or someone.

Did I always want to be a mother? Definitely, maybe.

How would I describe motherhood? Bittersweet.

I am a mother. I am a lot of other things, but I am a mother, too. And for some people that can become my whole identity. For a long time, I thought that was my whole identity. Only recently my eldest child, the one I refer to as M in this book, said to me, 'You are a very un-mumsy mum.' I must have looked offended because she tried to reassure me that it was supposed to be a compliment. 'Isn't it an oxymoron?' I asked.

Oxymoron: contradictory terms appearing in conjunction.

I did it of my own free will.

How can a *will* be free, and free of what?

We are frequently aware that we can choose from a number of alternatives. We like to imagine either that we have free will, or that at least we can have it whenever it is needed. 'Will' implies the ability to overcome a certain resistance and reluctance in oneself, the ability to do what one knows is the proper course of action regardless of the fact that we may not feel like doing it in the present moment. And, in fact, this is precisely how 'will' is acquired, by consistently following a course of action which one knows is 'right' or 'proper' or 'expedient', but which one does not at all wish to take. But what if we don't know what the best course of action is? What if we are told that there is one best course of action and we start believing it somewhat, even if we don't want to choose this path? What if we don't even know of the other choices? What then? Do we have free will then?

I have often wondered if, even in this era of unprecedented freedom and choice, women are really free to understand their own reproductive options or have the autonomy to shape these decisions. But what is autonomy? Autonomy or autonomous decision-making is an individual's right to make a decision that is right for them, in light of their own views and opinions, as long as no one else is harmed. While we might believe that we are perfectly autonomous and free to make

4

our decisions at will, we are never free of our societal and cultural context. The primary criticism of the notion of women's autonomy when it comes to their own reproductive health is that we are never ever really free of the interference of the state and society.

The intersectional aspects of autonomy in terms of the complex and inter-related effects of race, class, ethnicity on the decisions that a woman makes about her body, and also the choices that are on offer to her, are also not always well understood or considered. There is still very little published information about the reproductive needs of women of colour. Any discussion that does occur is also dichotomous, based in categories defined as 'white' and 'non-white', devoid of the diversity of different intersecting layers. And so individual choices and constraints are never discussed, the micro aspects of choice and autonomy ignored and dismissed.

This book is about the choices women have, or don't have, especially when it comes to reproductive autonomy. How much do we really know about our reproductive choices and possibilities? And are we free to make decisions that we really want without the weight of societal acceptations and norms? Whether choosing to have a child or not, either choice can be wrought with anxiety, shame and guilt.

•

'You are not going to defeat me,' I say.
'I won't be an egg which you would crack
in a hurry for the world,
a footbridge that you would take on the way to your life.
I will defend myself.'[3]

This is an excerpt from the poem 'Maternity' by Polish poet Anna Swir, in which she is speaking to her infant daughter. One day you are a mother, and no preparation seems enough. The layers and surfaces that we build around us, the reflections we see of ourselves staring back at us through our own eyes, and others, all start shifting and transforming. We begin metamorphosing into a being that does not seem to belong to us any more, a form that we could not have envisaged, even as we might have dreamt of becoming a mother hundreds of times.

Motherhood is idolised. The struggle between the self before motherhood, and the unpolished – often unrecognised, sometimes unimaginable – version after becoming one is not something we often see in literature or media. Rachel Cusk writes in her memoir *A Life's Work* that after her daughter's birth, her 'appetite for the world was insatiable, omnivorous, an expression of longing for some lost, pre-maternal self, and for the freedom that self had perhaps enjoyed, perhaps squandered.'[4] When one tries to talk about this death of the individual self, as one gives birth to a new human being, or the annihilation of what once was in order to raise a child, one is demonised.

Jessica Friedmann calls motherhood a feminist act. She says 'one-half of the workforce must be coerced into performing domestic labor in addition to waged labor and assimilating that labor as love. It is no wonder that motherhood is so pressingly marketed as feminine.'[5] As we acknowledge the privilege and the exquisite pleasure, and as we are told to cherish and revere it, we are made to ignore and dismiss that it is also unpaid and unwaged labour, feminised and weaponised against the very people who supply it. The paradox of motherhood is stark and brutal.

What happens outside this mainstream narrative in which every woman desires so deeply to be a mother, to serve a life's work? Guilt, anxiety, conflicts between our own desires and society's demands from

6

women, and our own internalised conflicts and ambivalences, are rarely documented. The poet Adrienne Rich wrote privately in her diary and then went on to publish these words in her much-acclaimed *Of Woman Born: Motherhood as Experience and Institution*:

> My children cause me the most exquisite suffering of which I have any experience. It is the suffering of ambivalence, the murderous alternation between bitter resentment and raw-edged nerves and blissful gratification. Sometimes I seem to myself, in my feelings towards these tiny guiltless little beings, a monster of selfishness and intolerance.[6]

The idea of motherhood is expanding. Some people want to be mothers, and some do not. But it is safe to say that no matter what decisions we make, and the choices that are on offer to us as women, the notion of motherhood shapes so much of our lives, whether it be deciding not to be a mother, or having the burning desire to be a mother by any means possible. A woman and her womb become one and the same thing, even as the concept of parenthood and gender identity become more fluid, and motherhood moves away from traditional norms, albeit glacially. The pressure of the body-clock ticking is a societal and cultural trope, and a genuine tool for oppression at the same time. Women and their fertility have become so inextricably interlinked that infertility is stigmatised and not something we talk about openly and candidly in our society. The silence around infertility and the centuries of ingrained socialisation around a failure to become pregnant mean that we do not have the vocabulary to articulate our grief at the loss of our fertility and the inability to give birth, this shadow land that we inhabit while trying to become a mother.

•

There are many books on motherhood, many good books, excellent books in fact, but these are rarely intersectional. We tend only to hear one kind of story, and one kind of narrative of motherhood, and what it means for women. The experience of motherhood differs across race and class, and if we take social, economic and historical differences into account, we could be more aware of the oppression, diversity and inequality amongst women. Women of colour do not experience motherhood in the same way as white women. Motherhood for women of colour is wrought with anxiety about racial bias and prejudice towards themselves but also towards their children. Motherhood while being othered is a wholly different ball game; maybe better, maybe worse, but how does one compare apples with oranges? Just different. But how often do we talk about the difference? *Same* is easy to process; the homogenous amalgamation of experiences into one colourless blob is easier to manage. And the bands, variations, gradations, the contours in the maps of motherhood are obliterated and smoothed out to the point of erasure.

This book is also therefore about the dilemmas of deciding to become a mother when you feel like an outsider, a dismembered body roaming in fractured landscapes of unspoken and unknown identities. How can such a body grow another human being, bring children into this world, when their own sense of identity is yet unclear, when they are still searching for home, and putting down roots? Simone Weil said that 'to be rooted is perhaps the most important and least recognised need of the human soul'.[7] A mother is a child's first home, its forever homeland. But can a homeless home be the cradle that a child craves? As an immigrant, and a perpetual foreigner and outsider, I have asked myself this regularly.

Our relationship with and our distances from our motherland then must surely preface any identity we carve as mothers ourselves.

8

Always living a life of two halves. For me that meant being never quite British, but not really Indian any more: a partitioned, fragmented, fractured self – looking for the glue to seal these cracks, covering them with glitter all shiny and sparkling, much like the craft projects I do with my children. Motherhood has no place for cracks. It ought to seal everything that has ever been broken. But we are too scared to admit that it seldom does. It is not a panacea, merely a pause in the journey ahead where we take forward our own cracks and fissures with us, hiding them from sight.

> *If only you'd been a better mother.*
> How could I have been a better mother?
> I would have needed a better self,
> and that is a gift I never received.
>
> Brenda Shaughnessy, 'Magi'[8]

It seems that, as mothers, we are always looking to the past as we look to the future. Our relationships with our own mothers, and the distances within those relationships – emotional and physical – can affect the kind of mother we aspire to be. I will never be my mother, I had thought so often during my teenage years. Now, I know that I would be fortunate if I could be.

While I have written *(M)otherhood* largely about my own experiences, of course, it is also about every other woman who has faced these questions in her life. Will I or won't I be a mother, and when? When is the right time? Why is this not so easy for me as others? And, what if I don't want a child? Will I regret this later? As I feel so desperate for a child, do I really want to be a mother? Or are these my hormones telling me that I ought to, acting in their sneaky subversive ways, reinforcing what everyone around me is telling me, society giving me messages that my role and destiny is to be a mother? If I don't, then am I not a complete woman? What if I do want to be a mother at any cost? What then? Am I being selfish? Should I not give in to the pull towards motherhood, because in doing so I am conforming to my biology, my body rather than my mind? And in doing so, am I not being a good feminist?

What if, in choosing to be a mother, I am disappointing all those women who went before me and fought for my right to exist and to choose, and to choose wisely, a life of freedom? Am I failing all the women who are contesting the pull of biology, saying that we are more than our bodies? I don't know how to choose wisely, and judiciously, and how to be a good feminist while I do so. What if that path to motherhood is only via someone else's body? What then? Am I being part of the culture that abuses and oppresses women and their bodies even when I know that this person has agency and is choosing to use her body to give birth to my child?

We might believe that a discussion of fertility only affects mothers or those considering becoming mothers, but as philosopher Mary O'Brien argues in *The Politics of Reproduction*, much of our social theories have been focused largely in gender divides and on the male half of the world, and a critical theory of reproduction that echoes with everyone who identifies as a woman is sorely missing. She says that:

> Woman's reproductive consciousness is culturally transmitted . . .
> It is a tribute to the indelibility of male-stream thought that we
> should have to make this point. The historical isolation of women
> from each other, the whole language of female internality and
> privacy, the exclusion of women from the creation of a political
> community: all of these have obscured the cultural cohesiveness
> of femininity and the universality of maternal consciousness.[9]

As our discourse around gender expands, we have to examine the notion of reproductive identity. The oversimplification of reproductive life and its impact on individuals denies the complexity of individuals, and has caused confusion by mis-categorising people into groups that they do not feel that they belong to. The current model of reproduction fails to take into account the diverse cultural experiences outside Western ideals. It creates these boundaries around the notion of motherhood, where only certain people can get involved in it. Meanwhile, the existing framework of reproductive identity has opened up a deep-rooted divide between those with children and those without. It serves to oppress everyone, flattering those who are being included by giving them a utopian vision of the adulation as part of this exclusive club, while completely ignoring the stigmatisation of being excluded. It narrows the social and political frameworks within which motherhood and womanhood can be discussed and analysed. By limiting the voices, it only serves those who want to keep others oppressed.

I write from the perspective of a cisgender woman where I acknowledge my privilege around reproduction. If I have sex, it can happen. It can be as easy as that. Of course, as we know, it does not always happen like that. But often we do not even consider the different layers and levels of agency women have depending on their biology, their sexual preference, their social and cultural context, and their financial status. I do not claim to understand what it is like for a woman in a homosexual relationship, where motherhood is always a conscious, deliberate choice: for many, one involving rounds of intrauterine insemination accompanied by financial, mental and physical toll. Ambivalence might exist, but there is no room for fuzzy boundaries around this decision to be a mother. I do not claim to know what it is for trans women, whose sense of self and identity is questioned, for whom being a woman is not about having a womb, and for whom becoming a mother is never uncomplicated. I do not claim to fathom what it is for non-binary individuals, for whom motherhood can be a time of upheaval, having to conform to one singular binary state, as they shape the life of another human being, especially if this involves giving birth.

Motherhood is inevitably a time where social and cultural norms impinge on our self, in a number of ways, and our internalised biases and perceptions of what a mother ought to be become heightened. I found an account of motherhood from Braiden Schirtzinger in the *Washington Post* really eye-opening as they recount the experience of taking on the most 'gendered role of all' and living '. . . in a body that felt more feminine, with its swelling belly and breasts, than [they] had ever felt inside',[10] and the distress of living in a body that didn't match their own gender identity. For Braiden, and many like them, 'motherhood' is often fraught with complications of using a non-binary name during sonographs and scans (and having to correct people), the surprise of colleagues at discovering that they weren't biologically male, the assumptions that people – even medical professionals – make about an intended mother, and worry about how their non-conformity could affect their and their child's care.

I am aware that this book is about motherhood and that I focus on the history of women's fertility in this book. This does not mean that fathers are excluded from parenting, or less significant. Or that there is only one way to be a woman. I fully acknowledge and accept the experiences of trans women. But this is my story, and I can only tell it in this way. I can only talk about how motherhood and my relationship with my womb has shaped me in so many uniquely wonderful and maddeningly bizarre ways.

Through my own experiences of motherhood and fertility

treatments, I explore the lengths people will go to have children, and why. Why do we have this primitive desire to have children? And what does it mean when we find out that we cannot? As a researcher, I often fall back on facts to ground me, especially when my emotions are highly charged, and so the book charts my journey, and the impact my fertility (and the loss of it) had on my mental and physical state and my relationships, while reflecting on the gender politics of the ticking body-clock, the scientific and evolutionary aspects of procreation, the history of (in)fertility and surrogacy, the moral and ethical (and feminist) issues, and the notion of the 'maternal bond'. This book delves into historical, social and cultural attitudes towards infertility, weaving in fascinating anecdotes from Greek, Egyptian and Indian myths, and attitudes towards fertility from the Middle Ages up to the modern period. I also aim to show that the choices we make are not black and white, and that being a mother is so much more than giving birth. By talking about this honestly and openly, we can (hopefully) break some of the myths and stigma surrounding womanhood and fertility, about surrogacy, and how we continue to assign a woman's identity to being a mother.

I firmly believe in sex as a spectrum, and not a rigid binary deterministic framework as we have been made to believe. I also believe that gender identities matter, and a woman is not defined by her sex. I believe that both sex and gender are bimodal and not binary. At the same time, I do believe that the body that one is born in, the sex of a person that is assigned to them,* also

---

* Many are born intersex and are assigned a sex at birth. I have made a conscious decision to not discuss intersex people in this book. Not because I don't think they are important, or I mean to exclude them, but because there is hardly any research and I did not feel equipped to do it justice within the scope of the book.

determines the oppression they face. Even though the female body has been imagined and put forward as a site of madness and badness since the time of Hippocrates, Michel Foucault in *The History of Sexuality: Volume 1* argues that the discourse around women's bodies really proliferated since the beginning of the eighteenth century, when medical experts subjected the female body to scrutiny and surveillance at the physical and biochemical level.[11] Recent discourse in body and sexuality also posits this century as the time when the idea of sexuality was constructed and concretised, pathologising and irreversibly positioning the female body as an inevitable place of weakness. As such, a tyranny of 'truths' as to what is normal or abnormal in terms of female identity has persisted over time.

In this book, I use 'women' to refer to cisgender women in most cases unless I specify trans women, trans men or non-binary. This is a conscious decision as I use myself as a reference point for most of the texts, and as much of the research in this area has been carried out on those who were born a woman. While I have spoken with some trans women, transmasculine and non-binary individuals, in the end I decided not to include many of these testimonies in this book, as it seemed tokenistic and superficial. Even as I can empathise, I can never claim to understand their experiences. Even if I speak with twenty, I can never announce these as an experience of a whole diverse community. Unfortunately, I am unable to fall back on hard science, data and research here, as so little has been done in this area. It is highly emotive and very sensitive as we learn, as a society, to navigate these identities that are firmly placed outside the binary, dualistic notions of humans that society has worked with for so long. I do not wish to use these stories and experiences, which I have been trusted with, as mere cursory, gestural nods to

14

a whole spectrum of experiences that I am myself still trying to understand.

•

Finally, as I write this book, I have to imagine the 'self' that experienced these thoughts. I have to recall the person to whom these memories belong. It is often hard to do. We are a composite of so many 'selves' – shifting, changing, overlapping – that it is so easy to lose sight of who we once were through the sheaths of time. When we don't even know who we were when we experienced the things we are remembering and recounting, can we ever recall these moments reliably? This is something I have pondered a lot through the writing of this book, narrating from the point of the 'self' that I was in that moment, rather than letting my present 'self' impose on these stories and memories, with the benefit of hindsight and experience (one hopes!). At one point in *The Situation and the Story*, Vivian Gornick says that writing a personal essay or memoir is like 'lying down on a couch in public'. I think it is much more than that. It is sometimes confronting our personas that we ourselves hide from – our undiscovered longings, our embarrassments, our undisclosed desire that we dare not tell ourselves. What if we don't like these selves? But we don't always have to, as long as we trust them, and we have faith that their stories and their perspectives mattered. This must be the point, I believe.

All that remains are the echoes of the past, and all we can do is to catch them before they disperse in the wind. It makes sense to write something that can help us make sense not only of us, and our past, present and future, but also of others, and the world around us. It makes sense to give some sense to the chaos of our lives so far. But then, aren't we all writing some sort of memoir anyway, rummaging amongst our daily travails and travels, ransacking our memories to create worlds that we have inhabited ourselves?

Life might seem to follow a linear path, but we are always navigating sliding doors, even when we might not see them. Memories come and go, uninvited, and time and space seem inconsequential. It jumps, bending space and time, twisting truth and fiction. Lives are messy. They don't just go from A to B, with prophetic moments of grand epiphanies. Instead, much of the significance is only realised in hindsight, through a metamorphosis of fuzzy jumbled memories into a sparkling pool reflecting back the best of our selves.

A set of seemingly random memories collected together is not a narration of my life, but much more than that: fragments of my existence so far, shaped by the staccato of my life, obstructed, interrupted, sometimes flowing, sometimes stagnant, still, but not calm. A life can only be a window to see the world, huge in its expanse. I hope that in using my own story to do so, I can help facilitate conversations that are more pressing and pertinent than ever.

Many of the scientific and social ideas around motherhood, and womanhood, emerge from cultural conditioning and bias, and many ideas around women's bodies have been shaped by misogynistic and patriarchal constructs.

Here and now is the time to examine them.

This is a book about motherhood. And the shapes it takes.

This is a book about bodies. And how some are less than the sum of their parts.

This is a book about choices. The roads we follow, and those we are not allowed to walk.

I.

THE AGE OF INNOCENCE

IT HAS BEEN ONE OF those rare days when everything seems effortless and easy. Speeding along the road lined with golden leaves, time seems to be moving slowly. Suddenly a little voice pipes up from the back seat. 'When I am bigger, I will have a baby in my tummy,' she says in her beautiful sing-song voice. She is not even three, and she speaks like a teenager at times, and acts like one too. I sometimes feel that my heart will burst open with the love, while at the same time, I am so exhausted that I don't even have the strength to pack up my bags before running away: the paradox of motherhood, where intense love jostles together with a desire to soar free, unencumbered and untethered. These trips to and from their nursery, driving across the countryside, can be so fractious at times, but today, she and her twin sister are in that most delicious toddler mood where I just want to squish them tight and imprint their soft corners on my soul.

'Susie in nursery says that when I am bigger like you, I will have a baby in my tummy,' she repeats in her giggly sonorous voice with that lilting Liverpudlian accent.

A familiar feeling rises up in my throat. It is a feeling that often returns, the sensation of my lungs filling up with water, and the wordless inaudible screams that cannot escape to the surface. The sun is now hurting my eyes, as it dips down on the horizon, and I squint, trying to focus on the road ahead, as a pheasant runs senselessly across to the other side, its auburn and orange feathers blending into the autumnal colours of the hedgerows.

The dreamy haze cracks, and I feel irritated. The annoyance sits right on the surface. I don't know the context, yet I feel angry with Susie for drilling this narrative into my child that every woman will be pregnant one day, and that her destiny is inextricably tied down by her womb. 'You can have a baby in your tummy if you want, sweetheart, but you don't have to.' My feminist ideals surge vehemently to the forefront. 'And you might not be able to,' I want to add but wisely choose not to. 'Or it might not be as easy,' I say quietly. It is a battle I fight every day to counter the messages my three-year-old children receive from the world around them, messages that tell them how a girl is to act, and what a woman's destiny is. I remember my own childhood and I want to hold them close and tell them that they can choose their own paths, that they don't have to walk this road lined with tightly packed hedges. The world is bigger and their dreams can be big too, beyond their bodies and biology.

•

In an article I discovered in the archives from 1925 in *The Iowa Homemaker*, Dr Florence Brown Sherborn from the University of Kansas makes a case for an all-inclusive preparation for motherhood that has to start from school.

I find a refreshing number of women college students who frankly say they want homes and they want children, but they want somewhere, somehow, to do something else worth while! What are we going to do about it? This, as I see it, is the real challenge of the hour.[1]

Sherborn talks about the ways in which women can make an impact without ever being involved in wars, treaties and diplomacy. Birthing a child is one of these four very essential ways that women can make a contribution to society.

The ancient myths of matriarchy are interlinked with the women goddesses; women were responsible for the continuation of the human race. The matriarchal system, with women holding a superior social, economic and political position compared to men, relied on their ability to produce offspring and create new life.

We women shoulder a huge responsibility. We have to fulfil our destiny of being the givers of life, and it seems like a huge cross to bear. For many reasons, we assign our identities to one small part of our bodies. In many cultures, a girl is perceived to become a woman when she starts her periods, and so we are encouraged to spend our lives believing that version of womanhood, with our fertility, our monthly cycles, at the very centre of our identity. But what this does is to restrict the notion of our identities and constrain the whole spectrum of human anatomy to certain limiting characteristics.

•

It has been a gradual realisation how little I know about my own body, this body that I have inhabited for forty-odd years. I studied biology at school – it was one of my favourite subjects. Since I was four years old, when I started dreaming of becoming a doctor, I have always been keenly interested in how we, as humans, work, why we work, what really makes each of us click. Yet all those years of learning and reading since then have not really educated me in how a woman's fertility works. How do we go through life without understanding or knowing our own bodies? Is it because we are taught to be inherently ashamed of ourselves, of what our body is capable of doing and desiring? Why is society so neglectful of giving this very basic and crucial information to young women, when its demands from them are so often non-negotiable?

I remember the diagrams of the female reproductive system that we looked at in biology textbooks, showing the 28-day menstrual cycle as if that is the norm,[*] with ovulation 14 days before each period.[†] These lessons were rushed and hushed conversations around male and female reproduction, ovulation and insemination, during which some of the boys tittered and sneered, and girls either looked completely embarrassed or belligerent. We were all pretending they were not awkward in the least, while all the time inside we felt

[*] Clinical guidelines still state that twenty-eight days is the median length for most cycles, with the majority falling between twenty-five and thirty days, even though research has shown that there is greater variability than this, with only 13 per cent of cycles lasting twenty-eight days according to a study published in *Nature* in 2019. In this study, 1.4 million cycles were recorded by 124,648 anonymised users, but still the data was largely centred in the Western world.

[†] From studies of more than 100 fertility-awareness based mobile apps between 2014 and 2019 it may also be seen that many are still designed with the assumption that our historic understanding of the menstrual cycle is correct (ovulation 14 days before the next period). Research shows that only about 30 per cent of women reach the fertile window entirely within the days of the menstrual cycle identified by clinical guidelines – that is, between days ten and seventeen. Most women reach their fertile window earlier and others much later.

acutely self-conscious and mortified. Mind you, this was the early '90s, in a small town in India, where even though boys and girls were now studying together in mixed classrooms, we were largely regulated by our gender – or rather the sex[‡] we were born with – and the narrow lanes and labels that society had pre-determined for us. We crossed boundaries and strayed from these paths but hesitatingly and very tentatively, quickly retreating to the safety of our boxes, and every act of rebellion had huge emotional costs. The fear of social ostracisation and stigma percolated our brains and bodies as warnings, the anxious refrains of 'log kya kahenge'[§] drilled into us, continuously policing our actions, glances, words. So, while we might be occasionally flirting and socialising with the opposite sex, timidly and cautiously, we were also sitting flushed, hot and bothered, with red faces and furtive glances, while one of the most important lessons of our lives took place.

I remember our teacher, one Mr Dubey, who looked as uncomfortable as we did, or even more so. The boys relished his discomfort, cracking jokes, playing pranks, as he stuttered through the chapter on the reproductive system. I learned nothing more than the simple mechanisms of the menstrual cycle, the names of hormones and the basic biology of my body, but nothing about

[‡] Sex refers to biological qualities characteristic of women (females) and men (males) in terms of reproductive organs and functions. Gender – a socio-cultural process – refers to cultural and social attitudes that together shape and sanction 'feminine' and 'masculine' behaviours, products, technologies, environments and knowledge, and is the identity that one presents to the world.

[§] '*What will people say?*' Many such statements – both external and internal dialogue – in the book are in Hindi. I have added translations in the notes, where possible.

what really makes me work and how. Nor did I learn that women are not designed to a standard template, though my lived experience taught me any deviations from the accepted standard would be seen as an undesirable aberration, not simply the result of a genetic uniqueness. And so our peculiarities and abnormalities become an oddness for ever, the root of shame and guilt. This was the age before the internet. There was no tap of information at our fingertips.

Much of the language in these textbooks was very gendered too – and still is. It has been thirty years since Emily Martin published a landmark paper in which she first discussed how gender roles are imposed on the way reproduction is talked about in school textbooks.[2] Eggs are passive, while sperm is active. Things do not seem to have changed much. Lisa Campo-Engelstein and Nadia L. Johnson in their 2013 article also remind us of that opening scene from the 1989 film *Look Who's Talking* where we see sperm inside a woman's reproductive tract moving towards her egg.[3] The scene is narrated by one of the sperm, though we can hear some of the other sperm talking, seeking entrance through the egg membrane – a difficult task as evidenced by the lead sperm stating 'Kinda tough here'. The egg then envelops one sperm as it cries, 'Ohhh, ohh, I'm in, I'm in'. Our cultural and social values, and systemic gender norms, determine how science is taught and understood and this was never truer than in the case of reproduction. As Martin points out, the sperm was a 'knight in shining armour' and the egg was a 'damsel in distress' waiting to be rescued. The idea of fertilisation is set up as an old-fashioned courtship and romance, with gendered personalities – and roles – assigned to the gametes to bypass any awkwardness associated with the physicality of the act itself.

The role of the eggs, although proven to be as crucial as that of

THE AGE OF INNOCENCE

sperm, has often been ignored in scientific literature.[4] The sperm 'fertilises the egg' but the egg never 'takes part in fertilisation'. Rather than 'fertilisation is the fusion of the egg and the sperm', often only a passive role is assigned to the egg, as in 'the egg is fertilised', with no agency accorded to the egg. In reality, the fusion of egg and sperm – two highly specialised gametes – to form a zygote is a series of complex physiological and biochemical processes. In order for the sperm to become 'fertilise-able' both egg and sperm first undergo a series of transformations collectively termed 'capacitation' which ensures that appropriate proteins have been released and there is enough motility for fusion to take place. When the egg and sperm first collide, the egg's zona pellucida, the extracellular coating outside its plasma membrane, fuses with the sperm. This initiates a series of processes called 'egg activation' where the egg releases calcium and zinc transients from internal stores causing fluxes in metal ions that then prevent additional sperm from fusing with the egg's plasma membrane. It also starts the early process of embryonic cell divisions.

The scientific reality that both gametes play an active role in fertil-isation is never taught to us, and we start to believe that our destiny is to drift along passively as women, 'transported' and being 'swept away', submissive, docile and dutiful, and waiting to be discovered by a man. Men on the other hand, are supposed to be the real go-getters, the ones who have to take the lead and make the important decisions in a relationship, 'penetrating' and 'entering', being aggressive, determined and assertive. Linguistically, this also removes any sense of agency and autonomy from the egg, and hence the female. The sperm is the smallest cell in the human body, but most textbooks omit the fact that the egg is the largest. The sperm is almost always mentioned first, regu-larly and consistently, a conqueror on a 'quest' of rescuing the egg before it dies, much like an odyssey, the hero on an adventure. When the male is mentioned first, and given more agency, this naturally confers a higher status[5] on it, and sets it up as the norm, reinforcing traditional stereotypes about men and women.

Additionally, many biology and medical textbooks[6] still use biased language[7] that creates a perception that the vagina is a hostile environment, where the sperm has to be protected from the 'acidic vagina', focusing only on the damaging aspects of the female anatomy, and not on the vaginal lubrication facilitating sperm migration. Discomfort and embarrassment around our own selves start here: our sluggish bodies, all murky, foetid and unpleasant.

Language does not exist in a vacuum, but is always a reflection of social norms. The problem with the use of sexist language in scientific textbooks is that it not only reinforces gendered roles and biases but also affects students and teachers negatively, impeding understanding of science in a non-gendered manner. Even at the level of undergraduate pre-medical and medical studies, the female biological system is presented as a comparison to the male one, often in reverse, such as 'sperm production' vs 'egg degeneration', and the amount of information is skewed disproportionately in favour of the male reproductive system. A discussion of anatomy textbooks between 1890 and 1989 showed that male bodies were always discussed first, and the female anatomy treated as a subset.[8] The imbalance in treatment, with not enough discussion of female infertility and sexual arousal, also creates an impression that the male reproductive system is more interesting or complex. There were sections in our textbooks on male sexual arousal, since erection and ejaculation are the primary facilitators for the act of fertilisation. But there was no mention of female sexual arousal, no indication that this was even a factor during sex, hence giving a clear message that it was not pertinent.

So, despite my official education, sex itself remained a mystery for me and, I suspect, for many others. The word 'sex' was taboo, although I would roll it around my lips silently as if this' was a sexual act in itself. The words that are most taboo have the most power psychologically, sociologically and emotionally. It was easy to see these black and white diagrams of the uterus and ovaries in a mildly detached way, to learn them for exams, painstakingly drawing out the diagrams neatly in pencil, labelling the parts, but still seeing them as alien. It was easy to dissociate ourselves from these mechanistic representations; it was hard to imagine that we were the sum of these parts, or even much more than that. Our desires, our childish attractions, our hormonal surges were a distraction, and I did not have time for these.

My memory of these diagrams are a bit hazy so I looked up some of the recent textbooks again as I coached some sixteen- and seventeen-year-olds in biology. The female reproductive system is often misrepresented. Even when other anatomical parts which are extraneous to reproduction (such as urethra and anus) are labelled, the clitoris is not acknowledged even when it can be seen in the diagram. In 1995, Lisa Jean Moore and Adele E. Clarke had observed the same trend in their examination of twentieth-century anatomy texts.[9] Failing to acknowledge the clitoris silences female sexuality and reduces women's genitalia to just their reproductive functionality. This also reinforces the dominant gender norms of female sexual passivity, and a woman's lack of agency in any reproductive decisions. Virginia Braun and Celia Kitzinger write in their 2010 article 'The Perfectible Vagina' that heterosexual female sexual pleasure is never placed on an equal par with male sexual pleasure.[10] Women's bodies are always defined in relation to heterosexual male pleasure rather than their own pleasure. A male orgasm is discussed in many textbooks; a female orgasm is only ever mentioned in the context of its value to transporting sperm or aiding fertilisation, views that were held in the late nineteenth century and earlier but have since been debunked.[11] The failure to acknowledge female orgasm beyond its role in fertilisation reinforces the myth that women have much lower libidos than men,[12] that they are the ones responsible for setting acceptable boundaries, that any sexual aggression and misdemeanour on the part of a man is because of his naturally higher sex drive, thereby absolving men of responsibility for their actions. The misrepresentation in these scientific textbooks bolsters the illusion that female sexuality is only for the purposes of reproduction.

Sex education and biology textbooks have also been very heteronormative, and much of Western culture, in particular, relied on two-sex models, oversimplified and stereotyped.[13] And it still does. The complete focus on heterosexual vaginal intercourse as the route to fertilisation means that any other way is considered abnormal or unnatural.

•

Infertility was never a part of the curriculum, and never a life plan. No one really talks about struggles to get pregnant, or even pregnancy itself, in these formative texts and classes. It is as if pregnancy is the culmination, the ultimate goal and there is only paradise thereafter. What is worth discussing once a woman has been impregnated? The man's role is over, and the woman becomes the vessel and the vehicle. I learned nothing whatsoever at school about what happens to a woman's body once it becomes pregnant. I had seen pregnant women, in real life, on television and in magazines, carrying on their womanly duties, shopping, cooking, looking after their families, but never a pregnant woman working – except if they belonged to a social class where their bodies and their labour were indebted to the state in service to other, higher classes of society:

the underbelly of society, where women had to continue working even as they became pregnant because they had no other choice. In other, more economically advantaged scenarios, women rested; they moved around slowly and uncomfortably, glowing, being cherished and adored by the rest of their family. They would never go out to work. I did not know what pregnant women did for nine months. I often wondered if they just rested and slept all the way through pregnancy, then magically gave birth as easily and painlessly as I had heard in all those mythological stories that my mother had read to me since early childhood. 'And then a child was born.' That is how most stories ended, but never began.

Motherhood, and the glorification of it, has played a huge role in Indian societies: considered obligatory, a role every girl was born to fulfil, shaped by the patriarchal constructions of mother goddesses. The ancient *Upanishads* and Jyotish Sanskrit texts, filled with representations of feminine divinity, have numerous instances of rituals and prayers women were supposed to perform to beget a child. Fertility symbols and rituals are ingrained in the daily life of the Hindus. Hinduism, like Buddhism, is bursting with fertility associations. I grew up with these stories, and even though we were not religious, it was impossible to escape completely. Women were referred to as 'fertile land', and 'mother earth', but only an earth that is abundant and prolific, sprouting and flowering. In a society where women are already discriminated against, and do not hold as much power or authority, a woman who is unable to conceive is seen as being on the lowest level of hierarchy. She is an untouchable, someone who is ostracised and holds no value for her husband or her family. Infertile women are called bhanj or waanj (barren) and childless women receive taunts and hostile behaviour from others too, often being made unwelcome at family gatherings and weddings.

In many communities they are still not allowed to be present at auspicious ceremonies, because their presence is thought to cast an evil eye on a newborn child, and even result in their death.

While this ostracisation is not common in larger cities and towns any more, and so many of my friends are choosing not to have children or to delay having them, there is a large population of India that still resides in smaller villages and towns. Here talking about fertility treatments is taboo, and natural remedies and prayers are resorted to when a woman does not give birth soon after getting married.

Most of the girls among friends and extended family were dutifully prepared for childbirth from a young age, their destiny etched out for them since they were born. My mother did not want this for me, or for my two sisters. And so she never talked to us about it. That said, I do not know if she would have, in any case, because women are supposed to be born with some innate sort of knowledge. 'You will know what to do when you become a mother,' we are told. And we believe it; we believe that we know how our bodies work, because weren't we born in them? Empowering people with more knowledge and information will help them make better choices and decisions, of course, but does society really want this? Is ignorance just another way to maintain oppression of women? We are unleashed on the world at eighteen as adults, and we are supposed to just *know*. And we muddle through the years, pretending to know, making mistakes, fumbling, awkwardly hiding our mistakes and foibles, ignorance evoking shame and guilt. Feeling guilty about not knowing all, carrying the guilt close, until it is encoded as part of us. So much said but so much left unspoken. Wondering in the solitude of our agony if we would ever find a co-conspirator in our shame.

•

Emotional and physical intimacy were not aspects of relationships I saw modelled within our house growing up. I never saw my parents hug or kiss in public or affectionately hold hands. When we walked down a market street, my father would walk ten steps ahead, while my mother walked behind. I wanted to be the one striding ahead, not following behind. And in that moment and for ever before then, I had wanted to be a man: not demure and quiet like my mother, but laughing out loud like my father, chewing paan, with his flashy sideburns and loud shirts. 'I wish she would walk faster alongside him,' I would think every time. Now I wonder why I had never considered that he could walk more slowly beside her.

I never knew my parents to share a bed. My mother and I slept in a room that functioned as our bedroom and our TV room, where we spent most of our time. There was a small kitchen next to it and adjoining these two rooms was an open, partially covered courtyard that also acted as our dining room. My mother insisted that we ate at the large dining table sometimes, but most days it sat unused, covered with a big, embroidered tablecloth that she had made, and a plastic dustsheet. I used to work and study there most evenings, while everyone walked by and life happened all around me.

My father slept on the divan on most days, sometimes when he came home drunk, and sometimes not. I would dread hearing his footsteps, wondering whether he would be reeking of alcohol, staggering, his eyes bloodshot. He was never ever physically violent but seeing him like that made me feel nauseous; this was not the man I wanted him to be, not the kind of father I thought he could be.

I would usually go to bed before he was back home, pretending not to know that he drank. If I didn't acknowledge it, perhaps it wasn't real. But then he would get drunk and call my mother names for allowing boys into the house when I had my friends over.

He was under the influence of alcohol, and he did not know what he was saying, I would tell myself every time. I kept wondering if women were born to feel this way, humility and indignity seared into their very core. I wondered if I could escape this, wishing so desperately that I were a man. I wished someone would say something, but at the same time, I was glad they didn't.

I remember making Father's Day cards and writing in them that he was the best father in the world. I remember smiling at him just after he had screamed at us, as if our collective love could soothe his soul and any childhood traumas that he carried with him, hoping he would understand that I never blamed him. I wondered if things would be different if I had been a boy, and if he had a son. Maybe he would feel less alone in this house surrounded by women. Yet he was the same man who had celebrated the birth of his third daughter, distributing laddoos to the baffled medical staff and our relatives who believed that my parents were cursed for having three girls. The same father who also gave me the freedom of an education, who laughed indulgently if I dismissed any religious or patriarchal traditions, who had never expected me to conform to anything that others expected of me, and who said that I *was* his son. The same father who was snarled up in knots made of his ingrained social norms, mingled with the poison flowing through his bloodstream. I wanted to be his son so that he would feel less alone, not stopping to think why I couldn't be a daughter and mean the same to him. And I knew that there would be a day when he, and I, would both know that I was not a boy. That one moment could mark our relationship for ever, his desperation and solitude amplified by that one moment I would start my periods and for ever be seen to be stepping into womanhood, closing a door between us.

I blamed myself for not being the one who could give my father the solace that he perhaps needed and deserved, the succour that might have hurled him out of the pits of despair where he used alcohol to liberate himself from throttling hopelessness. Maybe he was running away from a life that he never wanted either.

We all continued on our own solitary paths yet so intertwined with each other, so tangled, so mired in troubled solitude, with things left unsaid, a conspiracy of silence. Me, rejecting everything woman-hood represented but for ever trapped in it; my mother quietly, softly and unobtrusively imbibing everything that I began to detest in its cloying oppressiveness; and my father not being the man and father he and I both wished he could be. And so I lived with no idea of what a man and woman ought to be, the reality conflicting so harshly with my own ideals of it.

I was so tied to the desire to make my father happy, with his huge temper tantrums and his staggered relapses into alcoholism, that I dismissed my mother, who held the fort, bolstering us quietly in the background. She represented everything I never wanted to be and what I would run away from for a very long time – from being 'just a mother'.

I remember that my mother talked to me about becoming a doctor from the time I was two or three years old. The same mother who would get angry if I did not conform to the notion of a good girl; the same mother who wanted me to be independent but also not *too* independent. Once again unable to shake some of her life-long conditioning, even as she raised us to be fearlessly independent, she was fearful of the backlash if I stepped out of my box too much, uncomfortable with my rage and searing opinions. She had seen a life of submissiveness, of not being financially independent, and as she entered marriage, she had held my father close, encouraging him to study for his undergraduate and then his Masters, to enter civil service competitions. And there he was. There she was: always the wife and the mother, dependent on her husband to buy her things, to seek permission from, to tell her what to be and what not. Hyperaware of how girls have to shrink, become invisible, and not be seen or heard, I grew up angry and rebellious, wanting so desperately to be a boy, and not 'just a girl'.

Maybe we are born like this, because I don't remember reading any feminist literature, or watching any films except the Bollywood ones where every female actor conformed to the narrow roles predetermined for them, with a standardised notion of beauty. I wanted to play cricket on the street corners with all the boys in our neighbourhood, to have my hair cut short and run around in shorts. So I did. 'I am a boy,' I would reply any time anyone called me a girl, and they would laugh affectionately.

Ancient Indian writings mention sixteen major sanskaras or rites in a person's life. These are the values a Hindu should live by, and that take him closer to the Truth. Karnavedha, a Vedic ritual, in which a girl's (and often a boy's) ears are pierced, is one of these. My ears had been pierced too, and I remember walking home after the piercing with a bag of pedhas, those milky sweets that I adored, feeling grown up and proud. As I inched towards puberty, I took my earrings off and hid them in a box where my mother couldn't find them, refusing to wear them as they marked me out to be a girl. These artificial ornamentations, markers of femininity, these trappings of womanhood, felt so tyrannical to me.

Growing up being so acutely aware of the boundaries around us as women, being allowed to venture out, but being pulled back again

THE AGE OF INNOCENCE

and again if we put one step wrong, is confusing and disorienting. In the years when our sense of self is being shaped, this constant tug of war creates fuzzy images of what we can be, constantly being superimposed and over-ridden with those of what we are allowed to be. And the sense of belonging that we so desperately seek and need remains just a little bit out of reach. I was a romantic, even though I imagined myself to be a harsh pragmatist, worn down by the cynicism I imbued in all my associations. Constantly seeking something that would make me feel fine with who I was, I kept searching for someone to give me permission to try and be who I could be without shame, guilt, remorse. I had this feeling that I was just a pale shadow of who I was supposed to be, an imitation of what I was meant to become.

Eventually though the day arrived that I had feared, where I could no longer declare myself a boy, nor my father declare me his son. Just talking about menstruation or knowing that we had to go through it every month was shameful enough. When I had my first period, I wondered if I was the only one, because I never talked to anyone about it, not even my closest friends. It was just after my eleventh birthday, as I was lifting my youngest sister up and swinging her on my legs, that my mum stopped me abruptly. I remember that panicky look on her face. I didn't know what had happened. And I now wish I had marked that moment, that day, more clearly, because so much changed in that one moment.

It must have been the holidays, as I had been playing outside somewhere and had just come back home, on one of those most glorious of summer evenings where the cool breeze soothes the intensity of the day. The sun was setting, and we were in the room that passed as our living or sitting room, the one that my father slept in most days.

33

I was wearing a dress that day for some reason, a cotton dress in yellow and red. Even though I have never consciously tried to remember that day, the moment is evidently seared into my memory. I must have read about periods in one of the books that I picked up from the one small bookshop that we had in our town, because I remember not being very surprised. My parents didn't really monitor what I read so I probably read things that I wasn't supposed to at a very young age, filled with feelings and words bigger than me, not understanding it all but feeling so grown up and sophisticated at the same time. My mother hurriedly ushered me to the bathroom and pushed a small bundle of cloth folded onto itself into my hands. I remember that it was an offcut from part of my school uniform from the previous year, a dark blue cloth.

'Use this,' she said, 'you've already started your periods.' She sounded abrupt and distracted. Did she seem disappointed in me? I wondered. Had I failed her in some way? I couldn't figure it out. The next five days felt surreal. My mother hadn't had a mother as she had adolescence looming over her; her own mother died when she had just turned thirteen. I have to try and remember this now. Her own experience must have shaped this moment for her, as her first born suddenly seemed to be stepping into womanhood before the time was right; it wasn't supposed to happen yet. However, I already had breasts sprouting and the rest of my body had been changing shape somewhat; I had also started feeling strange emotions that I could not explain and so it was just a matter of time.

Nevertheless, I was her child, and this change in me must, surely, have suddenly made her fearful of what lay ahead of me. She told me many years later that the moment that I was born she had been ecstatic – a child after six years of marriage and a miscarriage – but the very next thought had been that I was a girl and that

I would have to face everything that she had faced as a woman. It wasn't an easy life, she said to me. And she didn't want that life for me. Maybe as she saw me standing at the cusp of womanhood, bloodied and sullied in the eyes of her god, and not as pure any more, she was fearful of what would – and could – come next. Perhaps she was worried about how she was going to protect me from this world. I really don't know, because she never said these things out loud then.

As I became a mother myself, I tried to imagine what was going through her mind that day. How strange it is that one little biological change can alter the perception of a person so much. Suddenly a spot of blood made me a woman in my mother's and society's eyes, rather than the child I had been until that very moment. A split second and it all changed. Well, almost everything. I had to stop playing cricket on street corners with boys at once. 'It is not right for you to do so,' my mother said to me gently and rather sadly, as she could see my body growing breasts and curves, making me more visible, conspicuous and vulnerable. I was unmistakably a woman now, unable to hide behind my 'boys' clothes' and short hair, my femininity palpable to predatory eyes. I knew I was a girl, but I continued to exist in my wishful world where, by crossing over into an identity that wasn't mine, I could assume boys' freedoms and opportunities, and become visible. I continued to exist, not belonging in either world fully, until I had to firmly choose one. And thereafter I was both visible and invisible, not seen or heard except to silence and tease, a provocation and titillation. Catcalls grew, as did those hungry unabashed stares on the streets, weighing, measuring, taking account of me and other girls as women. In turn, we were expected to lower our gaze, wear clothes that hid any womanly curves, talk softly, walk quietly, bring no attention to ourselves. Don't unfurl, collapse, shrink. Don't walk alone after sunset, don't travel alone on public transport, don't look at anyone. Or it really is your fault. This is when a girl realises that her body is not truly her own, but instead a canvas for men to inflict, impose, imprint on. For the very first time I really wanted to be invisible.

Women often breathe a lonely existence, wrestling with paradoxical needs to be seen, heard, wished for and desired, but also to withdraw, shrink, disappear. For the first five days of my first period I had to stay in the spare bed in a corner of the living room. The room became simultaneously my refuge and my prison. It also made me realise that I was now different. I was different from my two younger sisters, and as they ran around me, I couldn't do so with as much freedom and abandon. I wasn't sure how I was supposed to act now that I was a woman, and not a child any more. I felt disgusted by my own changing body. Puberty is marked out to be this completely transformational period of life, but the surprising thing is that I don't remember much of my experience as a girl before this time. Only that the age of innocence was over and I had to start preparing for the next stage of my life. I wanted to escape, but did not know where to since it wasn't just the physical, geographical space that determined my claustrophobia. Illimitable space can sometimes free us, but at other times it becomes a trap.

•

When I was growing up, women were considered impure when they menstruated, so they were not allowed to go into the kitchen, nor prepare food for others to eat. Things changed somewhat as I grew older, but even now, women on their periods are not permitted to take part in any religious ceremonies, be near the altar, nor enter a temple.

36

Although many temples only ban menstruating women, the Sabarimala Temple in Kerala bans all women between the ages of ten and fifty, deeming them of 'menstruating age'. They are forbidden on the grounds that their presence dishonours the celibate Hindu god Ayyappan. On 1 January 2019 in Kerala, a 'women's wall' was organised in which women from across the state formed a 620 km (385 mile) human chain to protest against the ban. In the very early morning of 2 January 2019, something incredible happened: Bindu Ammini and Kanakadurga, two women, entered the temple. The temple closed its doors immediately. The women's presence had polluted the holy site and cleaning rituals must be conducted with urgency.

Nestled high up in Western India, there is a temple dedicated to the menstruating goddess Kamakhya Devi, one of the fifty-one shakti peeths in India. The temple has no sculpture to worship, only Kamakhya's yoni, a stone which is kept moist by a natural spring through the year. The garvagriha or inner sanctum of the temple houses the mythical womb and vagina of the Hindu goddess Shakti. But even though the temple has an annual fertility festival, Ambuwasi Puja, marking the yearly menstrual cycle of the goddess, women are not allowed to enter the temple when they are menstruating. Mythical goddesses are worshipped; women stigmatised for the same.

Sixty-eight undergraduate students at Shree Sahajanand Girls Institute in Bhuj, Gujarat, run by a wealthy and conservative Hindu religious group, were made to strip and show their underwear to female teachers to prove that they were not menstruating. These students were accused of breaking rules banning women from entering the temple and the kitchen. The school rules also state that menstruating women are not allowed to touch other students during their periods, they have to sit away from others at mealtimes, clean their own dishes, and sit on the last bench, away from everyone else, in the classroom. Videos of a priest from the same sect show him proclaiming that women who cook while menstruating will be reborn as dogs. This was not in some distant past. It was in February 2020.

According to data released by the Indian government in 2016, there are 355 million menstruating women and girls in the country (almost 30 per cent of the total population), and only 36 per cent have access to sanitary towels.[14] In India, as per a report in 2014 by the Indian NGO Dasra titled *Spot On!*,[15] nearly 23 million girls drop out of school annually due to lack of proper menstrual hygiene management facilities. A horrifying 71 per cent of the girls surveyed for this report were not even aware of menstruation until they reached menarche, and 70 per cent of the mothers believed menstruation to be dirty. In rural areas, 81 per cent of women use unsterilised cloths and many tend to use the dirtiest piece of cloth available, because to them menstruation is synonymous with dirt.[16]

People bleed every day. Life goes on. But menstruating women are dirty. When the boundary between the inside and the outside of women's bodies blur, they are deemed unsightly. Growing up, I would be mortified if anyone knew I was bleeding, wrapping up pads in newspapers, hiding them in the folds of my skirts as I navigated my way to the toilets, eyes lowered, heart beating fast, palpitations growing stronger. We become quite expert at these acts of subversion from a young age, living dangerously, in terror every day. What if anyone saw? What if I bled and left some evidence on my clothes? Bleeding is seen to herald the dawn of womanhood when a girl can finally be married off, have children and gratify the lascivious thoughts of men. But the very process that instigates the other, more desired and anticipated roles, is considered dirty and unpleasant.

Hinduism is specific about cleanliness. *Mānava Dharmaśāstra* ('Manu's treatise on dharma'), written around 200 BC, states that menstrual blood belongs to the twelve bodily fluids considered dirty:

> . . . oil, semen, blood, bone marrow, urine, excrement, snot, ear-wax, phlegm, tears, the discharge from the eyes, and sweat; these are the twelve human defilements.[17]

But it is not only blood that produces the stigmatisation of menstruation. Menses occupy a unique place in some Hindu scriptures, which outline ways in which a man can become polluted simply by being in contact with a menstruating woman. Semen is okay, and while a man becomes polluted after ejaculation, he can be 'healed' after taking a bath. On the other hand, being in contact with a menstruating woman leads to a man losing many of his faculties such as wisdom and strength, something that he is unable to regain and heal from.

> Even if he is out of his mind (with desire) he should not have sex with a woman who is menstruating; he should not even lie down in the same bed with her. A man who has sex with a woman awash in menstrual blood loses his wisdom, brilliant energy, strength, eyesight, and long life. By shunning her when she is awash in menstrual blood, he increases his wisdom, brilliant energy, strength, eyesight, and long life.[18]

Menstrual cycles have been stigmatised and women shamed for having their periods around the world in many different cultures since the dawn of time. In Nepal, women have to go and live in a separate menstrual hut outside the house so that no one comes in contact with them – a practice called chaupadi – and women are not allowed to be involved in the gardening lest they ruin the growing plants merely by their touch.

The Old Testament of the Bible also claims that women are unclean when they menstruate. The story of Genesis sees Eve as someone who is not central to the narrative, only as peripheral support. Adam is created first, and God creates Eve only when Adam becomes lonely, hence setting the premise in motion that women are only second-best. But then as Eve dares to defy God in the Garden of Eden, she is punished with painful monthly menstruation and child-birth. This gendered foundation of menstruation as the 'curse of Eve' persisted through the Middle Ages.[19]

> If a man lies with a woman during her menstrual period and uncovers her nakedness, he has made naked her fountain, and she has uncovered the fountain of her blood. Both of them shall be cut off from among their people. (Leviticus 20:18)

Through the Middle Ages, menstrual blood was also seen as some-thing that did irreparable harm. *De Secretis Mulierum*, or *The Secrets of Women*, is a book written in the thirteenth century. While it is not a medical text, and there have been questions on its authorship,¶ it was used by doctors in Europe for a long time and has been considered 'an influential text in the history of medieval scientific attitudes toward women'.[20] Kate Clancy in an essay in the *Scientific American* quotes the book's claims that menstruating women even give off harmful fumes that 'poison the eyes of children lying in their cradles by a glance'.[21] This text also forbade coitus during menstruation and even though the Church also castigated sex during

¶   There has been some discussion and evidence of the book being written by a pupil of Albert Magnus, and the book also refers to Albert Magnus in a few places, although other researchers have called it pseudo-Magnus.

pregnancy and lactation, it was intercourse during menstruation that carried the most severe penalty, with the birth of a hideously deformed child, or one with epilepsy or leprosy because of the venom in the menstrual matter, and even cancer in the man who dared to take such a risk.[22]

In Europe, as late as the '50s, it was believed that menstruating women could turn wine to vinegar. It is probably when we need wine most, don't you think? James George Frazer, a Scottish anthropologist, describes in his book *The Golden Bough* that it was widely held in various societies at that time that wells run dry if a menstruating woman draws water from them; men become ill if they are touched by or use any objects touched by a menstruating woman; and beer turns sour if a menstruating woman enters a brewery.[23]

In the 1920s Dr Béla Schick believed that menstruating women produced a toxin called menotoxin, which could wilt otherwise normally thriving flowers. Science is not without bias; neither are scientists. And here is one prime example of how science can be contorted to fit a person's worldview. Just because one man decided that there was something inherently dirty and toxic about menstruating women, enough to wilt fresh flowers merely by touch, he launched a whole field of scientific study in it.[24] He, and others who took up this cause, really wanted to believe in this, and so they very easily ignored all negative results, only accounting for the results that confirmed their hypothesis. They discounted any cases or studies that did not corroborate their beliefs.** He was not alone in this belief in the existence of menotoxins, spurring on a whole plethora of studies, which were then published widely in reputable scientific

** This is confirmation bias, something I have discussed in extensive detail in my book *Sway: Unravelling Unconscious Bias.*

journals for almost sixty-odd years. The mind boggles. A paper from 1923 published in the *Journal of Pharmacology and Experimental Therapeutics* reaches the conclusion that 'The blood serum, blood corpuscles, saliva, sweat, milk and other secretions of menstruating women contain a toxic substance' that has an 'inhibitory effect on the growth of roots and stems of whole living seedlings, through its blighting effect on cut flowers, through its distorting influence on the geotropic properties of seedlings, through its inhibitory influence on the growth of yeast and through other phenomena.'[25]

As I was writing this book, I spoke with several young women who laughed at me for talking about any stigma associated with periods or women's bodies. We are all empowered now, they said. On the other hand, I remember how even as recently as 2009 comedian Joan Rivers was censored for using the word 'period', a commonly used reference for menstruation, in a television show. In a 1999 study, Paul Rozin and colleagues from the University of Pennsylvania asked 250 college students to interact with an unopened sanitary tampon on a clean paper plate in front of them.[26] All were willing to pick up the wrapped tampon, and fully 97 per cent were willing to unwrap it and hold it in their hands. However, only 54 per cent were willing to touch it to their lip, and even fewer (31 per cent) were willing to put it in their mouth. A study in 2002 showed that when a research assistant subtly dropped a tampon or a hair clip in front of a mixed group of participants, she was seen as less competent and less likeable while she was perceived to be menstruating.[27] A study as recently as 2018, for those who doubt that menstrual stigma continues, conducted in the USA and polling 1,500 women and 500 men from across the country, found that 58 per cent of women polled felt a sense of embarrassment simply because they were on their period. Forty-two per cent of the women had experienced period-shaming, with one in five being made to have these feelings because of comments made by a male friend. Half of men studied (51 per cent) believed it inappropriate for women to openly mention their menstrual cycles in the workplace. Hardly a surprise that most women admit to having felt that they had to actively conceal the fact they were on their period. Almost three-quarters (73 per cent) of women surveyed in this poll had hidden a pad or tampon from view on their way to the bathroom; 65 per cent had worn specific clothes that wouldn't show a leak if it were to happen; and 29 per cent had cancelled plans, like swimming or exercising, that might have exposed the fact they were on their period.[28]

It is so strange to think that in this era of extraordinary freedom, girls are still having to endure the feelings of shame and confusion I did that summer day when I was eleven. Lara Freidenfelds, in her 2009 book *The Modern Period: Menstruation in Twentieth-Century America*, discusses how the stigmatisation of the female body for being smelly, and for having cramps, is significantly shaped by racial attitudes too.[29] The way that puberty is more visible in bodies of colour, with earlier menarche, darker hair sprouting, and body shape maturing sooner in many cases, has meant that women of colour are brought up to shrink away more and hide their periods to avoid any undesired attention towards their bodies. They – we – grow up thinking that our bodies are ugly and disgusting, that we aren't good enough.

As a cisgender woman, I talk about the shame that women have been made to feel for menstruating, or not. It is a strange paradox. Because not all women menstruate. There is also ingrained shame for women who suffer from amenorrhea or do not have periods for other reasons such as early menopause, polycystic ovary syndrome, eating disorders or cancer treatments, many of which have lacked medical attention and research, showing the paucity of concern for women who do not fit into the typical boxes. There is a mistaken notion of femininity that has been associated with the start of the menses for so long, with its monthly cycle of bleeding, even though we have to hide it away.

There are also the experiences of transgender men and women. While they might have been mentally transitioning for many years, and finally get to inhabit the body that feels right for them, they often struggle with the biological markers of what being a man or a woman means. As 'Alex' shares in her story in an article in Refinery29, she has felt 'less of a woman' or merely an 'aesthetic woman' at times, especially to others, because she cannot fulfil the 'practical elements of womanhood'.[30] Trans model and activist Kenny Jones has spoken widely from his perspective as a transgender man about how not everyone who gets periods is a woman. As he suffered gender dysphoria from a young age, he internalised the shame, silence and stigma of having a period that made him feel less masculine, and so his '. . . ego and internalised expectations of male dominance' were enough to convince him to bottle it up and speak about it with no one. 'I felt isolated; everything about periods was tailored to girls, yet me, a boy, was experiencing this and nothing in the world documented that,' Jones has told *NBC News*.[31] It is difficult to overlook how such ideas are rooted in patriarchal structures, and rigid binary thinking. Gloria Steinem wrote in 1978 that if men could menstruate, the menses would be a badge of honour, not a mark of stigma, that 'menstruation would become an enviable, worthy, masculine event. Men would brag about how long and how much. Young boys would talk about it as the envied beginning of man-hood'.[32] But some men do menstruate, and we tend to forget that, associating this bodily function so closely with being a woman, all wrapped up, pretty in pink.

It should be no surprise that the marketing of sanitary products feeds off and fuels these various existing stigmas and biases. The marketing of period products is so entangled in the belief that all women of a certain age, and only women, bleed that it can exclude non-binary, intersex and trans individuals who experience the same. The identity of a woman hinges on such parameters, women's unique experiences made universal and homogenised into narrow boundaries of monthly hormonal cycles. We forget that these are not all-inclusive parameters, refusing to account for those shades of pink and greys at the edges.

•

Joan Chrisler, a psychologist from Connecticut College, writes in the *Psychology of Women Quarterly* that the way menstrual products are marketed and placed in stores continues to perpetuate the myth that it is unseemly for women to bleed.[33] The use of the term 'feminine hygiene' products of course reinforces the idea that women would be dirty and polluted without them; their natural cycles considered debased and animalistic. Euphemistic words such as 'mother nature' or 'that time of the month' are often used, indicating that even a neutral word such as 'period' is unpalatable. Language matters, because words have the power to create threat and fear. It can create divides and barriers where none should exist. Words create the parable of menstruation being a 'women's problem', something to be feared, a burden, a dirty secret, and to be associated for ever with being a woman. Transversely, it then becomes that women are dirty and a burden, because they carry these 'problems' with them.

I remember in a chemistry lab class when I was fifteen years old, one of my experiments failed, the mixture turning cloudy rather than to a sparkling liquid. The lab instructor loudly asked me if I was on my period. I had not understood the insinuation then, of my being poisonous, releasing toxins through my touch, but I felt his glare upon me, and that of the boys in my class. I stood at my desk, eyes lowered, shame burning into my eyes and my back, glowing hot rods skewered into my sides, my ear drums exploding with a loud buzzing sound, pulsating and drilling into my skull, my fingers tingling. I refused to cry even as hot and humiliated tears tried to burst forth from my eyelids. With one sentence he had laid bare what we girls tried to hide. I did not have any great revelations or moments of prophecy right there and then. All I knew was that all the shame I felt as a woman had squashed itself into that one short moment; that one sentence had taken away any respectability I had tried to gain with my academic achievements amongst the boys in my class. I knew they would be talking about it and gossiping about it for days to come. I would be the butt of jokes, laughed and stared at. And even though other girls must have felt this shame, some sniggered and laughed at me too. I understood that women shame women too, so deeply ingrained in our cultures can misogyny be, the stigma forcing women to turn against our own, often solely for self-protection.

Although that moment in class was not as catastrophic in the end as it had seemed in my head, now that I look back, I feel sorry for that young girl who did not think her womanhood was something to be proud of. She only felt shame in her body, in her difference, in her lumps, hair and hormones, and internalised the stigma of her bleeding and blooming body that was merely doing what it was always expected to do.

Adolescence, or coming of age, is a pivotal point in human experience, accompanied by hormonal, emotional and physical shifts, where our perceived social roles and responsibilities change too. As I have grown up, I have realised how many burdens we carry as girls, and then as women. The burden of being a girl in a society that does not want you. And the burden of trying to prove ourselves, again and again – and yet again – to be worthy of a place, taking up space, deserving to breathe and exist. If you think of what a woman goes through in her life, it is no surprise that the first thing my mother felt after I was born was fear and despair. And then it seems natural that women internalise this shame around their body[††] and particularly their womb, while continuing to be inextricably linked to and defined by it.

It starts here. Or does it end? Evanescent childhood. Fluctuating, shape-shifting, transient. Hormones, plasma, bodily fluids. Womanhood beckons, in its narrow delimitations, even though no one feels ready for it, or knows what it entails.

[††] Studies have shown that shame around menstruation and sexuality are linked. Women who reported more comfort with menstruation also reported more comfort with sex. Evidence also shows that women who perceive their vaginas as dirty, smelly, and shameful reported lower levels of sexual participation and enjoyment of sexual activity.

II.

THE AGE OF DEFIANCE

'YOU ARE PREGNANT,' MY MUM says as she cooks. I feel sick. I have been feeling sick for a while. Maybe it is just exhaustion. 'Of course I am not,' I insist. And I shake my head and move away from the kitchen door. The test at the doctor confirms it. I sit with my legs closed tight together, as if that would help now, ankles overlapping, stomach knotted. 'Is this for real?' I ask her again, and the gynaecologist shows me the result of my urine test. Home pregnancy tests are still not common in India in 1996, and my mother has brought me to one of the best gynaecologists. She is the same one who delivered my baby sister all those years ago. 'I do not want this,' I want to say. But it feels wrong to say it. 'Is it a surprise pregnancy?' the doctor asks. You can say that again.

Most books I had read and most movies I had watched in my teens had created an idea in my head that every time a couple had unprotected sex, there was an equal likelihood of them getting pregnant, of the sperm inseminating the egg. How could I have debated this? I had become pregnant, suddenly, without trying, without lying on my back, without eating my greens, without raising my legs up in the air for half an hour after sex, without thinking, without wanting, without wishing. I think of this a lot. I cannot imagine not having my daughter, she who is the love of my life, the one whom I have loved and protected fiercely. But, no, I had not prepared for her. Does one ever really prepare for motherhood? Do any of the parenting manuals really tell you the reality of what it will be like?

When we are young, we feel indefatigable. We want to take on challenges, love fiercely and loyally, with a passion unencumbered by our own and others' limitations. But we begin to doubt ourselves, and our very claim to be free, when everyone around us tells us that we don't have the right to be. Reading books had filled my head with romance and idealism, they said.

'Maybe I am wrong, and they are right.'

We talk about coercive control in relationships, but we do not look at how intimate, close-knit families in some cultures create the same toxic, controlling situations. These families of generations living to-gether, the daughter-in-law expected to mould herself and fit right in, moving seamlessly from her father's house to her husband's house, a shapeshifting non-being. Class remains a huge barrier in Indian societies, and marrying across class, for love, was seen as a crime. I had to be punished for stepping into spaces that I should not have demanded a right to, and so I was. Those cloying gestures proclaimed as love, but that throttle and suffocate.

This book isn't about that relationship, or that marriage. But when I found out I was pregnant for the first time, I was very young, ambitious, and as my spirit and my sense of identity were being crushed by the weight of societal expectations, as I navigated marriage into a traditional large joint family, I could not imagine bringing another being into this world. I had just graduated and was begin-ning to find my place in life. I was so young, and so much in what I then believed to be love, and I wanted to enjoy life, study, be a force for change. I was looking, searching for meaning, for my purpose in a world that seemed cold and cruel, putting up barriers, breaking me down slowly and steadily until I felt it was easier to succumb and be someone everyone else wanted me to be rather than push against the very grain of society. I stopped crying, rebelling, speaking out, even though the screams inside me were not ready to die just yet. When wings are clipped, there might be no sound, but the screeches echo inside for a long time. Every step I took was monitored, questioned, criticised. I was stubbornly clutching onto some sense of self, even as I felt my self-esteem slip and shatter.

From the day I was married, the persistent questions from everyone of when I was going to have a baby felt like a tight hold around my throat. All the rituals and blessings centred on becoming a mother, overpowering, gagging, strangling my own image of myself, that doppelgänger that could still be seen at times. 'A baby will make everything okay,' I thought. 'If only you have a child, your mother-in-law will adore you. If you give them a boy, they will accept you unconditionally.' So many conditions remained.

Garbhadhan is the first of the sixteen sanskaras, the sacraments, the rites of passage in the Vedic tradition. This is the first coming together of the husband and wife to bring about conception. 'Garbha' means womb; 'dhan' means wealth. This sacrament is about attaining the wealth of the womb, with the man 'placing his seed in a woman' with the intent of having a child.

As mentioned in the *Rigveda*,[*] one of the oldest Vedas:

प्रजां च धत्तं द्रविणं च धत्तम्

bestow upon us progeny and affluence[1]

---

[*] The *Rigveda* is one of the four sacred canonical texts called the Vedas and consists of Sanskrit hymns.

It is the moral responsibility of a married couple to have progeny. The reason for this is given in the *Taittiriya Upanishad*. When the student ends his Vedic studies, he requests permission to leave from his teacher. The teacher then blesses him with some advice, which he should imbibe for life. One of the commands is:

'Prajaatantu ma vyavyachchhetseehi. . .' (Shikshavalli, Anuvak 11.11)

'Do not terminate one's lineage – let it continue (by having children).'

Garbhadhan sanskaar is carried out by the following mantra:

Oh Goddess! You give power to this woman to bear a child. May the God Ashwinikumar and the deities such as Mitra, Varuna, Guru Brihaspati, Indra, Agni, Brahma fill the womb of this woman.

I did not even know whether I was truly enjoying sex, but this seemed irrelevant in the face of duty. I did not know my body. I had never experimented. I had never explored my sexuality. All I could think of every single time was that I did not want to get pregnant, that I must not get pregnant.

And then, I did. Growing up in a place where there was no sex education – well, I knew roughly how things worked from the awkward school lesson and the basic information in textbooks – no one had explicitly talked to me about it. I had no magazines, no social media, no internet to read about other people's experiences of their own bodies and of intimacy and sexuality. The pull of hormones and desire is strong, and you somehow manage to make sense of it all. My periods came and went, sometimes regular, sometimes not. I was often quite pleased when they were late, as it meant freedom from the drudgery, from hiding away, from pretending my body wasn't bleeding, from the embarrassment, awkwardness and discomfort. I revelled in those days, as if I had somehow challenged patriarchy and won. It seemed like a victory, especially as these were so hard to come by. So when I was late, I was too happy about it even to consider the possibility that a late period could mean I was pregnant.

'Unintended pregnancy' means, clearly, pregnancy without intention. But it is wrapped up in multiple layers of meanings, and there is an inherent, unresolved paradox within this term.[2] Unintended, or unintentional, does not always mean that the mother-to-be is unhappy about the outcome, or that the pregnancy and the child are not desired. Labels about unintended pregnancy are also deeply rooted in the hegemonic white cultural models of reproduction, which are more strictly regulated by contraception and family size. Largely emerging from questionnaires in the USA around the baby boom era, surveys aimed at women about unintended pregnancy were meant to measure surplus pregnancies beyond that of the stipulated or planned family size.[3] In doing so they were indeed measuring how much a woman *intended* to extend her role as a mother (does that role ever end though, if you have children?) rather than considering whether – and how much – a person was prepared to step into this new kind of social role, i.e. if they were prepared for motherhood.

Kristin Luker, sociologist and professor of law at the University of California, called this a 'threshold decision' over twenty years ago, with 'a much more complicated decision tree'† than we assign to it. It is a decision not just about fertility but a broader choice

---

† A decision tree is a simple way to visualise a decision, a predictive modelling technique used in statistics and data mining, where each branch represents the outcome of the test.

about parenthood within a specific social and cultural climate, which becomes fraught with anxiety as the notion of motherhood becomes increasingly linked to a judgement about broader lifestyle choices. It can become a battlefield of political arguments for and against family values, as if a family is one only with children. Unintended pregnancy exists as a misnomer, because often continuing with an accidental, unplanned pregnancy can be a way to prevaricate from these life-changing decisions, sidestepping persistent enquiries from well-meaning family and friends and letting fate decide when it is the 'right time'.[4] But, no matter what the reason might be or how a pregnancy happens, it isn't as much about whether we, as women, are prepared for it or not, but whether we are prepared for what follows, whether we are ready to be mothers. But this unprepared-ness is so often cloaked, the anxiety of being found out dripping through our pores. We want to be ready.

Was I surprised, shocked, stopped in my tracks knowing my life would change in unmeasurable ways when I found out I was preg-nant? Yes, of course, yes.

Have I felt guilty and tried to make up for that every single day, trying to prove to her and myself that she was never unwanted, undesired, unplanned? Perhaps, yes.

Was she a mistake? Never. No.

No ambivalence there.

•

In *Of Woman Born*, her 1976 analysis of motherhood as both ex-perience and institution, Adrienne Rich describes herself looking at her own mother and thinking, 'I too shall marry, have children – but not like her. I shall find a way of doing it all differently.'[5] I felt this too; I just didn't know what that different way would be.

Motherhood had already appeared in different shapes and forms around me. My mother, her love unspoken at times, but always a safety net, so reliable but not always agreeable to my own temperament. And there were others. Dedication, dependability, devotion supposedly personify motherhood, but there was also a whole generation of children being raised by ayahs and nannies who left their own children behind in their villages to care for those of others. The many layers of privilege in the way motherhood manifested was played out again and again in front of me: from the women whose motherhood was not legitimised because of their social class and economic status, to those who benefited from these mothers, and exploited them to their own advantage. Even as we bemoan the vast inequality between men and women, the gulf between certain women, and certain mothers, remains, with some more equal than others.

There was no one model of motherhood to learn from for me; all seemed so lacking in the intense, boundless love I had read about in books. The reality seemed a shapeless and formless pale ghost, which never came close to the ideals my young mind had conjured up. Motherhood was so central and pivotal in society, yet so peripheral and inconsequential at the same time. I searched for that model of love that would transform a mundane but tumultuous existence into a content and glorious one. I looked for mothers who were seen, really seen for all their foibles and their potencies. But there were none. How does one know what kind of mother one will be before one becomes one? Anne Enright writes in *Making Babies* that '. . . most of us come to an accommodation between the 'MOTHER!' in our heads and the woman who reared us.'[6] The mother in my head was an apparition, with no bodily functions or subsistence, and the distance to the woman who reared me seemed insurmountable.

What does the word 'mother' even mean? How does one know how to embody it completely? 'Ma', 'mater', 'amma', 'meme', 'mama' . . . Across the different language divides, it is the first word a child is supposed to utter, the word that is naturally formed on our lips as we first begin to speak, the connection we have to the land, the tongue, the language and customs of our forebears. Penn State etymologist Philip Baldi calls this 'an articulatory extension of the sucking impulse, a nasal consonant, in which the air flows through the nasal passage . . . and the lips come together.'[7] The accumulation of first sounds, the process of language acquisition, is through small units of sound called phonemes – a consortium of clicks, vowels, consonants – original and unique for every language, and also for every child, and not merely imitating adult speech as people often believe. In English for instance there are around forty-two phonemes even though there are only twenty-six letters in the alphabet.

Fffllo-o-op.

Chraaaan.

Jraggggn.

The linguist Roman Jakobson terms this 'tongue delirium', in which gradually all sorts of conceivable sounds are uttered until they slowly start becoming impressed on a child's memory.[8] This period of non-lucid existence sounds like something parents and babies share, the rapture, ecstasy, frenzy of ardent love, mapped out in pheromones.

My mother tells me that my first word wasn't 'ma', or 'mumma', or 'amma'. And as I become a mother myself, I remembered this when M's first word was 'mittens': not a primordial call for me, but a word that she loved rolling around her tongue.

Having a nebulous sense of what motherhood meant, in a rather idealised way instead of a concrete, tangible notion, I was aware as a young mother-to-be that not all mothers and children have close relationships. Some are wracked with frustrations on both sides. What if there were cracks in my own relationship with my child? What if I curled up like burnt paper at the edges, unfurling and unravelling, blown away at the mere suggestion of an outward gust? What if I couldn't hold her safe?

Even as I grew, through days, weeks and months, my ambition for my unborn child grew too. The Tapuat, the Hopi symbol for mother earth or labyrinth, is seen as the symbol for mother and child. The lines represent stages of life, the umbilical cord, and the path of moving – always within the watchfulness of the mother. The centre symbolises the amniotic sac – the centre of life – the beginning, carrying us through the journey of life. Was this really the world I was going to bring a daughter into, the world that had used up all its kindness in raising boys? Where boys were venerated, girls were being fed into the production line as soon as they came of age. Of course, I didn't know it was a girl. But I wanted her to be. In a country with deep, insidious roots in patriarchy, and where female infanticide (and foeticide) is illegal but carries on,‡ it was a brave choice to desire a daughter. It was my act of rebellion.

> In any case, you are always there,
> Tremulous breath at the end of my line,
> Curve of water upleaping
> To my water rod, dazzling and grateful,
> Touching and sucking.
>
> Sylvia Plath, 'Medusa'[9]

‡ The UN State of World Population report from 2020 states that India accounts for almost 31 per cent of the 'missing females' in the last fifty years.

•

Sometimes things that derail our lives also have the potential to transform them in unexpected and astonishing ways. The moment I heard the first heartbeat, beating outside and inside of me, I came alive. Pregnancy was alien and comforting. In a body that had not felt like my own for a long time, I was beginning to inhabit my whole self completely, assuredly, decisively.

The feelings of self-consciousness and inadequacy that had absorbed my being for some time in my role as a daughter-in-law, where I felt I had never been accepted fully, where I seemed to remain persona non grata, always seen as an interloper, had been peeled off like old skin. I was giving birth to the essence of my existence. Suddenly I was not just eating for two, but also living for two. Sometimes it felt like I was just living for one: I sang to her, and talked to her, recounting all the hilarious things I had seen and heard that day.

As my middle expanded, and my short frame filled up from head to toe, looking like a protuberant sphere, there was nothing remotely glamorous about my pregnancy. I did not feel beautiful or divine. I was not glowing as films and magazines had said all pregnant women do. 'This is not what a pregnant body ought to look like,' I kept thinking, judging myself. But I hadn't really come across a pregnant body in the media that hadn't been airbrushed, never seen the no-holds-barred forms of a woman's body changing closely, the corporeal, primordial, raw forms of maternity that I was encountering now, and it was easy to imagine mine to be an oddity.

Even in pregnancy, women are often expected to shrink them-selves, become smaller, their expanding girths offensive as they start taking up more space. The media often monitors how much weight

57

a woman should gain during pregnancy and how they should manage their bodies. When pregnant for the first time in 2013, Kim Kardashian was twice tagged as a 'whale' as a result of the weight she had gained.[10] She was also shown in juxtaposition to Kate Middleton in the magazine *YOU*, comparing 'Kate the Waif' vs 'Kim the Whale'. We have seen this with Meghan Markle, who struggled with the intense media scrutiny while she was pregnant and after giving birth and admitted to feeling 'vulnerable' and unprotected.[11] Even as a thirty-seven-year-old, she was called a 'geriatric mum' repeatedly in the media, scrutinised for how many times she was touching her pregnant abdomen, and how she was carrying herself.[§] Bodies of colour are monitored more than white bodies, expected to conform to a narrow societal view of what an ideal woman and mother ought to look like – slender, tall and delicate, even in pregnancy.

Representations of pregnant bodies in popular culture and media are either censured or glorified. The portraits of visibly pregnant women through history can also give us clues to how the politics of the time shaped women's identities and sexualities. The cultural historian Karen Hearn, who curated an exhibition at London's Foundling Museum, discusses in her accompanying book *Portraying Pregnancy* how in paintings from the 1600s to the late twentieth century, portraits of pregnant women are virtually non-existent, and every attempt was made to hide any evidence that the sitter might be pregnant, by using folds of clothes or props cleverly.[12] According to Hearn, childlessness also played a role, as maternal mortality was

§ The term 'geriatric pregnancy' is used officially for anyone over the ages of thirty-five years old, although the term is now considered outdated and insulting. However, this term was repeated in numerous bylines about Meghan's pregnancy.

very high, so the anxiety of death also surrounded the portraiture and representation of pregnant bodies. While there is a dearth of pregnant bodies in artistic representations, as the subject of pregnancy was considered too indelicate for public domain and eyes, and maternity was tied in closely with the virgin birth in art and literature, sometimes women of aristocratic families commissioned their paintings to gesture towards their fecundity and herald a hopeful claim to the throne with a possible male heir. This kind of scrutiny often proposes that there is something unseemly about the physical act of growing a child inside one's own body, dissociating the act of maternity from the inherent sexuality and visceral animality, while focusing on the spiritual aspect of it, with the valorization of motherhood as a woman's true purpose.

In the late twentieth century, the American painter Alice Neel painted a series of sexualised pregnant nudes, and though she did not clearly attribute this as a feminist statement, she saw this as a retort to the prevalent male gaze that did not depict pregnancy even though 'it was a basic life's fact'.[13] Annie Leibovitz's image of Demi Moore from the cover of *Vanity Fair* in 1991 also comes to mind, which unintentionally became a symbol of women's empowerment while also mobilising a highly divisive debate around sexuality and pregnant bodies. That issue of the magazine was sold shrink-wrapped on newsstands, much like a porn magazine, and a number of newsagent chains refused to sell it, deeming it unsuitable. Yet the maternal but erotic image made it the bestselling single issue in the magazine's history and made headlines on news bulletins around the globe.[14] This prompted many celebrities to unabashedly photograph their bump, rather than hide it, and as white motherhood took centre stage, it also heralded an era of increasing self-regulation and self-objectification for pregnant bodies.

In recent times, it has become more common to see pregnant bodies on our screens, in our social media squares and timelines. Nevertheless, when Beyoncé announced her pregnancy with a series of photographs in 2017, symbolically drawing from a range of cultural and historical sources, with subliminal references to Botticelli's *Birth of Venus*, and reminiscent of Renaissance portraits of the Madonna with her blue veil, it created a sensation. Perhaps particularly because it brought into focus how women's bodies have historically been marginalised and violated, while also continually objectified.[15] The re-appropriation of the image of the Virgin Mary was particularly telling – and controversial. The predominant depiction of Mary is that of white superiority, of positioning whiteness as pure and divine, and as a black woman Beyoncé not only posited a sexualised, heavily pregnant body but also challenged these cultural norms with what cultural critic and theorist bell hooks calls 'oppositional gaze':[16] to see, name, question and ultimately transform oppressive racialised images.

Hearn says that 'The visible pregnant body demonstrates that a woman is sexually active and that is hugely problematic . . . When men wrote about pregnancy portraits they used a euphemism, the French word for pregnancy, "enceinte".' Enceinte translates as 'an enclosure or the enclosing wall of a fortified place', immediately dehumanising the person who is pregnant to be seen only as a vessel, as an enclosure for the growing baby.

I only have a couple of photos from the time of my pregnancy, I think, but even as I grew heavier, bulkier and more burdensome, there was a lightness of being, and I felt the weight of my existence leave my limbs for the first time in a long time.

•

Motherhood is all-consuming and, paradoxically for someone who had resisted it, criticised it, seen it merely as shackles and drudgery, it rescued me from the bereavement of my own self.

> Bright yellow sick in the sink every morning
> bright yellow sick and I'm constantly yawning
> like the gold at the end of the rainbow, you're calling
> and I'm sick and I'm crying as the birds call the dawn in
> Hollie McNish, 'Sunrise Sickness'[17]

Motherhood had become my act of resistance. For so long, I had thought that by rejecting motherhood, I was rejecting subordination, not fully acknowledging that the moment I was born into this sex, a script had been written out for me. No matter how many times I had presumed I was making my own choices, they were never my choices to make in the first place. In devaluing motherhood and mothering, I myself was conforming to the patriarchal construction of sexual differences, where mothering came naturally to women. In rejecting the notion that mothering was second nature to women, I had also rejected the possibility of motherhood, because for me both seemed inextricably linked with each other.

Certain feminists, including Simone de Beauvoir, asserted that women are complicit in the heteronormative and phallocentric constructs of society, because motherhood makes a woman 'othered' and ties them to immanence, and so foregoing motherhood is the only way that a woman may hope to achieve equality and liberate herself from the constructs of patriarchy. By choosing motherhood, they argue, women are choosing an enforced maternity, one that essentialises women. This argument posits that motherhood is never undergone with freedom and liberty, and that it reinforces women's position as 'objects'; their bodies – and their offspring – belonging to men, the church, to society. This radical feminist discourse encouraged women to reject motherhood, and the universal vision and image of women as mothers, as an act of resistance. By rejecting the strict gender roles and the expectation that a woman must be a mother, many of us want to say that we are more than our female self; we extend beyond the neat lines within which we have to navigate our life paths. We want to say that we are human, too, and perhaps by rejecting the one role that defines women more than any other, we are reminding ourselves and others that we are ultimately equal to men.

Yet here I was doing the opposite.

•

The universal views of motherhood and of a mother's love were recounted to me through those months of pregnancy in images, actions and words. Yet no secrets were divulged regarding how one becomes a mother from not being one. Is it merely the act of having a child that can be so revelatory? All women, all mothers become one universal category, their experiences and stories homogenised into one narrative of mothering being innate to their nature. The love and devotion you will feel for your children is expected and unquestioned; the woman becoming a mother and nothing else.

I was determined that the act of carrying a child in my stomach would not define me as this single entity: mother. In India, in upper-class circles governed by large patrilineal families, the mere act of stepping outside to work and study – to try to continue to carry a pregnant belly into the world unashamedly, forcing it unapologetically and determinedly into spaces not meant for women, and definitely not for mothers – was seen as the worst form of insurgence and defiance by some. I was a renegade, a maverick, an enigma. Motherhood could not contain my spirit. As my growing belly rammed into the crevices of patriarchal and social constructs of motherhood, it was seen as rebuffing and ridiculing the neatly arranged patterns of the hierarchical power structures, and unsettling the delicate balance of gender roles that society had constructed over the last centuries. With swollen ankles and feet, I stomped klutzily on the images of motherhood projected onto wider sensibilities all around me.

Ignored, dismissed and derided for this behaviour, I sought solace in my lonely conversations with my growing child, and we communicated through the many layers of fat and blood with that visceral connection that had previously seemed mythical to me. I sang tunelessly and laughed as she kicked me hard, punishing me for afflicting her yet unborn ears with the discordant atonal droning. I would tell her about my day, the mundane dreary details and the fascinating riveting rarities that had been mine alone for so long. Surrounded by people in a busy household, I was never really alone, but I hadn't realised how lonely I had felt for so long. Now there was someone to share my thoughts with, someone who was hearing my voice, and knowing me, the real me, unfiltered me, who I felt was accepting me as I was. When we live with watchful eyes monitoring every move, judging, belittling, condemning, we can forget how to hope, and to trust. We can internalise these condemnations. We can form a shell around us, and we can become a shadow, a muted version of ourselves, shrinking and hiding from any scorn and derision. But now when I retreated into myself, I could also glimpse a version of myself that I hadn't seen for so long underneath the armour I had slowly built between the world and me.

This unbreakable trust that I suddenly felt through the mere act of carrying my baby was a revelation to me.

'Hello, I am your mother,' I would say to her often during those days and months, whispering it gently, not knowing if it was the vibrations of my sound, or the rhythmic pulse of my heart that she could hear. I slowly breathed in the word 'mother' as if by osmosis I would learn how to be one. But in those moments, the word 'mother', which I had loathed and disparaged, now felt like a comfortable blanket, even with all the aches and pains, the drudgery and the sluggishness, the immodesty of my bodily functions, and the corporeal animalistic physicality of pregnancy.

•

The twinges had started that morning, pulsating rhythms, as I left to spend the day in the archive for another day of research. Just the belly expanding, the pregnancy book said, and so I put it aside. My body was making so much involuntary noise of its own these days that the extraordinary had become ordinary. I had not heard any stories of pregnancies that hadn't been 'normal'; only of women who sauntered into hospitals right on cue and delivered easily and effortlessly. No one had talked to me about pain, or of troubled pregnancies: if you looked after yourself, and did as you were told, there was no reason that it wouldn't be straightforward. The onus was, and is, always on women to behave, to do the right thing, to follow the rules, so when something goes wrong, if ever anything goes against the plan, we are quick to blame ourselves.

I counted twenty-six weeks in the small diary I had been carrying with me. This could not be right. The immediacy and urgency of that moment suddenly made the loneliness so much more acute, and I was a mother and a child at the same time, desperate for my own mother to come and hold me and whisper comforting sounds to me. Dull, throbbing pain continued to surge through my middle as I was standing in the middle of a large room back at home later that day, a family wedding to go to, my jewellery and my lehenga laid out on the bed, diamonds and rubies sparkling and glittering. Amongst the riches, I felt needy and pitiable. So often we see the lustre, but not the empty shell.

'I cannot come to the wedding. I am in so much pain,' I had said softly to my mother-in-law. Unsure and anxious, I wanted to be held, to be reassured that it was all going to be okay.

'It's only gastric trouble. You are just making excuses.' She had walked off with a shrug.

These few words are imprinted on my soul, carried with me for eternity. Because in that one moment, as the large house emptied of all living souls, leaving me alone, in the dead deafening silence, with twinges that had now become sharp pulsating rhythms of agony and pain, the realisation that I had to save my child from a future like this became a resounding mission.

The pain had become strong and persistent, as if I were being torn in half. At times through my life, I have lain in bed at night with my eyes closed, imagining how I would react if someone I loved was in mortal danger. 'You never know until it happens,' my mother had said with a laugh when I admitted this to her one day. I would lie there and imagine I would be strong enough to do the right thing and be brave enough to step up. But I had also worried I would be too timid, too faint-hearted. What if I was never heroic enough? I had no acts of heroism to speak of, nothing noble or brave that I had done in my life so far.

People say that a mothering instinct kicks in on giving birth, making you protect your child above everything else. One of our primordial centres is the amygdala, an evolutionary mechanism, a brain region that can generate fear and distrust of things that pose a danger, such as unfamiliar situations and places. The amygdala is our emotional learning centre, important for acquiring, storing and expressing cues related to fear and threat, and associated with strong emotions, including happiness, fear, anxiety and sadness. It is the centre of our threat response, receiving information straight from our senses. The fear and mistrust I had felt for so long, and the desire to protect my unborn child, all jerked into place at the same time as my body shuddered with pain.

Late nights are not safe in Delhi, least of all for young pregnant women in the throes of early labour pain and unsteady on their feet. How I managed to call a taxi and get myself to the hospital many miles away I will never know. 'Nothing comes without drama with her,' one of the sour-faced women in the family had said about me a few months previously. She would have been so pleased to be proven right.

The next few hours are very hazy in my memory. Sometimes we reconstruct memories, and often don't recognise ourselves in them. They become disjointed, like lost pieces of the puzzle that don't quite fit. The shocked look on my gynaecologist's face telling me how dilated I already was, the frantic phone call to my parents, and my mother's voice that immediately made me weep with relief and calm down, and the exhaustion and release of finally being in safe hands. Even as I felt so scared, I remember feeling secure for the first time in a long time.

I lay there alone in a hospital bed, drugged up, needles punctuating my veins, and the fluid interjecting and pausing the child in its imminent arrival into this world. It was too early, and she would have to wait. I understood her eagerness: she had some of me in her already.

The doctor was a woman, and I liked her. Her presence made

the clinically minimalist room seem like a warm cocoon, less threatening than the perfectly curated rooms I had been living in for the last couple of years or so. This was the kind of woman I could be if I had the opportunity. She asked me my thoughts about the current political situation, and asked me about myself, not merely as someone's wife or daughter-in-law, and I never wanted to leave. Suddenly it felt acceptable to express my opinions, which I had hidden for some time, kept buried and secret. 'Why do women have to hide their achievements and professional ambitions?' I asked her one day. She had told me her own story of a broken marriage, of male egos and frustrations within her career. 'The cross we have to bear as women,' she said. Sometimes it is only through listening to different stories, of hope and resilience, of struggles and strains, that we find resonance in our own experiences; only then can we see a light in the darkness, and we feel less alone. It was only when I looked back at that time in the hospital that I realised I was beginning to drown out some of the anxious nightmares in my head as I began to heal, and for the first time, there was a glint of possibility that maybe I could be okay as a mother. Maybe I wasn't completely broken yet.

I was only in week twenty-six of my pregnancy, which is extremely premature. There is an old wives' tale that pregnancy lasts for ten lunar months. This was derived from ancient Hindu literature, in which it was also considered that in the eighth month, the vital force was drawn from the mother to the child and back again repeatedly, so a seventh- or eighth-month child would never survive. Every pregnancy is of course different, but the general understanding is that the earlier your baby is born, the greater the risks to their health and survival. The risk of neonatal complications is lowest in pregnancies delivered between thirty-nine and forty-one weeks: the doctor wanted to try to hold the labour back until at least week thirty-six, if possible.

The terror of losing something that has become a non-negotiable part of their very being can make people go to extreme lengths. I found reserves of strength I did not know I had until then. I had the six to eight injections every day for the next nine weeks, until it was safer for the child to be born. On complete bed rest, but with no rest. The nurses would come regularly and insert this battery of injections in my buttocks every day, finding the fleshiest part where I would feel less pain, or spend hours looking for veins to transfer intravenous fluids: poking, prodding, jabbing. I imagined myself as a cocoon for the growing child, and sometimes as a lab rat, vacillating between feeling dehumanised and never more human. Twinges from the ghosts of those injections, some to delay pre-term labour and some to help the child's lungs mature, still come back every winter, when the weather is cold, reminding me of those days, and I am filled with sweet nostalgic aches.

For the next few weeks, time was measured in hours and minutes of keeping the baby alive inside me, nurturing and strengthening her, and my spirit healing and getting stronger with her. I had stopped spiralling, spinning, twisting tortuously; the terror and trepidation gradually rinsed out with the chemicals flooding my seams. There were times when loneliness would hit me, and I would crave fresh air. Then there were times when I would be reminded of the world outside the hospital room, and I never wanted to leave those four walls. Days drifted, seconds, minutes, hours, with no sense of passing time, besides a goalpost when the child inside me would be strong enough and I could finally let go of her and bring her into the world. Until then, I was a prisoner of my womb, yet I felt I had been set free. It is an absurd paradox, examined closely, because within this act, I was passive, with no agency, and no choice. But the mere act of stopping, merely lying on my back every day and focusing completely on being the vessel through which my child would emerge stronger, made me feel empowered.

External forces continued to conspire to stoke feelings of guilt and shame, however. My mother-in-law and her sisters would tell me stories of straightforward births when they came to visit. There was the daughter-in-law who gave birth on the exact date that she was supposed to, with minimal fuss, and was back to normal the very next day. The baby and mother were perfectly healthy. No complications. They stared at me as if I were an alien, as if I would contaminate their lives with my passion and oddities. They told the doctors and nurses that I was always too fragile, that I was too sensitive, not sturdy enough.

Every time they left I turned my head and cried, feeling like a failure again and convinced the unusual nature of my pregnancy was my fault: I had worked too hard, travelled by auto rickshaws and buses, not walked enough, walked too much, not eaten the right things, not rested enough, not fasted on the right days: the list went on. I was too sensitive and weak, which was why I had to stay in hospital. I cost so much money and was causing such inconvenience. I had been too stubborn, too modern, too rebellious. I had put the child's life in danger, a child that could be the male heir they so desperately wanted. A list of personal failures stacked up as notches on my bedpost.

As women have been through time, I had been deemed 'too much' or 'not enough'. The patriarchal traditional family structure can be both a barrier and a support for women's decision-making authority regarding sexual and reproductive health. But in this case, for the first time, this choice had been taken away from the family. Mothers-in-law in India possess a great amount of indirect patriarchal power over their daughters-in-law through their sons and husbands. Ambika Kohli in an article from 2016 discussing the reproductive agency of middle-class women in North India calls mothers-in-law 'benevolent patriarchs', where they are able to articulate power as love and care.[18] The power may be obscured by love but is no less powerful – or oppressive – than dominative power.[19] Often women accept this idea of benevolent patriarchy because it benefits them in terms of maintaining harmony and gaining social and economic capital in large joint families. And Indian feminist studies have shown how even though there might be an absence of overt forms of protest, it is not an 'absence of questioning inequality'.[20] Women were still challenging patriarchal structures to an extent through covert forms of resistance, especially patriarchal authority over their own bodies and reproductive decisions. Resistance – and feminist empowerment – within these social and cultural confines is often silent but silence, or quiet resistance, can be a source of great strength too. Ripples can be formed by a mere whisper or suggestion of defiance. By choosing to come to the hospital and stay here, where I and my child felt safe, I had also exercised control and agency over my own body without negotiation, compromise or strategic manoeuvring. But by not conforming to feminine ideals within the gender hierarchy, by actively voicing what I wanted for myself, I had publicly asserted myself as operating outside the norm of middle-class values. Any cultural capital I might have accumulated in the last two years through my passivity, or any symbolic capital that I might have accrued through my silence, had been quickly swept away in this tidal wave of self-protection. Being a self-sacrificing mother is central to Indian middle-class values. How would I be a good mother when I could not even be an ideal wife or daughter-in-law?

At times the baby would stop breathing. Then she'd stop growing. Inches were measured, her thumping heartbeat slowed down, panic ensued, then another crisis was averted somehow. She was plucky, for sure, fighting for her life, her right to exist, and I was fighting for her, with all my will.

•

The first month of my pregnancy had ended with blood. Sometimes even just a few spots of blood, striking in their crimson hues, can be a warning. Blood is life and death. Treachery and murder. It joins us across generations, connects us across time and space. Blood coursing through our veins and arteries, carrying memories and traces of our existence round and round. Bleeding in men is heroic, hard-earned through courage and combat. In women, bleeding is often a normal, monthly occurrence, and it is taboo, stigmatised, silent and hidden. When women bleed, it can signal disappointment for some, an end to their own expectations and hopes. Conversely it can mean relief for others, because that narrative is not part of their dreams. At other times, such as in pregnancy, the same bleeding can be a sign of a breakdown, an insufficiency to sustain life. The moment those spots appeared, I felt a primal desire to protect my unborn child, stronger than any protective instinct I'd ever had, a deeper desire forcing through from my gut, bursting open with the primordial rhythm of a heartbeat that I had not yet even heard.

I used to be fascinated by palmistry, the notion that our life paths had already been pre-determined in the lines on our hands. The crinkles on the sides, and the faint lines marking every progeny, the genetic code interspersed with the stars aligning to bring new life. I had been told that I would have five children and I had screamed with laughter, much to the disgust of the old man who was reading my hand outside the temple when I was just a teenager. 'You will have five perfectly healthy children,' he had said sagely in Hindi, blessing me with a mark on my forehead, 'and you will be a mother.' 'This is all such quackery. I don't even want one,' I had thought to myself, as I giggled with my friend, co-conspirators against patriarchy. I had forgotten about it immediately, lost in my big dreams of conquering the world. Motherhood used to have no place in those dreams, until my dreams for my unborn child started to merge with my own, connecting seamlessly across my blood and hers, our hearts beating as one.

•

The idealisation of motherhood is seen even in childbirth, where women are discouraged from using drugs. It is supposed to be painful: being able to bear pain is the sign of good mothering instincts. There is also a long tradition of encouraging women to practise mindful techniques, a sort of guided autonomy method where women give birth with ease, without any pain or hassle, very quickly and with minimum fuss. These women were the true mothers, the ones who were up and cooking for the husband and the family in the hour after they gave birth, which they often did smiling. Never grimacing, never screaming, never incapacitated after the ordeal of childbirth. This was the narrative I so often heard during this time. Childbirth is easy and is supposed to be. This was the story I was told.

Even scientific language around reproduction remains rooted in patriarchy, and in racialised hierarchies. Birth choices remain overtly politicised, and women's bodies remain public property, with everyone having the right to comment on and make decisions about them.

In Paula Michael's *Lamaze: An International History*, [21] we see that the history of natural childbirth is riddled with somewhat contradictory ideas about conscious control and animal instinct, where the ideas of physiological pain were taken from experiments on other animals and then used to develop cognitive training for women for them to become more like animals.

In many cultures, natural childbirth is still seen as primitive, ugly and an inconvenience, and rich women don't have to endure it. The upper echelons of society can choose and plan to have a scheduled delivery, one that is considered less violent, with more control. The term 'too posh to push' originated as a way to denigrate women if they had epidurals or caesareans, which also alluded to the criticism of middle-class, educated women having careers and consequently treating childbirth and families as a burden. Underlying these concerns were eugenic beliefs about race degeneration, with a falling stock of healthy and 'superior' populations. The eugenicists were concerned that the poorer and less healthy sections of society were having larger families while the middle-class women were shirking reproductive duties due to feminism and fear of childbirth. The idea of 'natural childbirth', on the other hand, emerged as a conservative reaction to women's emancipation and feminism, and was rooted in the idea that nature intended women to give birth easily and without a fuss. It became a motto for the health reformers who held similar eugenic views about enticing women of 'superior stock' back into the home. As eugenicist and health reformer Caleb Saleeby said in 1909: 'The history of nations is determined not on the battlefield but in the nursery, and the battalions which give lasting victory are the battalions of babies. The politics of the future will be domestic.'[22]

Valorization of pain, and the ability to feel everything, without any medical pain relief, was encouraged, so that mothers would be prepared for what lay ahead in raising their children. As the obstetrician Grantly Dick-Read wrote, women should be reminded that childbirth 'is nature's first hard lesson in the two greatest assets of good motherhood. Children will always mean hard work and self-control. Tell her the truth: motherhood is not fun, it is not a hobby.' The underlying message was that it is more natural to embrace the pain, be a servant to the baby, and emulate working-class women or women of colour, both groups not considered 'posh' but so often in servitude of others, who gave birth like animals, easily and quickly, while taking a 'break from scrubbing the floor or herding goats to slip a baby out like a bar of soap' and who were believed to have a greater capacity for tolerating pain.[23] These ideas had, of course, first emerged in England during the colonial invasion of the Americas, with reports that the unfamiliar indigenous bodies reproduced differently, that they could have quick and painless labour alone in the woods, get dressed immediately and 'trudge home' with the infant, thereby mimicking the reproductive behaviour of other animals, and not that of the English women whose own childbirth was observed in domesticity and revered.[24] These accounts also established the ideas – some of which continue to persist in modern medical healthcare and manifest in the form of biases – that women of colour experienced pain differently, and that they were not really women at all, since women had been 'blessed' by pain during childbirth by the 'curse of Eve'.

Dick-Read, whose book *Natural Childbirth* had really been prompted by concerns about the decline in middle-class fertility, proposed that the answer was a more civilised birth in a very dignified manner, with docility and submission to the attending physicians, and acceptance that motherhood was a sacred calling where the spirit of motherhood could only be awakened by the first cry of the baby.[25] In doing so, the idea was to appeal to notions of social responsibility in middle-class women, to remind them that a woman's true purpose and vital economic role was to produce babies, their bodies were made to give birth, to do so while fully conscious and trust their innate wisdom.

Fernand Lamaze, who was inspired by strategies he observed in Russia, also did not believe in pain relief during childbirth, though his basic philosophy was that pain was not an inevitable accompaniment to labour and primarily existed due to conditioned reflexes that were acquired and temporary. He encouraged women to undergo perinatal preparation through the psychoprophylactic method using a combination of breathing and relaxation techniques so that they could stay conscious and own their pain during childbirth. Women were told that if they prepared well, they could learn to re-programme these reflexes and create new and positive ones where they could eradicate the perception of pain.[26] This created a whole generation of guilty women who blamed themselves if they felt pain during childbirth, blamed themselves for not being natural, intuitive mothers, for not having prepared very well. So we see that while a woman does not have true autonomy when giving birth, whether she chooses pain relief or not, she is also held accountable for whatever happens to her during pregnancy and childbirth, and for even whether she feels pain or not. Responsibility *sans* choice.

There is also a suggestion that by undergoing a C-section, as opposed to a 'natural' vaginal delivery, women might also be endangering the possibility of any subsequent children, even though a meta-analysis shows that these effects are small and casual association cannot be ruled out.[27] According to a July 2020 study by Penn State

College of Medicine researchers, who followed more than 2,000 women for three years after they delivered their first child, women who delivered their first child by C-section were less likely to conceive a second child than those who delivered vaginally, despite being just as likely to plan a subsequent pregnancy. The researchers recommended that 'it is important that women who elect to have a C-section know that there is a chance they may have difficulty conceiving in the future'.[28] When women are making childbirth decisions, this is not the sort of information that is widely available to them; they do not have scientific data and facts at their disposal to understand the effect of these decisions on their subsequent fertility and their bodies, but they are culpable for the consequences. Of course, not every woman really has a choice in the nature of childbirth, but the language used in many of these studies is patriarchal, laying the blame on women's shoulders for these 'choices' they make.

This narrative around the ease with which mothers can give birth if they choose to also reinforces the myth around the primacy of a maternal bond, the notion that women who birthed more 'naturally' had a stronger bond than those who had delivered through C-section. A study by Yale School of Medicine recruited two groups of parents from postpartum wards. One group of twelve mothers had caesarean sections and the other delivered naturally (vaginally). All women were interviewed and given brain scans two to three weeks after giving birth. During the brain scans, parents listened to recordings of their own baby's cry during the discomfort of a diaper change. The researchers then conducted interviews to assess the mothers' moods as well as their thoughts and parenting. The team found that compared to mothers who delivered by caesarean section, those who delivered vaginally had greater activity in certain brain regions in response to their own baby's cry as measured by fMRI. The vaginal delivery is supposed to 'prime' the parental brain by producing more oxytocin, a hormone linked to emotional connections, while C-sections may alter these neurohormonal factors and increase the risk of problematic bonding, the study claimed.[29] However, other research refutes this idea and has since shown that there are no specific determinants of maternal bond, but that it unfolds over days, weeks, months after a child's birth, influenced by cultural and social factors, and levels of stress and social support that impact the mother's mental well-being. Miriam Spinner at McMaster University in Canada proposed that mothering is not a specific instinct or a pre-determined behavioural pattern, but instead a set of behaviours and feelings that manifest only under specific circumstances.[30] Nevertheless, the pressure for this maternal oneness, of feeling one with your own child from the moment one lays eyes on them, or even before they are born, is an idealised fantasy that women live by. Any deviance from this conjectural norm leads to self-reproach, guilt, shame. If only we had done something else; if only we hadn't done what we did.

•

The day before my scheduled caesarean section, my mother-in-law found out the sex of the baby. I had hidden it from her for a while, fearing the reaction. I could see from her face how disappointed and crestfallen she was. I was a let-down. I had failed her again; there was going to be no male heir. 'Never mind. It will be a boy next time,' she had said dejectedly as I lay there on the hospital bed, saddled with tubes and my body riddled with pain, fighting a long fight to keep my child − her first grandchild − alive.

During the Hindu wedding ceremony, the couple take a vow to

reproduce a male heir, and the woman is bestowed with blessings to create new life. In Hinduism, religious texts like the Vedas and *Upanishads*, epic poems such as *Ramayana* and *Mahabharata* and social commentaries such as Kautilya's *Arthasastra* have reinforced the belief that childlessness is a curse. Hindus believe that a child – specifically a male child – is needed to secure their rebirth. Only a male heir can light the funeral pyre and complete the funerary rites.

On the birth of a child, a boy is treated differently to a girl. Jatakarma is a sanskara performed at the birth of a male child. The father of the newborn baby performs a yagna and whispers in the baby's ear 'Your secret name is Ved' and blesses him:

> Oh son! You have been born from my limbs, your heart has been created from my heart, thus by name you are my soul. Oh my son, may you live for a hundred years.

As one of three sisters, I'd of course grown up knowing this, hearing that even though my mother had given birth to three children after struggling to conceive for the first six years of marriage, it was not a satisfactory culmination of her womanly duties: she had not produced a male heir who would look after my parents in their old age and secure their release from the eternal cycle of life and death. Sons bring moksha (liberation from the cycle of birth and rebirth; ultimate salvation) to deceased parents. Sons light the funeral pyre; take their parents' ashes to the holy River Ganga for moksha (locally called gati: a short form of the Hindi word sadgati – liberation of the soul). Sons organise mortuary feasts upon their parents' death. A male child is crucial to sustain the sense of kinship and ancestral connections and community, a chain without which a carefully constructed social and cultural establishment can crumble and fall apart. The desire for sons shapes so much of the society's attitudes around fertility and contraception.

And just like this, with a few words, women can enable and bolster the patriarchy. Here she was: a woman, like me. She was a mother, and I was going to be one. Even though she could have easily reached out across the patriarchal divide and held my hand, she chose not to. For the first time, I began to see, stripped of blinkered optimism and false hope, that my unborn daughter and I did not have a future here, that I could not save her only to offer her this: a life as a second choice.

And now here she was, the most beautiful baby I had ever laid eyes on. The first thing I asked when I surfaced groggily from the anaesthetic was, 'Does she have all ten fingers and ten toes?' and I fell back asleep contentedly on hearing that she did. She was alive and I was exhausted. I cannot remember and I doubt I even knew then why her digits mattered so much to me, yet this is now a quirky story I repeat to M every year on her birthday. I reminisce and she laughs indulgently; these peculiar rituals that we create to reach across the divide, these oddities that become part of the family lore.

The first time we gazed at each other, I knew that I already knew her, and hoped that she would love knowing me. As I whispered quietly to her, 'I will always take care of you,' all the other voices in my head were quiet for once.

> The contents of the universe
> Mother I am
> Identical
> With infinite Maternity
> Indivisible

Acutely
I am absorbed
Into
The was—is—ever—shall—be
Of cosmic reproductivity

Mina Loy, 'Parturition'[31]

•

I had not even recovered from the C-section, my body still broken from late night feeds and lack of sleep, but as I lay in bed breast-feeding, caressing those delicate fingers and toes, brown digits and tiny fingernails, the dam burst.

'She is all mine,' I thought, for the hundredth time. 'Look, we are here now, and I will always look after you,' I promised her once again as I looked around the yellow and white nursery that I had not finished painting properly before I went into the hospital all those weeks ago. No pink and blue, I had insisted, laying down firmly for the very first time an idea of how my mothering would be. 'Why yellow?' they had all wondered, both silently and aloud. 'Why yellow, and not a nicer colour?' Yellow is the colour of the sun, and of power, of optimism and joy, and I needed it. Like the Tuscan sun, and honey, buttercups and bumblebees, things that soar and inhabit my dreams. You will be like honey, and sway like the daffodils, 'Tossing their heads in sprightly dance'.[32] One day we will go to Tuscany and sit amongst the vines and the sunflowers. 'She needs this,' I had said hesitatingly to myself. To them, I had just nodded silently. 'I like it,' I had murmured, when they were out of sight.

Red, blood red, appeared again, this time as a cascade in all its fury. As I struggled with nightly shifts, and breastfeeding, I passed huge bright red clots as big as my fist. It seemed a tsunami, intent on destroying everything, with all the tiny pieces of my life that I had been somehow holding together with my hands, clumsily but tenderly, being swept away. My hands were tired, but I couldn't let go. Not just yet.

As I was rushed to the hospital, fading in and out of consciousness, I wanted to hold on tight to that tiny bundle. 'I am all she has,' I wanted to scream. I remember the long nightdress soaked in blood by the time I reached hospital, the wetness between my thighs, and not much after. Here we were, both back again so soon at the hospital. I was drifting in and out of life, and I do not remember much else. I do remember thinking, 'I can't go so soon; she needs me to be here,' and with that thought I knew that I was a mother. I didn't even get a chance to say goodbye to her while I fought as hard as I could to keep my hold on this mortal world, the world I had so often thought about leaving during my darkest times.

It is strange what being a mother does to us, making us completely responsible for a life that is not ours. Our children become our lifeline, and as we hold on to that love, it endows us with a mysterious belief in our value and our place in this world. So we fought again, for me, for us, I and my newborn daughter, alone in the hospital nursery, already separated from her mother. When I came around, a couple of days had passed. I had wandered between insentience and consciousness, I was told, and mysteriously had clutched on to the steep slippery slope of life with brittle nails, resolutely and determinedly. All through those hours and days, I held on to delicate fingers, their softest touch robust and insistent, holding me back firmly, keeping me from slipping away. I had woken up, but what seemed posthumously; it felt like I had knocked on death's doors and been sent back. I wondered then what my purpose was. I had not seen any bright light, only dark tunnels with smooth slippery walls. I have always been afraid of the dark, but for some reason that day I was afraid of what lay outside this cavern, how it would be, returning back to life. Of course, these are things that seem so significant in retrospect. At the time, all that was evident was the unsettling nature of hanging between life and death, in that moment of stasis, living in that timeless space.

Trauma lives on in our bodies. Tissues, cells, muscles have a memory of their own, remembering the lives we have lived. In the years since my first childbirth, I have focused on what came after, and never looked back. It has taken me more than twenty years to realise that I carried that trauma in my body, the pain and the anguish of almost losing my life and leaving my baby girl, and trying to hold on, reaching the brink of death and returning to life.

When we emerge back into life after near death, it is not always the same life as it was before. Some things shift, some become clearer, some move further away. Measures of success are altered, mapped out by no other yardstick than our own, and our self-worth becomes sharper and more iridescent. It might not happen immediately; it didn't for me. But something immutable did happen, as if I had grown into my own skin while shedding the old one. A metamorphosis, but with no perceived change of state. I had lived before that moment, but was I really doing it right? I had woken up, literally and metaphorically. I have since read 'The Epic of Gilgamesh' many times, a poem I had first read as a teenager. Gilgamesh explores the nature and meaning of being human, asking the questions that seem as pertinent today as in the author's times: what is the meaning of life, am I doing this right, and how do we cope with life's brevity and loss? In the poem, Gilgamesh is fleeing on an eternal quest. The scorpions grant him entry to a tunnel that the sun passes through each night, but to be able to get through it, he must outpace the sun. He starts out uncertain in the utter, enfolding darkness, and then runs for hours and hours. Only his steps matter to him, he is alone, nothing to be seen behind or ahead of him. He emerges successful, by a thin thread, into a garden, dazzled by the jewel-laden trees, all purple and red, sparkling.

> A carnelian tree was in fruit,
> hung with bunches of grapes, lovely to look on.
> A lapis lazuli tree bore foliage,
> in full fruit and gorgeous to gaze on.[33]

This transformation from the bleak darkness to a colourful paradise, the reward after being chased by our own souls, and chasing the unthinkable, makes it all worth it in the end.

•

I was given five units of blood to replace what I had lost; the human body has only about eight or nine units, I believe, although this figure varies. Humans are not built entirely on a template; although we are in a lot of ways, in many others we have nuances and quirks. It is easy to forget this. One unit of blood is approximately 525 ml, which is roughly the equivalent of one pint. So I lost more than five pints, which sometimes makes it easier for me to remember. The cost of a pint varies depending on where you are in the world, if we are talking about beer. When it comes to blood, who can say what the value of one pint is? It depends on who we are, I suppose. It depends on who is evaluating, and whom the blood belongs to.

How much money should be spent to save someone who is dying? This kind of cost–benefit analysis is not merely a financial issue, but also an ethical issue. Economists and lawyers have been doing complex calculations to estimate the value of a human life for years; statistically framing and managing risk to figure out what outcomes are worth a potential death, and how to compensate people for wrongful deaths, for example. The current UK method to value a human life is the 'value of a prevented fatality' (VPF).¶ This gives a single value for all ages, implying an illogical, much greater value of a future day for an aged person than for a young person. Researchers at the University of Bristol propose that the VPF is flawed and should be replaced by an alternative methodology, namely the Judgement or J-value, an empirically validated measure which provides an objective balance between the amount spent on a safety measure and the life expectancy it restores.[34] It allows for the difference in benefit to people of varying age rather than giving one single value for all people. The J-value has been used to assess responses to large nuclear accidents such as Chernobyl and Fukushima. As of 2011, the US Environmental Protection Agency, for instance, set the value of a human life at $9.1 million.[35] Meanwhile, the Food and Drug Administration put it at $7.9 million – and the Department of Transportation figure was around $6 million.[36] Thomas Schelling, a Nobel Prize-winning economics professor at Harvard, reframed this question philosophically and called this the 'Value of Statistical Life.'[37] We cannot put a value on life, Schelling says, but we can find out how much money people will pay to reduce their own risk of death. The VSL is supposed to be an equitable mechanism through which every life is treated equally no matter what a person's status in society may be, no

¶ Where a safety measure is designed to reduce the risk of death there will always be a question of whether it is worthwhile, whether on economic grounds, or some other. The VPF is a technical term used for cost–benefit analysis for safety decision-making.

matter what social, economic or symbolic capital they hold. All lives are equal, but are some lives more equal than others? Justin Landy, a doctoral student at the University of Pennsylvania, explores how we compare the relative values of human lives – and why we are able to do so at all, despite the frequently expressed sentiment that all lives have equal worth. Doctors and rescue workers regularly choose to save some lives over others in emergency situations, such as a mother's life over a baby's life, and organisations routinely apportion money to programmes for the young versus the old – say, research on attention-deficit disorder versus Alzheimer's. How does one know which is the right answer?

The question gets even tougher when we start thinking about what a future life would be worth. Is a life in India, amongst the poverty and a billion people, the same value as in the Western world? Is a woman's life allocated the same value as that of a man, especially in a society where female infanticide is one of the highest in the world? Mothers' lives are not always given a high value, either. According to the latest UN global estimates, 303,000 women a year die in childbirth, or as a result of complications arising from preg-nancy.[38] This equates to about 830 women dying each day – roughly one every two minutes. Bleeding and infections after childbirth are understood to be the major causes, and the majority of these deaths happen in developing countries. The maternal mortality ratio in the world's least developed countries stands at 436 deaths for every 100,000 live births, which is in stark contrast to the corresponding number – just twelve – in wealthy countries. India alone accounts for one third of global deaths.

I could have been one of these statistics, a data point so easily forgotten. So, as I grappled with life and death then, who is to say that I was worth saving?

•

In 2009, when this little baby had reached twelve years old, I visited an installation of a giant shipping container in Tate Modern, resembling a cavernous black hole, the work of Polish artist Miroslaw Balka. Titled 'How It Is', the installation was pitch black, alluding to the biblical Plague of Darkness; black holes in space; images of hell. As I felt my way around the container, slowly creeping along the walls, sitting with panic and discomfort, for the first time since being in hospital on the verge of death I came close to what I had felt that day, in that moment of waking up again. There was a light at the end of the tunnel and all I could do was to focus completely on it. One hundred per cent. There was just no other way.

I remember reading Samuel Beckett's *How It Is* after which this installation was named, and realising that even a stark and sparse space, a wholly minimal world with violent encounters, breathless with no pauses or punctuations, can evoke the most intense feelings of sublime love. He says in his 1953 novel *The Unnamable*: '. . . you must go on. I can't go on. I'll go on.' And so we do. And so I did.

Our first experiences can shape our lives. Giving birth to my daughter felt like first love, my only love. Not planned but wanted all along. Terror and elation. Turmoil and exhilaration. We were in this together and motherhood felt like a war. Me and her against the world. Tenderness hand in hand with resolution. This was a model of motherhood I could understand. Mothering would be my biggest gesture of defiance.

III.

HOBSON'S CHOICE

But the Hebrew word, the word *timshel* – 'Thou mayest' –
that gives a choice. It might be the most important word in
the world. That says the way is open. That throws it right
back on a man. For if 'Thou mayest' – it is also true that
'Thou mayest not'. Don't you see?

— John Steinbeck, *East of Eden*[1]

MEMORIES CAN COME TUMBLING BY without any warning
. Sometimes a memory can feel like home; sometimes it can
be a heartless friend, reminding you what you have mislaid along
the way.

I have this memory of me sitting on the floor of the office,
incapacitated, frozen in time, a tiny particle of dust suspended in the
ether of sunshine that came flooding in. Riffling through my medical
papers and records and coming across that paper, which I thought
he had ripped apart and thrown away when we moved. That paper
still sitting innocently and inconspicuously in the big red cardboard
folder. The paper that caused a paper cut and raked up all the

memories of a date more than ten years before almost to the day. The memory of how I still fell apart as I read the words typed out across the top of the page in 11-point Arial font: 'Pregnancy Terminated'. The memory of crying for something that once could have been and never was.

The pain we know we once carried, often forgotten, often discarded carelessly in exchange for joy, is often just right there waiting to spring its head up at the gentlest nudge. I am thrown back there, back to the moment in the Lake District, when I knew that my body was trying to tell me something.

I had never been to the Lakes, but I had always dreamt of them, so picturesque, fertile, lush in the Wordsworth poems that I lapped up at school. I roamed the farmers' markets, relishing my newly discovered fondness for milky cheese and crispy crackers. We negotiated and compromised effortlessly and seamlessly, hoping, trying, aiming to please each other. I didn't like walking and climbing that much, while that's all he had known since he was knee-high. I would rather spend hours in second-hand bookshops smelling the musty pages filled with words and wisdom, sit in cafes reading the newspaper with coffee and cake.

The sickness hits me like a giant wave on our last day there. As we drive through the snaky mountain passes, I feel nauseous. The mountains loom, and the road curls around the pass, and my insides twist and gurn, whipping into a rising tide of acrid bile.

'I always get travel sick,' I tell him, embarrassed, as I throw up on the side of the road.

We have not been together for long. I have only known him for a few months and as we drive on, I feel huge swells of nausea so bad that we have to keep stopping. Shame and humiliation swirls along with the nausea and creates a more potent concoction of mortification. Our bodies can get familiar but we still hide away the nuts and bolts, the quirks and flaws. The utter beauty and calm of these mountain passes feels treacherous and threatening, looming over dangerously, bringing news of something unwelcome and menacing. It is a stomach bug, I think, and it will just go away. I turn around, ill at ease that he has to see the dregs of my life so soon, seeing me buckled up on the side of the road, heaving with my hair matted. A flock of sheep look on curiously, heads cocked to one side, waiting patiently. I breathe in the fresh air. I am going to miss this silence. Sometimes we need to escape the noise outside to escape the constant whirring of our own mind.

'Just that awful pasty that you ate,' he says, patting my back. That must be it, of course. The excess of the weekend taking its toll. A heavenly weekend where we had connected and discovered each other, and my relationship with nature had been restored after a childhood of growing up in busy concrete urban islands, where I had only seen mountains and oceans in my imagination. There were occasional stares – heads turned, puzzled eyebrows – on seeing a short brown woman with a tall white man, hand in hand, a picture perhaps asynchronous with their own mental models of the world. But, I, for once – just for a couple of days – had existed in synchronicity with the present, no thoughts of future and past tugging at me, just a kaleidoscopic pattern of green, brown and blue from the landscape around us blinding my neural pathways.

I went back to my work, my mind occupied once again with data, and maps, and words, but every morning a wave of nausea hit me even before I had opened my eyes, wrenching me from the inside. It reminded me of that forgotten memory from a few years before when I had refused to accept the inevitable. Like then, the nausea refused to go away, yanking, tugging, twisting my mind and my body. For days on end, I barely managed to nibble on a dry cracker, sitting with my head leaning over on my desk in the small office that I shared with three other graduate students, the smells and sounds cracking open my skull. The mental juggling of trying to seem routine and commonplace while your insides are churning, grunting with the effort, can be exhausting.

It was the summer break, so only a few of us were hanging around – those graduate students who were too poor and too time-starved to travel thousands of miles back home. We walked around the silent corridors, soaking in the quiet solitude, talking to ourselves as we worked. The days were becoming longer, and my time with my research shorter. Time to contemplate 'what if?' was a privilege and a luxury. We all run and hide away from something that seems terrifying, even when it is inevitable that it will catch up with us. Sometimes it is too late to run away. There is no other way but to face the monsters in our dreams head on, even if they are the stuff of which nightmares are made.

The purchase of the pregnancy test in a chemist diminishes any claim to privacy that a woman would require or feel entitled to. In picking up the test, and taking it to the check-out till, there is a sense of trepidation; sometimes it's an act of secrecy, of guilt depending on the person's circumstances. An act that says loudly to the world 'I hope to be pregnant', and sometimes 'I am so scared that I might be pregnant', and in either case, there is nothing that blurs the boundary between the public and the private so explicitly. The packaging of these pregnancy tests is far from discreet, with huge lettering and bright colours that scream from a distance what they really are. Additionally, although the speed and the early testing that so many of these tests promote can empower women to look for options in case it is a result that they do not desire, it also can give misleading hope if it is a false positive or ends in an early miscarriage.

The extra miles between the shop and my room in my shared accommodation seemed very long that day. I had been living there, saving money, finishing my PhD, while my daughter lived back in India with my parents. Guilt is part and parcel of motherhood, I had long realised: written into the code. Every step we take, every decision we make for ourselves and for our children is uncertain and faltering even in the surest and most assured of us all. How do we know that this is the right thing to do for them, and how do we know that this will not come to haunt us years later, scarring them emotionally and psychologically? We brought them into this world against their will as they screamed their protestations blue and purple, and so the weight of this responsibility makes every step we take tentative and fraught with guilt.

Even though deep down it was clear that this separation from my daughter would be temporary, the pain and the grief of extending that umbilical cord across four thousand miles tortured my soul every day and night. There was hardly a day when I didn't cry for her, hardly a night when I didn't dream of her. I was too inured in the ways of motherhood to think any other way. Every step closer to completing my research was one step closer to giving her a good life. That was the mantra I repeated to myself even when things seemed insurmountable.

Those many long miles to my room in the student digs seemed impossible that evening: it was late, and I had, as usual, skipped most of the meals, due to a combination of nausea and work. So I walked over to his, knowing that he would be at football and the house would be empty. I had a key to his semi-detached house, along a row of similar houses all brick-fronted and nondescript. I always liked to imagine the lives – secrets and stories – lurking behind those thick twitching curtains. I folded myself heavily on the bed, wearily, knowing that I would have to get up soon, a moment of inevitability looming over me from all nooks of the room.

'How could you have been so stupid?' I remember screaming quietly in the menacing silence of the empty house, accusing myself, fists clenched, a punch in the gut. Blame and accusation used to sit lightly on my shoulders at one point. I had thought that I was past it, but evidently not. The Clearblue packet sat there on the side of the bed, questioning, probing, nudging me into action. Sometimes you just have to jump off the cliff with your eyes closed, because there is nowhere else to go.

The bathroom was one of the best rooms in the house, freshly remodelled. How often we get so attached to our walls, floors, the bricks and mortar, assigning meaning and emotions to these physically tangible materialities around us. Houses become homes as we create them in our personalities, forming attachments and setting down roots. We had softened the impersonal with our own peculiar aesthetics: plants, succulents and paintings for me; candles and soaps for him. He loved baths and candles, and it was something that first made me smile with fondness at how little he cared about prescribed gender norms. The bathroom now smelled of ferns and Imperial Leather soap, and lavender and jasmine, my spiky cactus sitting next to his razors.

The shininess of the room hurt my eyes that day. I dragged my bare feet across the tiled floor as if walking across burning coals. In Indian mythology, women had to walk through fire to prove their purity. Sita did. Draupadi also did after the end of the Mahabharata War, that had continued for thirteen years, to prove her virginity and her adherence to her dharma. Always the women. Being judged, assessed, evaluated, examined, punished. Never the men. Men somehow have been excused by history for any misdemeanours, being allowed to play the cad, the playboy, the 'ladies' man'.

I slowly ripped the plastic off the packet. So much waste, I thought, as my fingers seemed stiff and unwilling to cajole the tiniest rip into a tear. Numbness simmered like a volatile fluid in a dormant volcano. When we see adverts for pregnancy tests, it is always the women who are celebrating a positive result. But what about those for whom this test brings a whole cornucopia of mingled emotions? Sadness, confusion, uncertainty, indecision, insecurity. Those who know it is not the right time. Those who fear for the safety of their unborn child and for their own lives. Those who live in uncertain climates, in poverty, with no food or shelter, who cannot afford to bring another mouth to feed into the world. Those who carry their own monsters and addictions and know that they would never be a stable parent. Reproductive choice and freedom are not limited to choosing the right contraception or the right technology for monitoring fertility cycles, but also the freedom and choice to make these decisions – very difficult choices, never sureties but only improbabilities, mired with mixed emotions, hormones wreaking havoc on body and mind.

The seconds ticked away. Eventually the words appeared. It was unmistakable. The line had been drawn and I had nowhere else to look. I remember staring at it for a long time, willing for it to go away. Later, I would have given anything for that positive result, anything to see it again. Over the years, I have imagined that moment so many times, trying to manifest it by the sheer force of my will and desire, but it never happened again. Not in the same unmistakable way. But this was not part of the plan then. There could not be any diversions in my route from A to B. I was already a mother.

That space was already taken, and I could not think beyond that. The exhaustion of being a single mother had become imprinted into my weary bones, into the code of my being itself, carrying the weight of motherhood alone for so long. The weariness seemed unsurmountable, and I ran away with fear, afraid of derailing everything I had slowly stacked up in some sort of congruence.

It was not the right time. Not for me, and not for him. We talked about it a few times in the following days. After many awkward words and conversations, second-guessing what the other wanted, pauses and uncomfortable silences, I – we – took a decision that we thought best.

I had cried, and he had hugged me. Of course he would be there no matter what decision I made, he had promised honourably. But I didn't want him to only be there because of honour. I didn't want this just to be my decision. I wanted love. Complete and utter devotion. 'Honour can only take us so far,' I remember telling him. We both tiptoed around our own feelings, scared of saying them out loud, of acknowledging that this meant more than we had expected and accepted, and fearful of the other person not feeling exactly the same.

Our natural shyness is at times a barrier to honest conversation, the awkwardness of youth terrified of exposing our flawed selves. We shy away from saying what we really feel and think, instead assuming the worst of the other person, scared of not being loved and accepted. I put up walls, and so did he, both determined to protect ourselves from any heartbreak and pain in the future. We circumnavigated the truth, shirking saying what we felt; we circled around each other in a ritual of who cared the least. Our impenetrable shells kept our centres – soft, craving love and acceptance, but also so vulnerable and fragile – safe from any hard knocks. I didn't tell him that I could want this, that I probably wanted it, that I didn't want to be the one to choose. He told me many years later that he wanted it to be my choice, for my own body, but had wished that I had chosen the other door. We both waited for the other one to commit, and say out loud what we wanted. But life does not work like this. We were still far too young to understand.

•

Today, as we have wider and more open political and social discussions around women's right to abortion, I am still mystified by the persistent silence around termination. There is still so much stigma around the actual act of abortion in real life.[2] Women's bodies are politicised, of course. They are heavily policed and censured. To be against the right to choose an abortion is presented as a moral decision. Women don't seem to have a moral agency in these discussions, with the right to our own bodies denied, autonomy hindered by emotional manipulation, any rational decision skewed by pre-formed moral views enforced by society at large. When wombs are fetishised as existing to serve society, the framework within which women are making these choices is not an unbiased one. The information that is provided to the women making these choices is not unbiased either. Many protestations against abortions are binary: between good and evil, between right and wrong. Yet the landscape of these choices is not black and white, and never has been.

We refuse to allow for the grey spaces in between. In order for this discourse to be a bias-free framework, women need to be given information that reinforces autonomous decision-making, rather than encouraging guilt and silence to weigh heavily on their shoulders, swaying them towards what they feel they should do. The right to choose is an ethical one, and making this highly polarised debate into one only about morality is to diminish a woman's integrity and agency. Even if a woman is allowed to choose, the legal and political frameworks to empower and support her are often missing. Agency is not just the ability to choose, but also the ability to exercise that choice freely and openly, without judgement and stigma. Women choosing to have a baby, or women choosing not to, is not as binary a choice as it sounds, either. When societies regulate this decision, women are being given the message that they cannot be trusted to make this moral judgement on their own. Women can say 'this is my head', 'this is my hand', but they are never able to unilaterally say 'this is my womb'.

Even though I had the choice and I could exercise that choice, my choices were never mine alone to make; there were factors of expectations, constraints and regulations around me both socially and medically.

I tried to rationalise my sorrow. I had been so sure of my decision; so unsure of the hormonal swing that followed. So much of the discussion around termination is also framed around regret: grief, repentance, guilt. Yes, there can be all of that, but there might also be none. And sorrow and grief do not have to be a consequence of regret alone. They can stand independently of each other. Even when we make the best decisions possible for ourselves, we can always have regret. If only things had been different, of course the choices might have been different. But then at other times a choice might only bring us relief because it releases us from misery. A twinge of loss, a momentary nostalgia for something we once had and lost, an imagined vision of something that could have been, does not always mean a lifelong shadow of despair. Once again, the black and white narrative overshadows the grey areas where relief and regret can co-exist.

A study in 2015 showed that more than 95 per cent of women surveyed were confident that they made the right decision in having an abortion.[3] One of the largest five-year longitudinal studies in the United States to date on the topic, published recently in the journal *Social Science and Medicine*, found that most women described the emotion they experienced post-abortion as relief, not regret. Much of the regret and guilt were found to be exacerbated by their personal and social environments and the abortion-related stigma that they perceived or directly encountered.[4] A 2017 study published in *JAMA Psychiatry* found that 'eight days after seeking an abortion, women who were denied an abortion reported significantly more anxiety symptoms and lower self-esteem and life satisfaction' than women who received an abortion.[5] Once again, the debate becomes about relief and regret, a binary and polarised rhetoric. Instead, we need to reframe this discussion to be about agency and choice, and the right of the woman to choose for herself and to say 'this is my womb alone', giving women the frameworks and mechanisms which enable her to choose rationally and to exercise that choice.

There is a flip side to this abortion debate. Throughout the world, female foetuses are being aborted to feed the desire for a male baby at a staggering rate,★ creating an inherent imbalance in society, and making it more likely that violence and discrimination against women will increase. A large-scale analysis of birth data between 1970 and 2017 from 202 countries by Fengqing Chao of the National University of Singapore and her colleagues suggested that sex-selective abortions have led to at least 23 million fewer girls being

★ From Joni Seager's *Women's Atlas*: In 1995, male births significantly outnumbered female births in countries like China, India, Pakistan, Bangladesh, and South Korea. In 2018, over twenty countries have documented sex imbalances.

born, mainly in China and India.[6] The gender disparity is huge: although sex-selective technology is now officially banned in India, a male-heavy society has been created with 37 million more men than women according to its most recent census. A report published by the United Nations Population Fund in 2012 says that the masculinisation of demographic trends 'has serious social and economic implications'.[7] Abortion thus becomes a weapon of patriarchy too.[†] Adrienne Rich says in *Of Women Born*: 'There is nothing revolutionary whatsoever about the control of women's bodies by men. The woman's body is the terrain on which patriarchy is erected.'[8]

In some ways this argument constrains the complexity of this debate around abortion. Religion, lack of women in policy and decision-making roles, gender imbalance at the leadership level, misinformation about female physiology and about abortion procedures, ethical and social considerations of what constitutes life all contribute to this discussion. Nevertheless, this is unquestionably a gendered power struggle; as Gloria Steinem says: 'If men could get pregnant, abortion would be a sacrament.'[9] In May 2019, twenty-five white men in Alabama, USA, decided to impose draconian new anti-abortion measures against women's basic reproductive rights. This also won wide margins of approval in Georgia, Ohio, and Missouri. None of these men will ever become pregnant, and yet they have the authority to decide what women should be able to choose for their own bodies.

It is interesting to note, as we consider abortion a touchstone for the feminist movement today, and as women's bodies have

† I discuss a case study in my previous book *Sway* which showed how women who are reliant on their husbands and in-laws often choose to abort a child if it is a girl, because of the fear of being abandoned or, even worse, killed for not producing a male heir.

become a battleground in politics, especially in the USA, that many
of the early first-wave white feminists were against abortion, and
some also supported eugenics and racial segregation. The radical
feminists Susan B. Anthony (of the same name as the most active
anti-abortion advocacy group[‡]) and Elizabeth Cady Stanton, the
architect of the suffrage movement in the nineteenth century,
published a newspaper, *The Revolution*, which included articles
referring to abortion as 'child murder' and 'infanticide', that would
burden both a woman's 'conscience in life and soul in death', and
were a means of exploiting both women and children.[10] Marjorie
Dannenfelser, the president of the Susan B. Anthony List, also
quotes Elizabeth Cady Stanton (from a personal letter written to
Julia Ward Howe on 16 October 1873[11]) saying: 'When we consider
that women are treated as property, it is degrading to women that
we should treat our children as property to be disposed of as we
see fit.'[12] Elizabeth Blackwell, the first woman to receive a medical
degree in the United States in 1849, wrote in her autobiographical
sketches in 1895 that 'The gross perversion and destruction of motherhood by the abortionist filled me with indignation.'[13] They have
been adopted as poster-children for the pro-life anti-abortionists,
although their positions continue to be contested by many feminist
groups, who claim that there are no facts or evidence that support
the idea that these women were explicitly against abortion.
Nevertheless, many feminists continue to proclaim that pro-choice

[‡]   From the Susan B. Anthony List website: 'SBA List is a nationwide
network of more than 837,000 Americans. SBA List's mission is to end
abortion by electing national leaders and advocating for laws that save lives,
with a special calling to promote pro-life women leaders.' They also
announced that the November 2020 election saw a historic number of
pro-life women elected to the U.S. House of Representatives.

and pro-life women can exist together, and that it is a false dichotomy.[§] Abortion is declared to be an oppressive tool of the patriarchy, whereby men can use women as playthings and discard them without any accountability. Conservatives and Republicans continue to lay their own stake on the suffrage legacy, and the anti-abortion groups manipulate these views and choose quotes from select suffrage pioneers to bolster their claim that the pro-life movement is a feminist movement, that they have as much claim to history as the pro-choice groups. While abortion is made the moral centre of the debate, it can be seen as sidestepping some of the other significant issues around women's equality in the workplace, free childcare, abuse and coercion. But it is not one or the other. Acknowledging the hurdles women face, and arguing for gender equality, and for women to have choice and control over their own bodies, but nevertheless forcing women to choose a pregnancy sounds like an illogical contradiction to me.

A huge data gap still exists in how abortion laws affect people around the world. Abortion laws and access to proper medical care also affect transgender men and gender non-conforming individuals but we don't even have an in-depth understanding of the issues nor is anyone discussing this. Even though we live in a world of data explosion, and there is more and more gender-disaggregated data being collected, there is still surprisingly a lack of data on women's agency and autonomy, and on reproductive rights. For instance, the World Health Organization has a database called GenderStats, and one of the datasets is whether women get to

§ One such example can be read at the website of the group that calls itself 'Both Lives Matter' and claims to be reshaping the debate around abortion in Northern Ireland: https://bothlivesmatter.org/stories/bexs-story-i-am-a-pro-life-feminist.

make decisions about their health. This dataset is completely empty. No data has been collected, even though it was considered important and interesting enough to have been separated out. The Gender Info database from the United Nations Statistics Division has abortion rates per 1,000 women across various countries but some have not been updated as far back as 1998.¶ It also shows the wide range of grounds on which abortion is permitted. 'To save the woman's life' or 'on request' is not a basis on which abortion is allowed in many countries. While there is paucity of data, it is also indicative of the systemic biases that mean that such data is not considered important enough to allocate resources towards. Feminist geographer Joni Seager who wrote *The Women's Atlas* has also talked about how much of the data that is being collected is still set in the male-focused methodology, where the experiences of women are ignored and dismissed.

Once again, it comes down to how little interest there is in women's lives, and that they are not considered valuable enough to dedicate time and energy, resources or analytical acuity towards them. When women and women's bodies and concerns are not counted, they do not count. Only what is counted counts, and what is not becomes invisible and insignificant. The underlying reason is also the gender divide in teams that are making decisions about what data is to be collected and mapped, and how. Many of these teams are solely comprised of men, and there is a lack of women in data

¶ Gender Info 2007 describes itself as 'a global database of gender statistics and indicators on a wide range of policy areas, including: population, families, health, education, work, and political participation. It is an initiative of the United Nations Statistics Division, produced in collaboration with the United Nations Children's Fund (UNICEF) and the United Nations Population Fund (UNFPA).'

science.When data is not disaggregated on the basis of sex – and gender – then it renders women invisible, and their bodily autonomy is further diminished. When data is not disaggregated as per social and cultural context, there is a tendency to sweep every experience with the same brush. In most cases, it is merely complacency; in some cases, it is lack of resources; or in some cases, gender is not considered a significant delimiter and marker for difference.Whatever the reason might be, data scarcity harms women more than we realise. And we do not have enough data on women's reproductive rights, their bodily autonomy, their right and access to reproductive choices and health, and the way the different socio-economic factors affect their reproductive agency.

•

Decisions do not absolve us of uncertainty. Even as I stood firm, mayhem and commotion were wreaking havoc inside me, opposing forces to the calmness and determination I exuded externally. Even as I took each decision deliberately and consciously, I remember being caught up in a whirlwind, swooped up in a tornado ripping through my heart, the conflicting emotions causing a torque trying to bend my stubborn will, so resolute to go through with it. It was the right thing to do. It was the only thing to do.

When we make a decision with a heavy heart – however clear the head – it hangs around, questioning you, poking and nudging you in uncomfortable places in your consciousness. 'Are you sure?' these nudges say again and again, and the answer is often no. No, I am not sure. Of course I am not. But this is what I must do. The chasm between *should* and *could* widens further and further.

I remember going through the process as if in a dream, a hazy nightmare in a small private clinic in the Midlands. I was not offered any counselling. I did not speak with anyone. I found some infor-mation on the internet and picked up a one-page leaflet at the local health centre. This now seems so surprising in hindsight, as even buying a kitchen appliance can often include more research and consultation. A big decision such as this could have – should have – included more clear advice and guidance.

Women are not involved in many of the medical decisions about their own bodies, and are often given very sparse information. So even when it seems that we are making consensual choices, we are doing so with little to no knowledge about the possible consequences and alternative paths. A woman's decision to terminate her pregnancy might be determined by the laws of the state and/or the affordability of the service, and availability of and access to state-owned abortion clinics. So, really, any decision a woman makes is never free of the socio-legal framework that she is situated within. When there is state-supported affordable childcare, for instance, a woman might make different decisions about becoming a mother. When there is no fear of judgement or stigma, women are free to choose completely autonomously. In this case, the decision would be a woman's alone and determined by other factors in her life, but at least there would be a level playing field, and the conditions of inequality that may affect her decisions would be addressed and fixed. There can be a framework of reproductive justice that removes the barriers for making well-informed choices about reproductive health.

The NHS had a long waiting period, the process seemed cumbersome, and I could not face seeing my GP, a face that I knew well, and he mine. The shame demanded invisibility and anonymity, and so we found a private clinic. The Asian doctor★★

★★ Such a stereotype, I know, but true in this case.

asked me gently but in a matter-of-fact manner whether I was sure and I nodded, looking closely at him, his lined face reminding me of my own father back in India. Homesickness can hit at the strangest times, little triggers as electric shocks through the core of the body, suddenly displacing us from one place and back into another, until we don't completely belong in either. I had held back tears for so long, telling myself that this didn't mean anything, that it didn't matter, and that it wouldn't. But as the doctor asked me to climb up on the bed and pull my legs apart at the knees for him to do an internal examination, something burst open inside me. I sobbed uncontrollably as I lay there: unsaid grief flowing away, the shame of having to spread out while an unknown man touched me in the most intimate parts, and the relief and pain of having finally made a decision. He looked on with a kind face. A contradiction: I was a mother, but I couldn't be a mother. Not then.

I was very lucky to have access to resources which allowed me to bypass the waiting list, make a quick and early decision without the agonising wait hanging over my head – and heart – every second of those long days. Abortion is still stigmatised in South Asian communities, and legal frameworks and access to services are severely limited in many countries in the Indian subcontinent. I feel lucky that I was in the UK at the time, where I had the anonymity. But social and cultural pressures have long hands, and these can also throttle us across thousands of miles. I paid my dues with silence, the internalised shame and humiliation compounding to weigh me down with guilt: at being pregnant while not married to the father, and then deciding to have an abortion to terminate this pregnancy; both censured and both liable to condemnation.

Any woman who is less financially privileged and legally protected

104

does not have similar access to choice. It is often on their bodies that abortion policies are forged. Due to other systemic inequities, reduced access to contraception and sex education, poor women experience unintended pregnancies at five times the rate of their more affluent peers. There is a long history in the USA in particular of social conservatives attacking not only funding available for abortions, but also the clinics where women could access abortions, putting hurdles in to delimit a woman's ability to make her own decisions about her reproductive health, framing these choices as 'non-essential'. For instance, in the USA, women are not allowed to access Medicaid health insurance to have an abortion unless it is deemed medically necessary.[tt] The Hyde Amendment[tt] is a prime example of how a policy can not only violate reproductive rights and principles of gender equity but also severely undermine racial and economic justice by targeting vulnerable women. This is an ambush, a deception and as Justice Thurgood Marshall said, 'this is

---

[tt] Medicaid.com: 'Medicaid provides health coverage to millions of Americans, including eligible low-income adults, children, pregnant women, elderly adults and people with disabilities. Medicaid is administered by states, according to federal requirements. The program is funded jointly by states and the federal government.'

[tt] As per the report by Jessica Arons and Madina Agénor in December 2010 for the Center for American Progress, the Hyde Amendment is, perhaps, the most punitive and inhumane regulation imposed upon the reproductive lives of low-income women. Each day, scores of low-income women are forced to make a choice between using scarce resources to take care of themselves and their families or use those dollars to pay for an abortion. The landmark decision in Roe v. Wade may have held that women have the constitutional right to determine whether to carry a pregnancy to term, but the Hyde Amendment stripped that right away from low-income women, especially low-income women of colour.

an undeniable fact that for women eligible for Medicaid – poor women – denial of a Medicaid-funded abortion is equivalent to denial of legal abortion altogether.'[14]

The Hyde Amendment adversely affects minority ethnic women who are more often in the lower socio-economic groups and more likely to be insured by Medicaid. It targets disabled women who qualify for Medicare, indigenous women who use the Indian Health Service, and women incarcerated in federal prison. Incarceration of any form is an impetus to denial of basic human rights. Women in immigration detention and in prisons have their rights violated repeatedly, because they are in captivity, dehumanised as a single group and 'othered', coerced to choose options that influence their freedom and sentences through the cycle of abuse, neglect and denial of comprehensive healthcare. While we might think, and it is indeed legally so, that women being held in prisons have an equal right to make decisions about their pregnancy as those who are free, it is often not the case. There is an entirely different discussion to be had around how much of our individual human rights are still maintained while we are in a legal correctional facility, but understanding these challenges is paramount to understanding and acknowledging women's right to their own bodies and their ability, or inability, to access reproductive health. The right to choose abortion should not be compromised merely because a woman is being held under criminal punishment. Incarceration increases the threat to already fragile and precarious reproductive choices and rights. Given that, due to systemic and structural racism and social inequities, there is a higher proportion of black and other minority ethnic women in prison, these policies – or the lack thereof – unmistakably affect the already marginalised women more than others.

Pregnancy and reproductive rights of women in UK prisons remain severely under-researched even though there are approximately 3,800 women in prisons in the UK (5 per cent of the total prison population) as per data published in June 2019.[15] Surprisingly, pregnancy and birth numbers are not recorded but estimated at approximately 600 pregnancies and 100 births per year. In one of the very few research projects carried out in English prisons looking at pregnancy and childbirth, published in January 2020, researchers from the University of Hertfordshire found an acute sense of detachment and denial amongst the pregnant women (collectively called 'pregnants' by the prison officials, hence further dehumanising and 'othering' them) towards their experience of pregnancy as a way of coping with the feeling of disempowerment resulting from being pregnant while being incarcerated.[16] Some women exercised their agency by rejecting natural birth and choosing a medical birth so that they could control the time, and lessen the fear of commencing labour in prison. The apparent complacency towards pregnant women by the prison staff seems to be to avoid being seen as offering special treatment to any woman prisoner, which, compounded by lack of counselling and adequate information, means that often women are not even aware of their rights and entitlements. They feel frustrated and disempowered and it can be difficult for them to assess the consequences of their choices due to this lack of information. However, lack of privacy and the institutional ignominy and dehumanisation remain women's primary concerns, over-riding any disquiet about the lack of agency or autonomy.

The lack of access to abortion due to costly healthcare provision, religious stigma or legal bindings inevitably affect women of colour much more. Women of colour are more likely than white women to be low-income and to be enrolled in Medicaid in the USA. As

2015 data from American community surveys (for women aged 15–44 enrolled in Medicaid) from the Guttmacher Institute shows, more than 52 per cent of the seven million women on Medicaid and of reproductive age were women of colour, with 31 per cent of these black women and 27 per cent Hispanic women, compared to 16 per cent of white women.[17] When there are laws restricting late abortions, these also disproportionally affect poor women and women of colour because often these are the ones who do not have access to early abortion. These are the ones who have to choose between putting food on the table for their family or paying for an abortion. This choice can involve pawning jewellery and personal items, or scraping together money by any means possible, or continuing the pregnancy against their will and better judgement because they cannot find the money or get to a clinic in time. And it is they who are continually ignored by policy-makers but who must live with the consequences of political decisions over which they have no control. Motherhood – or the right to choose whether or not to be a mother – in women of colour is already an uncertain prospect, and this is just another blow further heightening the gap between white middle-class women and those from minority groups, and producing inequities in reproductive decisions.

The law – and choice – often remain the prerogative of a select privileged few.

•

It might seem that discussions around racial justice and reproductive justice are two different camps, two different agendas. As a woman of colour, I have personal experience of the racial bias in medical healthcare, and I am very aware of how racism and issues around women's agency and autonomy are very much interlinked. Ethnic disparities in women's health outcomes also extend to the reproductive domain. Differential access to treatment and consequently a lack of trust in the medical establishment lay down the racial and ethnic divides with regard to reproductive health. Sexual oppression and racial mistrust often go hand in hand; both relying on an outright denial of agency and dehumanising individuals into a faceless homogenous mass who cannot be trusted to make their own decisions. Ibram X. Kendi is quoted in the *New York Times* in July 2020 saying, 'There is no such thing as a nonracist or race-neutral policy. Every policy in every institution in every community in every nation is producing or sustaining either racial inequity or equity.'[18] The notion of autonomy is often treated from a very Western, Eurocentric perspective without understanding or acknowledging that a woman is individually as well as socially and culturally situated.

The links between reproductive justice and racism are not new. Margaret Sanger, an early feminist activist for women's reproductive rights, has faced accusations for her support of eugenics by promoting use of contraception to control the population of minorities who she deemed 'undesirables'.[19] In 2015, a number of Republicans campaigned to have Sanger's bust removed from the Smithsonian's National Portrait Gallery and in July 2020 the Planned Parenthood office of New York removed her name from their Manhattan clinic because of her harmful connections to a movement that believed in selective breeding and targeted people of colour, immigrants, disabled people and other vulnerable groups.[20] In the USA in particular, racist origins of the anti-abortion movement date back to the ideologies of slavery. Just like slavery, anti-abortion efforts are rooted in white supremacy, the exploitation of black women, and placing women's bodies in service to men, and anti-abortion efforts have nothing to do with saving women's lives or protecting the interests of children. Racism and reproductive coercion have been central to the US government's efforts to control population growth and to justify slavery and oppression of black women for many decades. Medical evidence has shown that 'an abortion is as safe as a penicillin shot'[21] – and yet abortion remains heavily restricted in states across the country, making reproductive healthcare inaccessible for women from minority and marginalised communities.

There are unmistakable links between anti-abortion campaigners and white supremacists which stem from the 'great replacement' conspiracy theory: a racist belief that rising immigration and low birth rates amongst white people are causing a crisis for the white population by 'replacing' the white race across USA and Europe. Their solution for this is to actively canvass against women's bodily autonomy and restrict abortion, and replace it with incentivising procreation. Much of extreme right-wing anti-abortion rhetoric and policies are less about religion or faith but increasingly based in this belief that white women need to have more white babies in order to stop the demographic decline of the white (superior) race. According to Sian Norris in *Byline Times*, Jim Dowson, the founder of Britain First, a far-right British fascist political party, is also the man behind anti-abortion group Life League, as well as being the pro-life figurehead, for the extremist Knights Templar International, a group that claims that changing demographics in the UK are the 'result of fifty years of contraception, propaganda and economic necessity making women work rather than have children, and literally millions of abortions'.[22] Women's reproductive rights are being weaponised in the fight against immigration, using women's bodies as the battlefield to create a legion of 'racially pure' soldiers.

In the UK, the Centre for Bio-Ethical Reform (CBR-UK)

recently hit the headlines after posting billboards featuring graphic pro-life imagery of unborn foetuses near MP Stella Creasy's constituency office. Its #StopStella campaign has specifically targeted the pregnant MP over her role in liberalising the law in Northern Ireland, where abortion had been banned since 1861. This group is a branch of a US organisation, and aims to end abortion in the UK within five years, even though it has been legal in this country for more than half a century. Many of these right-wing and anti-abortion campaigns of course also evoke the spirit of nostalgia to hark back to the 'olden times' when things were so much better. As the founder of CBR-UK Andy Stephenson says: 'Regarding the end of abortion, we think there is an opportunity for this nation to turn back to a civilised society'.[23]

'What kind of country are we living in?' I ask myself again and again. As an immigrant in this country, as a woman of colour, this nostalgia for the 'old way of living', the political and media campaigns to keep the outsiders out, the bias against immigrants is acutely distressing for me. But when it also ties in so closely with rescinding women's rights to their own bodies, procreation being used to counter the influx of immigrants, tropes around racial purity being used freely, I feel that we are living in a time-warp, where not only my own identity and sense of belonging but the future autonomy of my children is very much under threat.

•

In *Politics*, Aristotle says: '. . . when couples have children in excess, let abortion be procured before sense and life have begun; what may or may not be lawfully done in these cases depends on the question of life and sensation.'

It seems very clinical to talk about such an emotive subject in this way, and therein lies a problem, because emotions have to be considered. We cannot absolve this choice away from emotional entanglement. Choosing to be a mother or not has to be a woman's choice, and the emotions interwoven with this choice have to be given space.

The idea of monitoring women's bodies is not new. It is disguised as sanctification of a woman's body, where the law – and men – can control and monitor it as a valuable resource. But what it does is to make women's sexuality shameful. Research shows that hostile sexism is related to the belief that men have the right to monitor and constrain women's reproductive choices while benevolent sexism can also create a coercive control where women are considered as weaker, and hence deserving of a man's protection.[24] In this case, the discussion around abortion is often framed as a desire to protect women from negative emotions, grief and exploitation, which is why the recent debate around choice is very much focused on the women, rather than on the foetus. Consequently, as Duerksen and Lawson showed in 2017,[25] women who decide to have abortions are framed as poor decision-makers and pitiable, perpetuating harmful stereotypes about such women and about the effects of abortion. There is also a long-held hostile sexist belief that women are somehow leveraging their sexuality to extract resources from men. In some countries such as Turkey, Japan and South Korea it is even written in the law, with spousal permission required for women to have an abortion. Male control can also be exhibited in forms of withdrawing certain privileges and financial support from their partners if they do not agree with their decision. In a 2017 survey with over 27,000 Nigerian women, only 6.2 per cent were reported to be making their own decisions about their reproductive health-care.[26] Women's reproductive choices and autonomy are therefore often subverted by cultural factors too, with some cultures conferring more power to men.

Amnesty reported in 2015 that a ten-year-old girl and her mother arrived at a hospital in Asunción, Paraguay, with stomach pains.[27] The doctors quickly discovered that the girl was twenty-one weeks pregnant, the result of having been raped by her stepfather. Her body wasn't fully developed to carry a child, and this young age is of course deemed high risk by the World Health Organization. In Latin America, the chance of maternal death is four times as likely in girls under the age of sixteen. Paraguay however has one of the strictest abortion laws in the world, permitting the procedure only when the mother's life is in danger, without exceptions, not even in the case of rape, incest or an unviable foetus. Even though such restrictions to abortion access violate international human rights law and standards, and even with the risk to the health and life of the girl, Paraguayan authorities denied her access to a safe and therapeutic abortion.

In the end, when it comes down to it, most − if not all − laws governing abortion are based in a desire to control women's fertility with an underlying mistrust of their decision-making abilities about their own bodies, and the belief that their consent does not matter. They are also a drive to vilify women's sexuality, and to make them atone for their bodily desires. Whether it is a ten-year-old who has been raped and forced to carry a child to term, or a thirty-year-old who does not have the resources to bring another child into this world, or a woman who does not have access to contraception, or another whose mental or physical health is under threat due to a pregnancy, the right to an abortion becomes a question of privilege, access to opportunities and resources, bodily autonomy and trust. And it becomes a question of agency, beyond the religious and cultural rhetoric.

And while we talk about abortion rights and choices, we have to remind ourselves that this affects not only those who identify as women but also trans men and non-binary people. Nick T. writes in *Out* in March 2020 about their experience and confusion around getting an abortion as a trans person.[28] It is these stories that we don't even hear, the gendered nature of the medical forms, the gender dysphoria being pregnant causes in those who do not identity as women. All abortion restrictions disproportionately impact people of colour, and LGBTQ+ people of colour are particularly vulnerable because of the intersectional nature of prejudice and bias against those who present differently to heterosexual or cis women, and the stereotypes and assumptions that are held about people who do not fall clearly on the binary gender spectrum.

Making abortion illegal only makes it unsafe. But, even in states where it is not illegal, it is shameful and stigmatised, a dark alley that we bury away in the deepest corners of our selves. Laurie Penny writes in the *New Republic*: 'If we commit the cardinal sin of having a pregnancy terminated, we are supposed to be ashamed, to whisper it, to make a show of shame – just as we are supposed to be ashamed of consensual sex, just as we are supposed to be ashamed of surviving rape.'[29] Men trying to get women to stop having abortions, and women prodding other women to have children: the goal seems to be the same in the end, to fulfil our destiny as women, to bear children.

Trump came to power in 2017, and in the first week of his presidency signed the 'global gag rule' prohibiting any foreign-aid organisations who take US family planning money from using any of this money, or funds from any other donor, on abortion-related services, even in countries where abortion is legal. Called the Mexico City Rule as it was first announced in Mexico City in 1984 by

President Ronald Reagan's administration, it was subsequently rescinded by Barack Obama in 2009. The NGOs were not even allowed to advise on or endorse abortion as a method of family planning if they wish to receive federal funding. There were widespread concerns about the unintended impact of previous gag rules with research in 2011 by Stanford University across twenty countries showing that the rate of illegal and unsafe abortions (which result in 13 per cent of maternal deaths across the globe) actually went up by 40 per cent the last time such a policy was implemented by George W. Bush.[30] We all saw the photo of seven white men standing around Donald Trump as he signed this executive order, a stark reminder of how men get to control women's reproductive choices. What I particularly remember from this time was a meme that went viral soon after showing Hillary Clinton surrounded by seven women signing a ban on any ejaculation by men that was not for procreative purposes. This satirical meme was created by a French activist group called '52' because women make up 52 per cent of the French population, and highlighted the absolute absurdity of our current societal structures where men hold the power to dictate to women, but women would never be allowed to do the same to men.[31] While it amused, and provided some short-lived respite from the crushing blow to women's rights, it is a disappointing, disheartening, desolate reminder of the sexist ideology that underpins the reproductive justice framework.

•

The memory of the surgical procedure is hazy: conscious disremembering of the sorrow muddled along with the numbness from the anaesthesia they had given me. We drove back, lost in our thoughts, me clutching my bottle of pills.

'Take one every day, without fail.'

'I don't want to be reminded of this with each pill that I take,' I had said weakly. The nurse had nodded. But that was it. Just a matter-of-fact, efficient conversation with very few words, and a sugary lukewarm cup of tea: both very much what I needed. No kind word, no gesture of love or affection, no hug: all of which I really wanted.

He drove silently. He had bought me some flowers. It was sweet, but flowers are neither here nor there. I have never cared that much for flowers. Sometimes people use flowers as a crutch. Say the words. Say them out loud. Don't write them in a card. Don't hide them behind flowers, to be put away in a vase and then dried into oblivion. Just say them. But we don't. He didn't. And nor did I. I remember sitting down on a pavement at the services on the way back and feeling suddenly weak and teary. He looked uncomfortable, helpless, forlorn. I wanted to be the strong one. Always the strong one. So I didn't cry. I held the tears back, and they melted away, the caustic drops slowly eating my now-empty insides.

Every year, I have counted the years and the imaginary candles on the birthday cake that was not meant to be. I can still close my eyes and imagine green-blue eyes like his and dark hair like mine. In a parallel universe, that child would have been a teenager now. Maybe they would have been going to university, maybe travelling. Over the years I have often thought about this, particularly as we were going through a rollercoaster of heartbreak and loss, when I tried again and again to become pregnant once more and failed.

As a woman making an empowered choice about my body, I knew that by carrying the guilt around with me, I was letting my ingrained cultural and social conditioning gain the upper hand. But it is tough to argue with the hormonal shifts that tell you that one

116

day you are a mother, and the next you are not, even if it was merely a clump of cells with no sentient thoughts. I wish I could go back to that one moment in time when we refused to discuss it further. I could not see any other option for me on the table because there was none. I wish I had thought and considered that it might not happen ever again for me. And I wish that I had known then as I know now that I would still be with him here, loving him as I do. But one can never know.

A choice can sometimes be an illusion, a something and nothing. These two sides of the argument are never equivalent; neither equally desirable, nor equally undesirable. In Thomas Ward's 1688 poem 'England's Reformation', not published until after his death, he wrote:

> Where to elect there is but one,
> 'Tis Hobson's choice; take that, or none.[32]

There are scars that will always remind you of the pain, a visceral feeling of having something so close that you could feel it and then for it not to be there any more – gone before it was even really yours. Is it a strange paradox to grieve for something that you never really had, and that you thought that you did not want?

Perhaps – just maybe – the idea of a choice is just a myth.

IV.

TICK-TOCK, TICK-TOCK

W<small>E HAD NEVER TALKED SERIOUSLY</small> about having children, though we had been together for more than five years now, and so it wasn't just a flash in the pan, a summer romance. It might have been something we tiptoed around together at the start, but then our circumambulation became a ritual. We had fought, and we had loved, and had seen each other's hard edges and soft corners. 'I don't have time!' I had wanted to shout. It is unfair that a woman feels this sense of urgency when a man has all the time in the world. But he was in no rush. It was hard to tell whether the pressure I was feeling was coming from inside me, or from societal expectations. Our cultural and societal narratives are filled with the stereotypes of women desperate to become mothers, and stories of women tricking their partners into becoming fathers. I had to keep reminding myself that I was not one of them. I didn't want to be one of them. Our minds and hearts play tricks on us; we start believing that the metaphorical sandglass is an unembellished truth.

I had a highly demanding academic position, and I was commuting. I was already a parent, and I was parenting, dealing with the pre-teen seasons of moody days. M was almost thirteen years old. She was growing up fast, and I missed that sense of closeness we had in her earlier years. She was pulling away and I wanted to pull her in. Perhaps it was that. This is the paradox of motherhood: our desperate desire for them to be independent and grow up, side by side with the acute desolation we can feel at not being needed, the yearning to be the most important person in your child's life. As we go through the tumultuous pre-teen years, when they are pulling away, is all that remains the sad demise of an ideal of motherhood? The pedestal that our children placed us on is suddenly and very cruelly yanked away from under our feet, and we find ourselves anchorless, searching for the solid ground of that mother–child bond that seemed so indisputable and undeniable just a few days, weeks, months ago.

This seems to be especially true of mothers and daughters, that interminable intimate bond that is also so fraught with tension. The peculiar paradox of a daughter pulling away from a mother as she starts becoming a woman herself, the primal desire to stand apart even as every pubescent change in her body brings her even closer in semblance to the woman who is her mother. An attempt to protect fragments of herself from becoming blended with her own mother's identity, a primeval desire to be her own self, away from the fractal frivolity of her genes. As the girl starts becoming a woman, there is a scream that ascends, 'I am my own person,' slowly at first but then a tidal tsunami that can often drown the mother in perpetual perplexity. I did this with my own mother, and my daughter now to me. Life loops around; circles are closed.

As I was questioning every parenting decision I had made with my now-teenaged daughter, every motherly instinct that I had felt was so fundamental to my whole being, it made me unsure of becoming a mother again. What if I made the same mistakes again, and what if I messed it up? There is nothing quite like a smidgen of a hunch that we might not be well-suited to the parenting role that we are auditioning for once again to make us feel like an impostor. 'Am I a good mother?' I asked (ask) myself again and again, and wanted someone to tell me yes, that I was, and that I would be again. But no one pipes up. In the end, we just have to know within ourselves that we have done the very best we can, and hope that if we are given a chance to do it again, we would do the same. Or that we'd know what to do differently the second, third and the next time around. Mothering can be fraught with guilt, panic and a lot of fear at times. As I heard the stomping of sullen teenaged feet, and the petulant resentful tones from my once angelic child, with her hormones raging and shooting across her teenage brain, I sat there and wondered why I would want to do this all over again.

Living in a small – picture-perfect and anchored firmly in history – cathedral town in Middle England, with my partner and daughter, our rescue dog and cat, life seemed complete. Zora Neale Hurston said that 'Love is like the sea. It's a moving thing, but still and all, it takes its shape from the shore it meets, and it's different with every shore.'[1] After what had seemed like a lifetime of drifting in choppy waters, I felt like I had found my shore.

But being 'the only brown person in the village' and at work, had also bit by bit toppled that self-possessed sense of belonging that I had been slowly building up all my life. I had recently been stopped and searched, accused of being a 'gypsy' shoplifter, and in one sweeping statement branded an outsider. How does one become a mother again when you feel unanchored? How does one bring new life into a world that does not fully acknowledge your own? I had done it once. I wasn't sure that I was prepared to do it again.

120

Then there was the fear, the terror that lived just behind my eyelids, the memory of the first birth. What if the birth was as bad as last time? The trauma of the birth of my first child so many years ago lived in my blood, a constant reminder of how my own body had failed me. Of course I don't remember any of that, I kept reminding myself. That was an anomaly, my rational brain would implore. 'You almost died, beta,' my mother would remind me across the four thousand miles, her face crisscrossed with millions of tiny lines, most of which have existed since those weeks and months she spent sitting by my bed in the hospital in Delhi, praying and demanding, beseeching and haranguing her god.

But I was also acutely aware of my body-clock ticking. I had this sense of impending doom that perhaps I would not be able to conceive. 'There is no reason that you wouldn't be able to,' P kept telling me. 'We have done it before; it will be straightforward.' He was so cheerfully optimistic, and I really wanted to believe him. On one level, our life was settled, in a content pace. We danced around in movement and in stillness, through years that did not ask many questions, and I did not feel the desperate pull to be a mother again. But on the other hand, I didn't have the luxury of waiting to find out if I really wanted more, and when. His complacency at times seemed like a rejection of my turmoil. In a relationship we do not have to agree always, or be on the same page, but a couple always have to be willing to read from the same book.

•

I envy the men who are allowed to spread their legs and desires, hopes and aspirations. Women squeeze themselves into the narrow boundaries between the rails, hesitant to take up space, their ambitions ugly and abhorrent to society.

In an article in *Vogue* in 2011, a thirty-five-year-old single woman talks about choosing to freeze her eggs because 'she knew she was coming dangerously close to the age when eligible men might search her eyes for desperation, that unseemly my-clock-is-ticking vibe.'[2] Living with a ticking time bomb is torture enough, but at the same time having to hide the urgency, not put the throbbing pain of a ticking uterus and ovaries on the open table for all to see, and hear, is a form of persecution and oppression that we don't talk about enough.

Ambivalence is not prized in a woman, especially when it comes to having children. Society sees this as weakness, indecisiveness, selfishness. 'Surely you don't mean it?' we are told as if we don't even know our mind in the first place, or have no right to. 'Are you sure?' is another thing that I hear so often. Of course I do; of course we do. I mean everything I say. How can I not? Who says things without really meaning them? I might change my mind later, but surely that's okay, isn't it? Then I might say something that means something completely different. And I will mean it too. Do women have the luxury or the freedom to change their minds?

So many women I have spoken to have referred to the same burning desire to become a mother suddenly coursing through their mind and body. It's as if the sudden call of the siren sounds one day, beckoning them to motherhood, the broodiness taking over their day and night, as the ringing of the body-clock becomes louder and louder in their ears, and there's no snooze button. 'Once the clock starts ticking, there's no way to stop it,' these women tell me. 'But why do men not feel the same panic?' they ask me, and they wonder why men have the freedom to wait and delay, with life stretching out before them, and the space to breathe, to stretch their legs until they are hemmed in by fatherhood.

So what about men in all this? You might say that men don't have it easy either. But do they feel the same pressure to be a father, a parent? Surely not. I don't think so. Most men don't feel the sense of urgency, because society does not tell them to catch the fatherhood train. They don't hear the clock; there is no alarm that goes on around them; there is no regret for the time they have wasted not finding a good partner who would help them achieve fatherhood. No, there is none of that. Not in the same way at least.

A survey of 1,000 young people in 2016 by the British Fertility Society in partnership with the Royal College of Obstetricians and Gynaecologists revealed that almost two-thirds of those surveyed think men's fertility only starts declining after the age of forty, with a third believing that it doesn't begin declining until after the age of fifty. While nearly 80 per cent of the young women said that they would like to have children before the age of thirty, only about 60 per cent of the men had any desire or urgency to have children at this age.[3] There is definitely paucity of data about men's willingness and desire to conceive and start a family with several studies reporting the lack of male participants as a limitation. This in itself could be perceived as a sign that men are not as engaged with their fertility as women seem to be, and so in many studies the male view is only represented through the voices of their partners (particularly in a heterosexual relationship). Childbearing is often not an individual decision, or not allowed to be one, with the individual attitudes and social influence sometimes at loggerheads. Men, it seems, are more likely to succumb to societal pressures and have children to appease community and family, even when they have lower desire for a child, and are not ready economically or personally,[4] and even when they do not experience direct pressure often unreservedly handed out to women. This does not take away the difficulty that some men might face making this decision, especially if their decision does not adhere strictly to society's expectation from them: trans or non-binary men, gay men, men of colour especially lack the privilege that straight white men in heterosexual couplings might have when it comes to decisions about their own bodies and reproduction. Asian men, for instance, might encounter a large amount of pressure from their families to have children and continue the family line. It is often assumed that transgender people do not want children. However, research, even though limited for now, has shown that more than 54 per cent of the 50 transgender people surveyed desired children,[5] but as people are transitioning earlier in life with greater societal acceptance and awareness, they have to make very early decisions about their future fertility. Research studies show that many young people do not receive the necessary counselling before they undergo transition, which can have an irreversible impact on their ability to have children later in life.* A study from 2018 with 156 transgender and gender-nonconforming adolescents, for instance, showed that only 20.5 per cent had discussed fertility with a healthcare provider and only 13.5 per cent discussed effects of hormones on fertility.[6] Lack of information, access to these services, financial constraints and adequate counselling all play a role. They have to make demanding decisions about oocyte

---

* I write this while fully supporting a person's right to their gender identity and undergoing hormonal treatments and puberty blockers. As long as people are aware of the impact of any treatment, the hysteria in some quarters around it causing future infertility is completely unwarranted. A person's right to their authentic self and identity is of course much more important than their ability to have biological children. The discussion here is solely focused on the privilege that cisgender people have in delaying these discussions.

cryopreservation and uterus preservation for trans men, and sperm cryopreservation for trans women, at an early stage of their lives, as they consider the impact of hormones,[7] unlike cis men who have the privilege to delay these decisions and discussions.

Having children might be the most intimate of acts, and decisions, but it is patterned by societal structures and biases. Women, in most cases, carry the emotional load of gendered expectations of parenting, as well as the physical load of contraceptive decisions. Therefore they can be implicitly more invested in this – or are expected to be – and hold more direct and decisive fertility intentions as opposed to men who have more room to navigate reproductive ambivalence that can be in contradiction with the intentions of their partners,[8] and in some cases having 'more than year-long discussions to resist and negotiate their partner's desire to have a child'.[9] Unlike women, men are not conditioned to believe that their bodies are telling them to have children, and theories around evolutionary psychology assert that men are designed to have sex, women to reproduce and seek a nurturing role. This perpetuates not only gendered roles, but also desires. Women are maternal, and men are not brought up – or expected – to be. This does not just pigeonhole women, but men too. Men have had to conform to these notions to prove their masculinity.

When we talk about delaying reproductive decisions in a family, it isn't always the women who are making these decisions. Men can often put it off because they believe that they have all the time in the world, the common perception being that men do not face a decline in their fertility. This is true to a certain extent, as there is no gender equity when it comes to reproductive health. The menopause isn't a woman's friend. Men do not face the call of the menopause. Not in the same way. Even though we hear about 'male menopause'† it is really a myth. Men are like fish in that way. Like male fish, they continue to produce sperm through their life, often well into their eighties.‡ They do not face a precipitous drop in their reproductive hormones like women. Unlike women, who do have a dramatic decline in their sex hormones and egg reserves, men face less than a 1 per cent drop in their testosterone after the age of forty, and most older men still have testosterone levels within the normal range, with only an estimated 10–25 per cent having levels considered to be low.[10] It seems very unfair.

Women, from a young age, often as young as twenty-one years old – depending on cultural context – are reminded of their body-clock. Tick-tock, tick-tock. 'Your body-clock is ticking, you better hurry up,' they are told again and again. Much of this is unsolicited advice, but female fertility remains an open subject of public discourse. Female bodies are time bombs. Although female infertility – or fertility – has always been a subject of discussion since time immemorial, the term 'body-clock' first appeared in the late 1970s. 'The Clock Is Ticking for the Career Woman' the *Washington Post* declared on the front page of its Metro Section on 16 March 1978. The author, Richard Cohen, could not have realised just how inescapable his theme would become. It became the most commonly repeated trope about women's fertility window, this teeny tiny window squeezed in between 'too early', and 'too late', a narrow ledge which women have

† The term 'male climacteric' (from the Greek *klimacter*, the rung of a ladder) was used and is more appropriate because it suggests a decline and not a precipitous drop in hormone concentrations. Sometimes it is referred to as 'andropause' (from Werner, A.A. (1939). 'The male climacteric'. *JAMA*. 112, 1441–3).

‡ Rate of sperm cell production might decrease and there might be fewer living sperms in the ejaculated fluid.

to grasp on to before they lose their grip and fall off, their hopes of becoming a mother quashed forever. Originally coined by scientists to describe circadian rhythms, the processes that tell our bodies when we should rise, eat and sleep, interest in body-clocks started in the 1950s when the US air force began sponsoring research into how we could eliminate the need for rest. This was the era when the productivity craze had hit the country, and there was an eagerness to understand the human body and overcome its limitations. Suddenly in the 1970s the phrase 'body-clock' shifted to its current use and primary association with fertility and reproduction. Now that reproduction was re-established as a primarily womanly concern, it was easier to claim that men and women were scientifically and biologically different in all ways. Women, being limited by their rapidly declining fertility, could not be as serious about their career, or would be punished with childlessness if they stepped outside their traditional role. They had no right to claim and demand equal rights and positions in the workplace. The term 'body-clock' or 'biological clock' became a two-pronged stick that a woman could be beaten with, simultaneously celebrated for being a woman, and bringing new life in this world, while being penalised for doing the same.

In 2001, a provocative advertisement campaign across Chicago and Seattle on buses and public transport sponsored by the American Society for Reproductive Medicine cautioned, 'Advancing age decreases your ability to have children'.[11] One of these adverts depicted a baby bottle shaped like an hourglass. The window was small, and the sands of time wait for no one.

'Freeze your eggs now, before it is too late,' says an ad on the London Underground as I crisscross through the city for back-to-back meetings during the course of writing this book. 'Too late for what?' is my first thought. And my second, 'Too late for some.' I look around and see women of all shapes and sizes, colour and ages, engrossed in their daily lives, sitting with their own thoughts, staring ahead, possibly dreaming of a world where these constant reminders of their failing fertility would not surround them.

I wonder about the stomach-churning anxiety these messages induce in women while reminding them that they could be rid of all the stress and anxiety if only they chose motherhood now, before it's 'too late'. The particular Doomsday for women who fail to heed this warning presumably being a day of reckoning where they would be pulled up in front of friend and foe, accused of putting their careers before motherhood. The fictional hourglass rushes at exponential speed for women.

Are women hearing their body-clock ticking because society is telling them so? Of course. The science around the notion of a limited specific window of fertility that exists for all women is still hazy and vague. Moreover, there is now increasing evidence that men can also have a similar pressure on their fertility, even though no one talks about it in the same way. There is a standard template imposed on women, because everyone seeks comfort in a standard recipe. And, the standard milestone in this case is thirty-five, the age when suddenly a woman goes from being a throbbing, pulsating, lush and fertile individual to barrenness. That one day changes a woman from being in the prime of her being to a geriatric mother.§ That number in the calendar of life, where suddenly a woman is 'over the hill' of reproductivity and destined to be left weltering in the dark subterranean world of childlessness.

§ Used as a medical term for women who are pregnant and over the age of thirty-five. The term is outdated and there are efforts to use 'advanced maternal age' instead.

These are how many of my female friends have described the pressures they feel from everyone around them and the pressures they put on themselves. Media plays a role, of course, newspapers reporting on medical reports and research as 'landmark conclusive studies' with gross misinterpretation of results to suit a particular narrative[¶] and sensationalist reports of women who left it too late and had trouble conceiving at the age of thirty-four years old.[12] Bylines such as 'Dangers of delaying motherhood until 30'[13] ignore the fact that this particular research study was comparing risks associated with the maternal age of first-time births compared to smoking and obesity and concluded that the risks for individual women were very small.[14] Related research based in Norwegian data has also shown that older women seemed to have coped better with a C-section delivery, rating it as 'better than expected'.[15] These successful professional women are nevertheless worried that one day their bodies will yearn for children, but their body-clocks will turn around and say no. These women, who were happy being child-free, and in many cases single, suddenly start feeling the tug of broodiness, with anxiety that they might be compromising their own bodies and minds by not prioritising childbirth. I am not saying that everyone feels so, but we are all weighted down by the expectations. Often the nervousness and angst caused

---

¶ A report in 2009 by Dr David Utting and Dr Susan Bewley, a consultant obstetrician, in *The Obstetrician and Gynaecologist*, a peer-reviewed medical journal published by the Royal College of Obstetrics and Gynaecology, stated this: 'At the age of 25, just 5% of women take longer than a year to conceive with regular intercourse, rising to 30% in those aged 35'. The misleading headline in the *Daily Mail* referring to this report said: 'Women are six times more likely to suffer from fertility problems when 35 than 25'. These are NOT the same thing, as we cannot statistically extrapolate the results like this.

by societal pressure can also be falsely ascribed as broodiness, or there's always the anticipation of broodiness arriving anytime soon when least expected. What would one do then? What if it is too late by then? What if we are not prepared? The guilt of not doing the right thing, of making the right decision, weighs heavily on our shoulders. If we decide to be mothers, we face the motherhood penalty.** And if we do not decide to have children, we are seen as stepping outside our traditional roles, and hence are penalised and punished for it. It is a no-win situation at times in my view: a double-bind bias that often influences women's choices to be a mother or not.

John Reed wrote in a *Time Magazine* cover story in 1982 that 'For many women, the biological clock of fertility is running near its end . . . and [is] making successful businesswomen, professionals and even the mothers of grown children stop and reconsider.' And right there the box was drawn firmly to keep women within the narrow defines of their traditional role as the child-bearer, the notion of the body's biological clock asserted to remind women that they cannot venture very far from their role as a mother, even if they do not choose to become one. Or, god forbid, are unable to become one.

Heston Blumenthal, the Michelin star chef, says that women cannot reach the same heights as male chefs because their body-clocks start working, and that it is 'evolution'.†† Body-clocks have become a tool of female oppression, making women and others believe that they are certain to be lured by this, and therefore not as committed to their careers. They are used as a fact, rather than a metaphor, deployed to justify the 'weakness' of women compared to

** Motherhood penalty is the discrimination – often implicit but also explicit – that women face in the workplace after becoming a mother.
†† Yep, really. In an interview in *The Economic Times* on 10 September 2019.

men, as if the mere act of their bodies diminishing in reproductive capability also diminishes their physical and mental abilities, and that women are more susceptible to the pull of their ovaries and their wombs, controlled by their hormones. Once again, therein lies an inherent mistrust of women's ability to make decisions for themselves, as if they are merely subject to their bodily desires, helpless and weak-willed against the assault of their body-clocks. The ticking of the body-clock is a time-bomb reminding women that they will regret pursuing a demanding career if they do not heed this warning sound of their ovaries rebelling and shutting down. This number '35' becomes a bright neon signpost on the road of a woman's life, flashing indiscreetly, unashamedly, until it fills up every bit of the brain matter, a constant shouting in the ears. The idea that a woman might not even want children is immaterial.

The journalist Molly McKaughan, in her 1987 book *Biological Clock: Reconciling Careers and Motherhood*, writes about how women had become an army of 'clock-watchers'. While feminists were rebelling against these ideas in the 1990s and first part of the new century, there continued to be haziness around how much a woman's fertility really declined between the ages of thirty and thirty-five. And there still is.

As I weighed up whether I was ready or prepared to have another child, I felt like I was walking around with a placard around my neck saying time was running out, not just trickling through an hourglass but gushing forth, and I better do something about it. I was filled with panic and anxiety: what if it was too late, what if it could never happen again, what if my body was already broken beyond repair?

In *The Impatient Woman's Guide to Getting Pregnant*, Jean Twenge contests the widespread belief that one in three women over thirty-five will fail to get pregnant after a year of trying, noting that the claim is based on an analysis of French birth records dated 1670 to 1830. Luckily, medicine has made some pretty significant strides since the eighteenth century. In fact, from a much more recent study of 780 women across seven different European cities, about 82 per cent of women aged thirty-five to thirty-nine succeed in getting pregnant naturally, a slight decline from the fertility rate of women aged twenty-seven to thirty-four but significantly better than the 60 per cent chance estimated by the 300-year-old data.[16] We know that these women were actively trying to conceive, having sex at least twice a week, whereas we do not have this information for the historic data. In a 2015 biopsychosocial and genetic study of 551 families carried out at the Boston University School of Medicine, researchers even discovered that women who had their last child at 33 or older without the help of drugs lived longer than those who had their last child by 29 – a correlation and not evidence of causation, necessarily, but a notable phenomenon nonetheless.[17] Middle-aged mothers seem to live longer. A separate study in *Fertility and Sterility* led by Kenneth Rothman of Boston University followed 2,820 Danish women as they tried to get pregnant. Among these women, 78 per cent of 35–40-year-olds got pregnant within a year, compared with 84 per cent of 20–34-year-olds.[18] Another study led by Anne Steiner from the University of North Carolina School of Medicine found that among 38- and 39-year-olds who had been pregnant before, 80 per cent of white women of normal weight got pregnant naturally within six months. There was no significant drop seen until after the age of 40.[19]

So, what do these studies tell us? Yes, women's fertility decreases with age. But thirty-five is not a magical marker of a slippery slope into oblivion. It also tells us that women's bodies vary across a whole range, and the notion of a body-clock is only a mythical monster created (and then disproportionately distorted by the media) to seize agency and autonomy away from women. It is not an absolute truth. The baby panic is based in questionable data and statistics. It is a gendered construct, and we need more – much more – research into understanding women's bodies, especially their reproductive health. When we talk about women's bodies in terms of fixed templates and boxes, any outliers are not considered. They are dismissed and ignored. It is also significant to consider that most of these studies are based in white women in European countries and the USA. These women also had textbook fallopian tubes with no history of infertility, endometriosis or polycystic ovary syndrome. Even if we try and ignore the biological factors that might vary across different ethnicities, there are social and cultural factors that can contribute to how fertility is understood and dealt with.[20]

I personally found Twenge's optimistic account of getting pregnant with three children after the age of thirty-five upsetting, and not hope-inducing at all. I guess I wasn't looking for an 'and they lived happily ever after' story, because my road to being a mother had already been paved with too many setbacks and thorny obstacles. Yes, it worked for her, but what if it doesn't for me? While on one hand, we have the panic machine running in overdrive, we do not hear many stories that contradict these alarming statistics about thirty-five being the line between promise and overwhelming desolation. At the same time, any such stories of 'older' women falling pregnant naturally without difficulty are seen as an outlier and create a feeling of despair and trigger anxiety and loss in those who are still struggling to conceive. We also forget that much of the ideas of womanhood and women's bodies in obstetrics and gynaecology are based in an idealised white woman, rendering other bodies of colour as aberrations, even as ironically much of the early progress in women's reproductive science was based in unethical experiments carried out on powerless black slave women.[21] There is some evidence that the levels of estradiol, a form of female oestrogen hormone, is lower in black women in the USA compared to white women.[22] There are hardly any other reliable studies that have assessed the difference in levels of reproductive sex hormones across women of different ethnicities, and so their bodies are expected to conform to standards set by white European women. How race intersects with fertility has been left unexplored for a very long time. The experiences of brown and black women and their fertility rates have not been studied in any depth, so we keep falling back on a certain kind of woman as a template, projecting these data on the wider population, not considering the diversity in the population and women existing outside the global north.

As a woman of colour, I look for studies that capture the experiences of others like me, and I continue to find that women of colour are almost absent in these studies, their experiences not documented, the challenges they face not understood.

•

In April 2002, Sylvia Ann Hewlett published a book called *Creating a Life*, a book that gained enviable publicity and which counselled that women should have their children while they're young or risk having none at all.[23] Within corporate America, 42 per cent of the 1,658 professional women interviewed by Hewlett over the internet had no children at age forty, and most said they deeply regretted it. Just as you plan for a corner office, Hewlett advised her readers, you should plan for grandchildren. I went down a rabbit-hole – as one does – trying to find out more about Hewlett and her motivations for writing this book. It seems that with five children of her own, including a child conceived at the age of fifty-one after infertility treatments, her own personal longings and aspirations might have skewed her sociological undertaking to some extent. The notion of childlessness is always sidelined as something that happens to women involuntarily in all cases, rather than an active choice they might have made and been happy with. In Hewlett's book, for instance, she concludes that only about 14 per cent of these childless 'high achievers' actually chose not to have children, and the other 86 per cent had a life without children forced upon them because they had chosen career over motherhood. In fact, when I examined her survey, I realised that what she asks the respondents is if they knew in college whether they would have children, and only 14 per cent had admitted that they had actively chosen back then. How many of us really know what we want back in college? The way we envision our lives in the idealism of youth can change, and often does. The space between desire and regret is wide open – grey with blurred lines. They are not always mutually exclusive.

Personally, what was interesting for me in this book, even if the data seemed cherry-picked, was that amongst the people that she surveyed at the very top levels of corporate America, roughly half of all high-achieving female executives were childless, while only 19 per cent of their male counterparts had no children. Hewlett's survey of almost 500 high-achieving men found that only 7 per cent believed men could actually 'have it all'‡‡ while the women were more optimistic about their own chances with 16 per cent believing that they could have it all.

It seems to me, once again, that the real issue here is the gendered

---

‡‡ Which she defines loosely as a happy combination of marriage, kids and career. We can of course debate this endlessly too.

roles that we all are expected to play – at home and at work – and that women are still being told that they cannot really have it all.

Women are fed these narratives around pregnancy and their fertility, which means that so many women spend most of their twenties and their thirties being pressured, implicitly or explicitly, about the urgency of getting pregnant. I do not believe in these narratives. I did not conform to these narratives, but I realised that the more I started thinking about having a second child, the more I got caught up in this web of scientific theories and superstition weaving around me as an invisible trap, making me feel claustrophobic and panicky. It was a race I was determined to win. I don't like losing and god forbid I lose to my biological clock.

There can, of course, be a gap between the desire and ability to have a child. Some people call this 'baby fever', which is akin to the delirium that some can feel with a rising temperature, the loss of rationality, the chemicals altering perception of our own bodies and their place in the world around us. Feet firmly planted, but head in the air, the glassy gaze looking towards one unattainable goal – to have a child. But when we talk about this urge to have children, even as it merges with the psychological impulse to pass on our genes plus the societal pressure to do so, we are often only really considering middle-class Western women in our society. I wonder if baby fever manifests in different cultural and social contexts in the same way. There is a myth that non-Western societies, especially those in the global south, are prolific with children. In certain cultures, families are characterised by a lot of children; women expected to conceive naturally and easily. When they want one, they have one. But if you can't then it must be god's will. That's how it was meant to be. It is karma, and maybe I was naughty in my previous life, so this is what I am expected to be. This might be indeed true for

136

some socio-economic groups where access to sex education and contraception is intermittent or negligible, and women might not even realise the need to have autonomy over their reproductive choices. But this is not true for everyone in non-Western cultures. People in cities, caught up between the two worlds. Educated, aspirational, driven to succeed but still obligated to fulfil their traditional roles. Fertility decisions and choices never stand alone, determined so much by social and economic status, education and marital status, and relationship intentions.

•

Whatever my desire to become pregnant, I was surely fertile, I reasoned. I had become pregnant twice, without even trying. I was fertile ground. I had to be. But still, when I read the headline 'What science tells us about the ageing parental body should alarm us more than it does' by journalist Judith Shulevitz in *The New Republic* in 2012, it reminded me how I couldn't dismiss the notion that time was running out. The more I looked, the more I saw such headlines, grabbing me by the throat, shaking me up and down like a ragdoll, beseeching, begging, pleading me to take notice and act. 'It is okay if you just want one, because you already have her, but if you want another, you need to act now. Now, now, NOW.'

My disordered state of mind was compounded by my realisation that we were both conforming to our gender norms and stereotypes. I was a brown woman, and a traditional Indian woman who would of course want a large family, conforming to the role that I was brought up to play. I felt like I was failing my feminist sisterhood and ideals, and this made me guilty and angry. But surely being a feminist meant being able to make this choice. I hadn't felt this struggle as strongly as I did in that moment, this jarring incongruity between my identity as a feminist and what I believed to be my whole self, and that of me as a woman, governed by social norms and my biological clock telling me that I had better choose my traditional role, the one that I had been designed to fulfil. The cacophony in my head was growing louder every day. And even though I firmly believed with every fibre of my being that men and women were not different and that science is a bedrock for sexism, here I was, confused. Because even as my mind fully understood that when it came to reproduction, men were accorded a natural privilege – both biologically and socially – my heart was fighting this storyline where women are judged for choosing not to have children, but at the same time their desire to have children can also be dissected. A woman's path to this choice to be a mother or not is often tinged with so much sadness and anger. Not only are they expected to justify it to everyone else, they are constantly compelled to rationalise it to themselves too.

Even as my rational and scientific brain kept telling me not to believe the hype, I knew that I couldn't take the risk. And maybe there is some sort of primitive desire that women have more strongly than men, which make them broody. I don't know if it is true, because then again, I am generalising. And I could say that yes, most women I speak to have told me so, that they suddenly became broody one day, and that the pull of their biology was too strong to resist. But then again, I haven't asked my male friends, or male members of my family. No one appears to ask men if they feel broody too.

The men I know don't necessarily talk about the desire to have children. In large social and family gatherings, they are not asked directly and indirectly 'when are you having kids,' or told by their friends and parents 'you are not getting any younger'. They don't see adverts or articles on sperm freezing surrounding them, crowding them, because the number of sperm will diminish. Because of course unlike women and eggs, men are not born with a fixed number of sperm in their bodies. It's like we, as women, play a lottery, because genetics play a huge role in how many eggs we are born with, and how many will survive.

Things people regularly ask on Google:
How many eggs does a woman have at 25?
How many eggs does a woman have at 26?
How many eggs are left at age 30?
At 35?
At 40?
At 45?
At 50?
The numbers stack up (and vary) across different fertility websites and resources, magnifying ambiguity and confusion:

Up to 400,000: the number of eggs a healthy teenager has in her ovaries.
1,000: the number of eggs which die each month.
30 years: the age at which a woman's fertility starts to decline.
25 per cent: the chance a healthy fertile couple in their twenties has of conceiving.

We see these numbers. We glance at them, and we believe in them. Or sometimes, we don't. Most of the time these numbers do not really tell us anything.
Another medical website says:

Women are born with approximately two million eggs in their ovaries, but about eleven thousand of them die every month prior to puberty. As a teenager, a woman has only three hundred thousand to four hundred thousand remaining eggs, and from that point on, approximately one thousand eggs are destined to die each month.[24]

Even as a scientist used to working with data, I found it difficult to understand what this really meant for my fertility. There is no consensus on these numbers either, because of course women are not all built on a template. As a woman in her mid-thirties I could assume that I had plenty of eggs still left. But who can tell? I trawled through a number of medical journals and fertility centre websites from around the world, and spoke with medical professionals, but ended up feeling more overwhelmed than before I started. So much of the discussion around women's fertility is centred around egg prediction or the number of eggs available in our bodies. But that is not the only reason for infertility. It has a much more complex landscape than we are told about. The quality of the eggs matter too, not just the quantity, says Joyce Harper, professor of women's reproductive health at University College London.[25] Most of the headlines around fertility do not really discuss chronic illnesses, endometriosis, fallopian tube blockages, fibroids, peri-menopause. We don't have sufficient data on this. Neither do we know when the nuts and bolts of the machine start creaking.

•

There is some research now to show that, actually, men do have a body-clock.

Tick-tock, tick-tock.

Gloria Bachmann, director of the Women's Health Institute at Rutgers University, carried out a comprehensive review of medical studies from the last forty years, published in the journal *Maturitas*, showing that there is a downward trend in male fertility after the age of forty-five.[26] It is not clear why this might be the case, whether it is the number of active sperm or due to the degradation in the quality of sperm: there just isn't enough research in this yet. Men have long been considered immune to the ravages of age in terms of their fertility, both physiologically and socially; we continue to see rock stars and celebrities dating women much younger than them and becoming fathers even when they are seventy. It perpetuates and reinforces the societal myth that time does indeed wait for men. There is also, arguably, more shame associated with male infertility, because that is the ultimate sign of losing one's masculinity; ironic when men are not as associated with paternity as women are with maternity. A friend I spoke to told me that he would be devastated if his 'swimmers' weren't swimming anymore. 'The boys have to keep doing their work,' he told me rather crudely, with a laugh.§§

Researchers are also now showing that although sperm is being produced every day, there are more DNA mutations over the age of forty, and older men become less fertile because genetic defects build up in their sperm. In younger men, the damage is minor and can be repaired inside the fertilised egg, another contribution of the egg that we do not hear about. But in older men the amount of DNA damage can overwhelm the body's natural repair mechanisms. There is a critical threshold of DNA damage and above that, the damage can no longer be repaired. And when this happens, there is a higher chance of miscarriage, or chromosomal abnormalities in the foetus. The mechanisms of producing sperm also slow down with age, and so their number and speed is impacted too. There is

§§ Unfortunately, yes, despite this, he remains a close friend.

also a loss of testosterone, and the sperm lose their 'fitness', much like humans tend to lose muscle strength and suppleness with age.

While women have been limited by a determinate number of eggs that they are born with, our mechanisms ensure that all the DNA-copying has already occurred at birth, and so there are no mistakes likely to occur along the way. Whereas men produce fresh sperm every day, and the mechanisms of DNA-copying can become erroneous with age, and there are more likely to be errors and mistakes. There is also some evidence that environmental factors over time – the oxidative effects – can cause damage to the sperm. So, a rock star lifestyle – smoking, drugs, partying, drinking – can cause chromosomal damage in the sperm. Which does make one wonder how certain male celebrities have been able to conceive successfully at a very advanced age. For all our advances, so much of human physiology remains a mystery. And it is worth remembering that while we might hear the stories where older men have had children, we are less likely to hear of the ones who have tried and failed.

And what of the babies born to older fathers? A 2005 study of 70,000 couples found a fourfold rise in Down's syndrome among babies born to men aged fifty and older.[27] They were also more likely to have limb deformities. Ageing sperm have also been linked to problems like schizophrenia, dwarfism and autism in children born of older fathers, according to Roger Hart, professor of reproductive medicine at the University of Western Australia. Dr Stephanie Belloc from the Eylau Centre for Assisted Reproduction in Paris studied the records of 12,000 couples who visited her clinic and separated out the influence of the mother's and father's ages on the chances of conception and miscarriage. The results showed that men's ages also affected pregnancy rates, which were lower in the over forties, and that women whose partners were thirty-five or older had more miscarriages than those who were with younger men, regardless of their own age. The risk of miscarriage was on average 16.7 per cent when the men were aged thirty to thirty-four, but it doubled to 33 per cent in men over forty.[28] Even though these results only show patterns, and even while we know that correlation does not always imply causation, this information is not well-known. It does not get disseminated in the popular cultural and social milieu, and the age of the woman becomes the only concern when a couple is trying to conceive. The guilt of a failed conception, and pregnancy, even in the case of assisted reproduction, lies squarely on the woman's shoulders. There is a reason that most sperm banks require donors to be between the ages of eighteen and thirty-nine. Some sperm banks even set an upper age limit of thirty-four. The Human Fertilisation and Embryology Authority (HFEA) in the UK set a limit of forty-five years. But men continue to believe in the 'Charlie Chaplin effect'[¶¶] and delay committing to having children. Perhaps because there are some scientists and researchers who continue to cling on to the idea of the omnipotent and indestructible sperm.[★★★] And perhaps because not enough men come forward to speak about the problems they had while trying for a child.

All that being said, a Google search for 'maternal age fertility' gives 24,100,000 results, while one for 'paternal age fertility' gives almost fifteen times fewer at only 1,570,000 results. We never hear of a prospective thirty-five-year-old father being labelled as a 'geriatric'. Women's reproductive health is big business, with companies cashing in on our subsequent fears around losing our fertility. I google 'how much to freeze eggs' and get around 53 million results, and when

¶¶   Charlie Chaplin became a father at the age of seventy-three.
★★★   Andrew McCullough, director of sexual health and male infertility at NYU Medical Center in New York City, for instance, is not convinced that age plays a role at all in male fertility.

using the same query for sperm, I get only around 4.5 million results. Egg-freezing costs are at least twenty-five times more than sperm freezing too, and the gender bias is strikingly evident. According to the HFEA website, the whole process for egg collection, freezing and thawing costs an average of £7,000–£8,000, including medication, thawing eggs and transferring them to the womb.[29] Storage costs are extra and tend to be between £350–£500 per year. Some US Fertility clinics put this figure around $30,000–$40,000.[30] These figures vary based on the age of the individual and the number of cycles needed. Women can store eggs for up to ten years for 'social reasons' but in certain circumstances may be able to store their eggs for up to fifty-five years (for example, when the woman is at risk of becoming prematurely infertile through medical treatments such as chemotherapy). So, the storage costs in itself could be many thousands of pounds, while sperm-freezing costs a mere £175–£375 per year as an average, with no additional surcharges. Egg-freezing is of course a lucrative business. The biology makes it so. No surprise then that the spotlight remains firmly on the woman's fertility, and efforts are focused on not only getting older women to use assistive reproductive technologies to get pregnant but also to generate disquiet amongst younger women, in their twenties, about their waning fertility, to urge them to worry about the future and start investing in egg freezing, to consider it a smart investment in their future. Women's fertility is a valuable commodity.

It is little wonder that, with the media and society perception and messaging around fertility being heavily weighted towards women's responsibilities and failings, I – along with plenty of other women, I am sure – wanted to learn more about male fertility when we were weighing up whether or not to have what would be my second child.

We did not talk any more about having a child. I submerged myself in my work, but I was drowning. Unspoken words often take a huge amount of mental and emotional energy to keep quiet.

With all the time pressure seemingly on me, I wanted to tell P that time was not necessarily on his side, either. I wanted to tell him that he might not realise it, but his body-clock was ticking too.

V.

A FRUITLESS CROWN

Days and nights shifted, and I kept drifting. In and out, up and down. Bobbing, coursing through my comfortable middle-class life, where I still feel like an imposter sometimes, living someone else's life that I have accidentally stepped into. I was the happiest I had yet been in many ways.

But then how does one measure happiness? Do we know if this is the happiest we could be, or would ever be? We weigh our smiles and the lightness of our limbs and hearts against an arbitrary scale in our imagination and memories, and then we decide that life has never been happier. Yet we have no way of knowing if life would just be the same as now, or if we have a capacity to be even happier, truly joyful and completely at peace, with no sense of looking backward or forward. We wonder if the pangs we feel at times, through lonely nights and soulful mornings, alone with our thoughts, when the bleakness of the world seems much darker inside than outside, suggest that perhaps, just perhaps, there is even more to life. On such occasions, I felt guilty for wanting more. What if choosing to have another child jinxed what I already had?

I listened to Bob Dorough sing 'Three Is a Magic Number':

A man and a woman had a little baby.
Yes they did
And they had three in the family.
That's a magic number.

We were not a 'traditional' family; we hadn't had a little baby together. But P was M's father, and we were three in the family. Maybe that was really the magic number. Maybe we didn't want any more. Maybe I shouldn't want any more.

There are always so many questions, and no easy answers. We grapple with the questions in our brains, and their echoes in our hearts, hoping that they will un-jumble one day, line up alongside each other in neat parallel lines. The non-stop whirring of the mind makes it impossible to listen to what the heart has to say. And the tremulous warnings of the heart drown out the rational musings from the brain.

Then there was always the virus that had been a part of me for so long that I mostly forgot about it, until it asserted its dominance and made me feel ill, weak, nauseous. That time ten days after the C-section when they had given me five units of blood, almost three-quarters of the blood that ran through my veins, pumping in and out of left ventricle and right. Then, as they hurriedly secured blood from anywhere and everywhere, I had also been given the virus, constantly reminding me that life is ephemeral, and that a return from the dead had come at a cost. The virus that had stayed in my body, hidden away – until it was found one day, suddenly discovered in an unrelated blood test, almost nine years after M's birth. I had been a chronic carrier for so long without even knowing it. When I found out, the news had come as a huge shock, and I sat there stunned, feeling disgusted with my own body. For nearly a decade it was a part of me, but without my knowledge, an unwelcome visitor staying close and taking over my body with an authority that made me feel repulsed, and repulsive. I was the carrier of 'polluted blood', a malfunction coursing through my veins. Hepatitis C,[*] a condition that remains shrouded in so much stigma, a disease so often associated with drug use, with 'deviance', thereby transforming those who have been affected – even by blood transfusion – into shamed bodies. Because more than 90 per cent of people in developed countries who have hepatitis C have a history of intravenous drug use, through sharing of unsterilised needles, or have a history of unsafe sexual practices, they are frequently blamed for acquiring the disease, and viewed as irresponsible, accountable and untrustworthy.[1] As a blood-borne disease, hepatitis C is also strongly associated with HIV, which carries its own stigma.

It is easy to internalise this shame and stigma, and so I did. The fear of disclosure, the consequent threat of discrimination at work and in social situations, the intrusive questions, the terror of being seen and considered differently than before, always hung around me menacingly, and so I didn't tell anyone. I had read stories of people losing their jobs, of not being accepted to graduate school, of being ostracised by their friends and family. Misinformation and poor health

[*]   Hepatitis C virus (HCV) is one of the most prevalent global chronic viral infections worldwide. It is estimated to affect around 3 per cent of the world population, about 170–200 million people. Hepatitis C is not spread through breast milk, food, water or casual contact such as hugging, kissing and sharing food or drinks with an infected person. Few people are diagnosed when the infection is recent. In those people who go on to develop chronic HCV infection, the infection is also often undiagnosed because it remains asymptomatic until decades after infection when symptoms frequently develop secondary to serious liver damage.

education is the framework underlying the general perception of HCV. Only my husband and my parents had known. I felt like I was carrying a secret around with me all the time, something personal and intimate, even as I myself constantly questioned whether I had bought into the stigma by doing so. But sometimes secrets become part of ourselves, and then they are impossible to let go. Instead, we waited for a cure for this illness because at the time there was none.

Then, suddenly, in the middle of one of the hottest days one summer, I got a call from the specialist and they had new hepatitis C drugs, still on trial, and they wanted me to be a part of the tests. The treatment would be intense, and so we discussed the side effects. I had the strain of the virus that is one of the hardest to shift and treatment would make me feel ill, much like an intense bout of chemotherapy. And it would also mean delaying any kind of decisions about pregnancy for another few years. So without talking, debating, discussing, suddenly we decided to forego the trials and to try for a child.† We started trying without really trying, believing like most heterosexual couples that it would just happen if we stopped using contraception.

Every month, there was a huge surge of excitement and antici-pation. Perhaps this would be the month. But then it wasn't. It felt like a huge rollercoaster ride, or a horror movie unfolding, depending on how you look at it. The visceral sensation of fear and thrill is the same, the excitement, the nervous energy, the anticipation, and then the huge crash every month. Yes, the sex was good, and even though it became somewhat perfunctory, it was still thrilling. But the real thrill was afterwards as I lay back with my legs up in the

---

† I finally underwent a more advanced treatment in 2018–2019 for HCV and was declared clear of the virus.

air. Every time I had a huge sense of anticipation, because this could be it. This could be that moment when the magical alchemy happened, and two worlds collided to create a new being. It was like jumping off a cliff, the wakefulness and euphoria immediately after and the corresponding raised levels of endorphins in the blood and the feelings of intense pleasure. We lived in a paradoxical world, where stress and fear lived hand in hand with pure bliss.

As time went on, we started to wonder if we needed help. But then we held back, always wondering if maybe just another month would sort things, because that could be the month when the flow of hormones would all align in a cosmic configuration. It was written in the lines of my hand, after all. Tracing the lines deliberately and languorously with a fingertip, I tried to evoke the spirits of my ancestors, those who resided in heavens above, hoping that they would nudge the stars and planets into place.

We continued to fumble for reasons in a muddle. I was frittering away time wondering why I was unable to get pregnant. We waited to see a specialist for a long time, as is often the case. We had only been trying for a few months, and the standard advice is to wait for 6–12 months before seeing a specialist. There was always hope, hope that this would be the last month that I would be infertile, that magically all the green kale juice, the good antioxidants in a very carefully monitored diet, absolution from any coffee and alcohol, would make my body a toxin-free, fertile ground where new life would be welcome and would flourish without hesitation and trepidation. The kitchen counter was flooded with all the herbal medicines that anyone had ever recommended, some to be taken twice a day, some more. It was bound to work, there was an unshakeable feeling of optimism and determination; determination to do the right thing; a firm resolve to make the next cycle successful.

The asynchronous nature of time is never stronger than when you are waiting for something: a palpable sense that time is standing still, but at the same time a rising panic that time is passing by too fast. In the meantime, there was nothing much to do except pretend that all was okay, while the failure to become pregnant stayed like an incurable itch with me every micro-second of the day. I would catch myself laughing at something, but it would sound hollow to me.

·

I remember that we started the first cycle of treatment with so much hope. 'No stress, remember,' the nurse told me. 'No stress,' people on all those fertility forums told me. 'Stay calm. Do yoga and meditation.' Trying to stay calm never really works. But staying calm while everything around me was bound to rake up a sense of restlessness was impossible. I had to remind myself continuously not to get anxious while in the middle of one of the most anxious phases of my life. This soon became a series of careful mediations, every action deliberate and measured. In my usually chaotic brain, used to a scatter-gun approach, not used to focusing my mental beam on anything so precisely, this was a new invitation. This was important. This was how it would work. If only I did all the right things.

No stress. Eat healthily. No coffee. No alcohol. Exercise. Drink a lot of water. Walk every day. And then some more. But do not walk too much. Do not exercise so much that it exhausts you. Have you tried acupuncture? It really works. My sister tried it and her IVF cycle worked the first time around. Have you tried Chinese Herbal Medicine? Yoga? Pilates? A friend ate only a vegan, gluten-free and dairy-free diet for a year and they were successful the first time around. They have twins now. Gaining weight can be a problem during a fertility treatment. Why don't you join the gym? I know a wonderful acupuncturist. My cousin went to her and it completely un-knotted her. Pineapples can make the embryos stick. Lie back with your legs in the air.

The waxing and waning of the moon determined fertility rituals for people in the past. I remembered that the first time I fell pregnant, soon after I had got married, a Hindu priest had told me to wear a moonstone ring on my small finger at all times, of a certain weight and size; its luminous milky-white aura would protect me from the evil eye, and keep all the celestial beings around me in the right place. Or was it me that the ring was supposed to keep in the right place? I couldn't remember. I thought I had put it away at the back of my small jewellery box, which still carried sparse remnants of that life that I had once lived, my mangalsutra still there at the bottom of the box, as if somehow getting rid of it would cause evil beings to bring trouble for the man I wasn't married to any more. These irrational fears that we sometimes hold on to. We want to believe in myths and superstitions. We want to believe that there is a world beyond the one that we immediately reside in, that there are things we don't yet know, that there are mysteries and secrets still remaining unravelled.

I woke up one night dreaming of the moonstone ring, and couldn't settle. It had worked that time. Maybe it would again. And once again the rational self was abandoned in exchange for desperate hope. It was not there in the jewellery box any more. I was more distraught than I could ever imagine myself to be. 'It was just a ring,' P said to me. He could not understand how these talismans can save us from ourselves in such times.

Women tie themselves up in knots trying to do everything and miss nothing. Once I had made this commitment to myself to become pregnant, there was not much of me left to give to anything else. Not to myself or to others around me. And as the lens zoomed onto one thing, everything else became slightly out of focus, blurry, distorted and confused. I knew work was suffering, but my personal and professional selves were kept on separate shelves, and they rarely overlapped.

'Why would you want another one when you already have one?' my boss had said with a dismissive laugh when I tried to talk to her about it one day. So I put my personal life out of sight, even though it was never away from my mind. It was always there as I lectured, as I sat in meetings and in conferences, but never spoken about again. Every month when the negative test came, I would sit silently with my head bowed, and then get dressed, go into work, and act as if nothing had happened, all my desperation and sadness shrouded in a professional veneer.

Amongst these vague disjointed realities, I was trying to fit together the jigsaw pieces of new life. We clutch on desperately to stories of those who tried something that worked. Lucky them. We don't hear of those who tried acupuncture for months on end and it never did anything for them. We don't hear of people who had kale juice and a specific diet but never saw the seeds grow. Perhaps we don't want to hear of these stories because what we most want is hope. Hope that something will work, that there is a way around the biological reality, and that the body and mind can be twisted and turned and coaxed into pliability. Most of all we want to believe that it all really works out in the end.

In an episode of *Downton Abbey*, a doctor tells Matthew Crawley as he worries that his injuries have rendered him infertile that 'anxiety is the enemy to pregnancy'. The paradox lies therein. Anxiety is not our friend, but it is our persistent accomplice as we navigate this path to assisted parenthood.

It is not the worry and anxiety of things not working out, month after month, but also the shame and stigma (oh, hello, old bedfellows) of not being able to reproduce naturally. There have been estimates that one in eight heterosexual couples have trouble getting pregnant or sustaining a pregnancy.[2] However, despite the prevalence of infertility, the majority of women do not share their story with family or friends, and so many face this alone, without much support, having to hide away pain and disappointment. The mental and physical trauma of undergoing a series of medical treatments compounded with the uncertainty and guilt can lead to isolation, psychological vulnerability and depression. The more we stay silent, the less we hear such stories, and the more we believe that we are the only ones.

Mental exertion of another kind has also been blamed for failed attempts at pregnancy – in women, that is. Dr. Edward H. Clarke, M.D., a professor at Harvard Medical School, wrote in his 1873 book, *Sex in Education; Or, a Fair Chance for Girls*, that when a woman works her brain over math, botany and chemistry, she will 'divert blood from the reproductive apparatus to the head.' Too much ambition in a woman would result in too much anxiety and this would inevitably affect her fertility. Ergo, too much ambition or education in a woman was determined to be an undesirable quality.

In the 1940s some of the medical professionals went a step further, believing and proposing that women who were educated unconsciously hijacked their own fertility. They termed this *psychogenic infertility* caused by too much ambition, anxiety and education, which led women to harbour anti-maternal thoughts that affected their ovaries and hormones.[3] Women who worked supposedly had unconscious bias against getting pregnant, and stories and myths abounded of women who became pregnant as soon as they stopped

154

working and became homemakers. Such thinking was steeped in deeply misogynistic views, of course, with no sufficient medical evidence, and was intended purely to keep women in their place inside the home.

The potential impact of emotions on pregnancy have since continued as urban myths, which many continue to believe in. I believed in them too. Even as a scientist, who was trained to look at evidence, and evaluate facts and fantasies. I tried to look at scientific studies, but half-heartedly, because I was so ready to believe and conform to anything that would make our fertility treatments successful. There was no second place in this race, it was either winning or losing, and so we put all of ourselves into it. I did find a 2014 study in the journal *Human Reproduction* which correlated the level of salivary alpha-amylase, an enzyme that is secreted by salivary glands in response to stress, with fertility in 400 women in the United States. Those who had the highest levels of salivary alpha-amylase were 29 per cent less likely to get pregnant after a year of trying – and more than twice as likely to be declared infertile – than those who had the lowest levels of the enzyme.[4] Even though I knew that correlation is not causation, and that this was a small sample, localised and based in one single parameter associated with stress, I took it to confirm what everyone around me was telling me. It was my fault if I was stressed and the fertility treatment did not work. I was not in control of my emotions; I was too emotional; I felt too much. Like so much to do with women, it always comes down to this. Hysterical, angry, excitable: emotions are always weaponised to denigrate women's feelings. They always have been. Therefore, women cannot be trusted with their own emotions, and neither can they be trusted to act rationally, logically, wisely. I remember 'faking good', putting on a brave face, because isn't it a little self-indulgent to show your worries, concerns, anxieties? I suspect many people do this, feel like this, and so we never know the frenzied paddling that goes on under the surface merely to stay afloat, to propel us forward by inches, to get through another day.

Not surprisingly, recent research documents that infertility patients consistently report significantly more symptoms of anxiety and depression than fertile individuals. Recently, I looked at the research once again, perhaps with a more objective eye, as I was not caught in the foggy mire of my personal infertility discourse. A 2004 study utilised a structured psychiatric interview of a total of 122 women, interviewed prior to their first infertility clinic visit. The results were striking: 40 per cent of the women were diagnosed as having anxiety, depression, or both.[5] In a large Danish study of 42,000 women who underwent assisted reproduction treatment and were screened for depression prior to treatment, 35 per cent screened positive.[6] In another large-scale study in 2016, 7,352 women and 274 men were assessed in infertility clinics in northern California. It was determined that 56 per cent of the women and 32 per cent of the men reported significant symptoms of depression and 76 per cent of the women and 61 per cent of the men reported significant symptoms of anxiety.[7] Finally, in a study on suicidality in 106 women with infertility, 9.4 per cent of the women reported having suicidal thoughts or attempts.[8] How do we define stress? It differs and affects people in different ways. Often people thrive on stress, and the level of stress that individuals experience in the same situation and circumstance also varies. So any such study on stress has a lot of unknowns in it. Also, as we know that many of the medications prescribed in assisted reproduction have side effects of depression, irritability and anxiety, the eternal chicken–and–egg question remains:

does infertility cause stress, or does stress cause infertility? It is impossible to unscramble from the broader stress-related emotions associated with an unsuccessful treatment in itself. How is one supposed to disentangle from the stress when it is such an inextricable part of the process?

None of the research studies, so far, have conclusively shown that stress has a hugely significant impact on the treatment or the outcome, as the level of stress and anxiety has an impact on how many women choose to continue with the treatment and how many 'drop out'. Most women I spoke to during the process of writing this book who had made the decision to stop infertility treatment after one or two unsuccessful cycles, and chosen to stay childfree instead, had done so primarily for a better quality of life. Stepping off the hamster wheel with nowhere to go is a survival mechanism, preserving sanity in an uncharted vast landscape of infertility. That's not to say that it always gives them the peace they so desire or stops the nagging questions – both their own and those of others. Surely it would have worked next time.

Would it have worked next time?

What if we have given up too easily?

What if this was not meant to be the end?

What if we could have been better, more resilient, more adaptable, less stressed?

What if?

•

Much of the discourse on infertility in popular literature and the media is around women who are much older, white and middle class. This shapes the narrative that it is white women who are more likely to suffer fertility problems. There are some poignant moments that stand out. Julia Child in the 2009 film *Julie and Julia* attempting to fill her life with hat design classes and cookery courses, with the melancholy of childlessness hanging over her and her husband. She breaks down as she hears about her sister becoming pregnant. In the 2018 film *Private Life*, we meet Rachel and Richard right in the middle of a fertility treatment. We see a raw, honest depiction of IVF, as these two forty-somethings, who haven't had sex for many months, navigate their nth cycle. The cycle of hope and despair continues, with promises of a miracle baby from each cycle – as Rachel says: 'A lot of women have babies at forty-one. I thought I'd be one of them.'

The popular image of infertility is also that of an upper-middle-class, white, straight woman in her mid-to-late thirties or early forties. It is a stereotype that erases the significant experiences of minority ethnic, working class and LGBT+ women, who often face the most barriers to diagnosis and treatment. Women who have used fertility services are likely to be white and married, with higher levels of income and education. When Michelle Obama revealed her own journey with IVF treatments in her memoir *Becoming* recently, I was reminded yet again that black and brown women are still invisible in discussions around infertility, while research has recently shown that fertility is declining most in minority ethnic women.[9] As I looked at online forums, I only found photos of white women. No one who looked like me. As I looked through websites and brochures of fertility clinics, the faces that stared back at me looked nothing like me. I furtively browsed pregnancy memoirs in bookstores and saw nothing from women of colour. Was I alone in all this? Was I the only brown woman who could not get pregnant? The brain starts playing tricks on you after a while, and the loneliness of being the only one, the fear of being a glitch – an incongruous outlier – is crushing.

Fifteen per cent of white women aged 25–44 in the United States have sought medical help to get pregnant, compared with 7.6 per cent of Hispanic women and 8 per cent of black women, according to data from the Department of Health and Human Services,[10] even though married black women have been shown to have twice the odds of infertility compared to white women, according to a survey conducted between 2006 and 2010 by the National Center for Health Statistics.[11] While a number of research studies have shown cost to be a major obstacle, it is not just economic barriers that are an impediment to accessing infertility treatments for women of colour. The existing literature and a great deal of the data is very white-centric, primarily stemming from the global north. But the reasons behind these 'invisible infertiles' – those who are missing from the data and stories of infertility – are more complicated than one may assume at first glance. Once again, the deep-rooted biases in healthcare – the fear of being stereotyped and of being misdiagnosed and treated badly by medical professionals – can prevent women of colour from seeking treatment. The mistrust of medical personnel persists, as we hear more stories of unconscious bias leading to prejudice and discrimination against women of colour in diagnosis and treatment.

Cultural stigmas of course play a huge role, as does the emphasis on privacy in certain cultures, where the societal perception is of huge importance ('what will others say?'). Among minority ethnic communities, infertility carries a big stigma, even though they are more likely to suffer from uterine fibroids, one of the major causes of infertility. In certain cultures, families are large, and it is expected that you will conceive naturally and easily, that women become pregnant as soon as they can and want to. Even if one does encounter problems, spirituality, religion and alternative treatments often play a bigger role in addressing fertility issues than, say, seeking IVF. Few openly discuss any problems they might have with conceiving. It is usually considered a source of shame for the family, and it is kept a secret.

Physicians may consciously or unconsciously make similar assumptions or possess biases about who deserves to be a parent and who wants or deserves treatment. Since women of colour are also often seen as hyper-fertile and as contributors to rapid population growth and crowding in inner-city areas, as is too often the case, public health initiatives for addressing infertility usually do not reach them. For instance, my own work with women in rural India a few years ago showed that a lack of adequate sex education meant that they did not know their bodies well enough to recognise their infertility problems for a long time. These women often don't have access to ovulation kits and apps to chart their cycles, which are now increasingly being used to monitor and map data about fertility. I did not use any of these apps either. Yes, they weren't as prevalent then as now, but I also felt fearful about my personal data being online, and about relying on technology coupled with a false sense of naivety and optimism ('It is my body. Shouldn't I just know about it?').

In some countries, fair and equitable access to fertility treatments is also impaired due to stigma against unpartnered (unmarried) individuals and same-sex couples. Although laws in many countries actively prohibit discrimination on the basis of marital status or sexual orientation, such laws do not exist at the federal level in every state in the USA[12] and in many countries around the world, and as we know, discrimination is not always explicit. These gaps in protection against discrimination dissuade many single and queer women from seeking treatment.

160

In the UK, fertility treatment on the NHS is still a postcode lottery with free treatment only available to couples depending on where they live. Thus, geographic unavailability may impede many from seeking or obtaining treatment. Geography can play a role in who has access to treatment and who does not, who has the resources to be able to travel to these clinics on a regular basis, and who has a supportive workplace that allows them to take time off for these repeated visits.

Many women from minority ethnic communities often face secondary infertility (being unable to conceive after giving birth in the past), a condition which is severely misunderstood, unrecognised and under-funded. In most of the Clinical Commissioning Groups (CCGs), free treatment on the NHS is not available if either partner in a couple has a child from a previous relationship. Even if 'three is a magic number', we had already lost the lottery before we had even started playing it.

When one has conceived so easily the first time, and then again, it is hard to reconcile this with the idea of being infertile. The notion of your body not being what it used to be, when not much else seems to have changed overall, can come as a shock. Yes, a few more wrinkles and curves, some sagging, but that isn't the same as accepting that our bodies do not work in the same way they once so carelessly and offhandedly did without assistance. A *New York Times* article from 2016 reports that more than 6 million women between fifteen and forty-four struggle to become or stay pregnant – whether they've previously had kids or not – according to the United States Department of Health and Human Services. Of those, one-third are estimated to have secondary infertility. It is still not researched or tracked separately from general infertility. It is easy in the vacuum of data to blame ourselves: we are too old; we left it too late; we carry too much weight, or not enough; we have too much stress and work too hard. No matter what happens, our bodies, and their frailties are always our fault, their shortcomings a consequence of our vices.

And there I was in my thirties, a brown woman. I thought that I was too young to have fertility problems.

•

'Don't think of the monkey. Whatever you do, don't think of the monkey.'

But the forbidden fruit is always sweeter. The monkey jumps and takes hold of all our thoughts. I was seeing children and babies everywhere. All the news that I read was about women getting pregnant and giving birth. And, while happy for friends, and people I didn't even know, my heart closed into itself, creating an outer shell, becoming resentful and bitter. I was constantly fighting this sinking feeling of loss for something that I didn't ever really have, this unborn child that I wanted but would never be able to conceive. A huge sense of despair and regret for a decision that I made when the time was not right. Guilt, loss, grief all come as waves. That feeling of being held under water returns. My lungs are filling up with water, the air sacs straining, bulging, blue and purple.

Today we wouldn't have had to try and fail. But we didn't go through with it then. And now we couldn't. Life is funny like that. I felt that I was being punished for that decision I made. I am not religious but sometimes I cannot escape my upbringing and all the Hindu scriptures and stories that were read to me while I was growing up. What if it was karma, what if I was being punished for taking a life that was not mine to take? Maybe I didn't deserve this now because I did that then. Rational thought and logic had no place in my life, even though all the medical information and websites say that there is no evidence of any link between induced termination and future secondary infertility if the abortion was carried out in a safe environment. Even as I pushed them away, they kept coming back, these illogical thoughts skirting the edge of rationality.

•

I was an 'inhospitable environment'. It would be difficult for me to carry another child. It isn't something that you expect to hear over the phone. I should not have called up, but I really wanted to find out the test results. The impatience weighed heavily on my shoulders. 'They will never tell you over the phone,' P had said. But I am always in a rush to find things out. It is this feeling inside me that things won't happen if I don't chase them up. Maybe it is how I am wired or maybe it was because of growing up in India. In India, there is a word *jugaad* that you are brought up with: a hustle, a fix, an 'I-have-to-make-things-happen' ethos. Being the eldest of three girls, in a world where things don't come easy for girls, the fire in the belly is lit very early on.

I called up expecting to hear the same old message that I needed to go in or speak directly to the doctor. It was the nurse on the phone, and she just told me there and then. Just like that. For once, when I was hugely unprepared, I was just bowled a googly. Anyone who knows me would know that I am not one to use a sporting metaphor. But I grew up on a diet of cricket, fed to every Indian child with their milk from the moment they were born – watching cricket, playing cricket on the streets, talking about cricket. We used to listen to cricket commentaries during school lessons, on small radios hidden in our wooden school desks. This was before iPhones, and network ubiquity, before the explosion of images, videos and sounds. Those seemed like more innocent times, with

163

the words on a small wireless device and peanuts during lessons our biggest acts of rebellion. I digress. But there can be so much comfort in nostalgia, remembering days before I had to consider my fertility, content in my ignorance of my own body, unaware of its limitations.

Oh and yes, there were fibroids, and other medical jargon that I couldn't quite understand. The only thing that suddenly stood out in bright neon lights was that I had an 'inhospitable uterus'. How was that possible? I had already had a child and I had been pregnant once more after that. It was a welcoming womb then, attracting and hosting even when it was explicitly barred from doing so.

'How is my uterus inhospitable?' I asked the nurse in a petulant tone, knowing full well that any of my physical fragilities or failures weren't really her fault. I stood there in my study, with the settled pace of my comfortable middle-class life, in a quiet village over-looking the stunning spire of the large medieval cathedral. The spire that always announced to me that I was home as it became visible over the rooftops and green canopy, when I drove in from my long commute every evening. I tried to keep my eyes firmly on that looming spire through my window, to anchor me. Holding on to that view, I could stop the ground slipping from underneath my feet.

'You shouldn't really be allowed to give this information over the phone.' I tried to sound stern, but the smallness of my voice betrayed me, obscuring the strength I was trying to muster. Healthcare practitioners are trained to deal with sensitive news. I have since revisited that very moment so many times, churning it over in my mind, hoping that the added distance has made me more objective. Memory can sometimes be a devious companion, and so I have tried to reason that perhaps I was unjustified in feeling as emotionally distraught as I did then. But time hasn't been the cool balm that I had hoped it would be. It wasn't as much the news or the way it was delivered but the utter disbelief that for someone, I wasn't worthy of basic human consideration and sensitivity. Honesty is the best policy, but a cushion would have helped, a furry cocoon to engulf me while I was dealt this blow.

'Thank you,' I told her out of habit, eschewing the fury in my gut. I remember standing there for a long time, my head bent in defeat, looking out of the window at the strawberry plants in my garden, until I saw a hedgehog run past, its spikes standing up to attention, scouring me out of my delirium.

I spent the next few days googling 'what is an inhospitable uterus?' on the internet. There wasn't much else to do. Sticking to facts and evidence often help when your emotions are unreliable. It helps me moor my thoughts and feelings, when I am trying to second-guess how I ought to feel. It seems that the internet is quite vague about it, but the medical verdict was clear: I could not provide a safe environment for a foetus to develop and grow.

Our bodies are supposed to be our safe homes, where we feel most ourselves, where we retreat when the world around us is spiky and threatening. It is what we are born into, and it is the only thing that is our constant companion, honest and sincere through our lives. For these bodies to betray us, to become unsafe, feels like infidelity, being cheated by the one we had most loved and adored, suddenly in our moment of deepest vulnerability. It is when we really need our hands to be held close, that they are pushed away. It takes so long in our lives to know the map of our bones, the curves and creases, the fingerprints of our existence. Sometimes it takes an eternity; sometimes we don't fully achieve it. For me, suddenly, that intimate partnership, the close comforting understanding, had turned sour. My uterus suddenly felt like red-hot lava, toxic and noxious. The rancid, putrid, foetid smell was now wafting through my arteries and veins, and I was a stranger to my own self. Lonesome and friendless.

In Shakespeare's *Macbeth*, infertility haunts Lady Macbeth and the king for most of their lives. As Macbeth ascends the throne, his sadness at the lack of heirs to pass the crown to becomes apparent:

> Upon my head they placed a fruitless crown
> And put a barren sceptre in my grip,
> Thence to be wrenched with an unlineal hand,
> No son of mine succeeding.
> (III. i. 63–6)[13]

Women have given birth since time immemorial. Evolutionarily this is what they were designed to do, to continue the human race. Any woman unable to give birth or conceive successfully has long been deemed a disgrace, the weight of 'barrenness' lying heavy on her head. Barren is such a ghastly word, the common term used to describe infertility in women, its roots well established in the Bible. The stories of eight biblical women, ranging from Sarah (wife of Abraham and mother of Isaac) to Hannah (mother of Samuel, the judge and prophet), and their respective struggles with infertility firmly established barrenness as a familiar parable in early modern‡ society:

‡ There is very little research to show attitudes to male infertility although there are indications that male reproductive failure was not merely focused on sexual failure and impotence as is widely believed. One such research paper which shines some light on male infertility discourse during the early modern period is Evans, J. (2016). "'They are called Imperfect men": Male Infertility and Sexual Health in Early Modern England'. *Journal of the Society for the Social History of Medicine*. 29 (2), 311–32.

the worst kind. During this time, ideas around barrenness and female infertility were becoming established, with references to the Bible used to bolster beliefs and perceptions about gender amongst medical scholars. To be called barren tells women that they are not fertile soil; they cannot create life; they don't have value or meaning; they are like the rocky untilled earth that is never going to bear any fruit. During this period, women became the main focus in discussions around medical infertility, which is particularly noteworthy as women were otherwise completely invisible and marginalised in much of our historical records. The early modern society's patriarchal and misogynistic fixations about the pathological nature of women's ailments meant that women's bodies were scrutinised obsessively.

I couldn't get my head around this idea of being barren. Suddenly, inexplicably, my body had decided it would not cooperate. I had been used to keeping tight control of my life and its course for the most part. I had tried to be a rock. Now the sand trickled through a gritted fist, me watching helplessly, trying to grasp the grains with trembling hands.

•

Finally, we got an appointment. Finally. When one has waited for something for so long, it can feel terrifying to face it head on. With its imminence I had an urge to run away. Yet I felt a corresponding sense of exigency at the same time; it seemed like the day of reckoning. Going into hospitals always reminds me of my childhood fascination with medicine and determination to be a heart specialist. My parents were eager for me, their eldest, to be a doctor, much like the stereotypical representation of an Indian family in the sitcom Goodness Gracious Me, and were disappointed when I chose to pursue engineering rather than medicine.

The long corridors of the women's hospital had the faint smell of chloroform and medicine mixed together with despair, loss and grief. Against the grey pallor of the freshly painted walls, the bright paintings and murals of tiny ceramic pieces decorating the entrance seemed like the painted smile of a jester, hiding the gloom underneath. The new mothers with their pristine new babies snuggled close in pink and white pretty woollen blankets and hats, satisfaction and exhaustion written in the lines of their face. The mothers-to-be walking proud, with a dream in their eyes, and a wobble in their walk. And then there were others of us, fragmented into tiny pieces, not daring to dream, but living through moments of long childless days building castles in the sky. Hope continuing to live hand in hand with despair.

The consultant drew a graph for us with a line zooming down across the page to show how my fertility had gone downhill. I stared at it, and so did P. I was perched at the edge of my chair, my short legs never reaching the floor, while P sat back with his lanky long limbs folded over him. The line showed a biological reality, right there in black and white. Being data scientists, we both deal with data and graphs, and so we glanced at each other and shared a secret geeky smile. These were the kind of amateurish graphs that we would normally laugh at. I pretended to be calm and detached, intrigued and interested in the data, asking insightful questions, appearing matter of fact, as if it were just another anonymous case study that I was discussing as part of one of my scientific experiments.

Raised eyebrows, scrunched-up forehead, narrowed eyes looking at me, the consultant examined me as if I was a curiosity. 'Are you a doctor?' he finally asked me. I wondered if he thought that I was acting 'too big for my boots' and I immediately became anxious.

168

With so much of our reproductive future in his hands, I wanted him to be on our side, wanted so desperately for him to like us, to champion us, and to want us to succeed. We wanted as many cheerleaders as possible right then, rooting for us, praying for us. I didn't want him to think that I thought of myself as clever in any way. It is often when women feel the most vulnerable that we feel the need to bolster a man's ego; not give him even an inkling that we consider ourselves on an equal par with him. This is a way we protect ourselves from the fallout of a man being offended, hurt, upset. What if he is unable to accept it graciously? Given that in the UK there are more than double the number of men compared to women on the specialists register,[14] this means that women are often at the mercy of male medical professionals, those who sometimes hide behind big technical words, words that are a deliberate attempt to make us feel small and them big, words that create barriers between us and knowledge of our own bodies. Women often have to navigate these shadowy pathways of medical jargon with men in white coats speaking to them as if they are children. I just wanted someone to tell me in the simplest words, without pretence, in an honest and transparent way, what was happening, why and what our options were. But it is never as simple. Everything seems clouded in mystery, women's bodies hidden from themselves as if knowing too much might allow them to weigh up choices and possibilities. Everyone presumes that 'everyone knows' and yet no one does. And no one asks.

'Inhospitable uterus' comes up again, as does 'incompetent cervix'. A uterus is just a uterus; a cervix is a cervix. But as we put ourselves through the scrutiny of these medical professionals probing and prodding the parts that have been ours and ours alone for so long, suddenly our bodies become public property. The patriarchal gendered language is so heavily steeped into reproductive science: a tilted cervix, an unreceptive uterus, and we are back to the classroom and the biology textbooks where women host, and men seek. Women passively wait, and men have to be welcomed, attracted, as we play the age-old mating game. I also notice how vulva, vagina, uterus are all called 'female' anatomy and I can't help wondering how someone who is intersex or identifies as another gender after birth would feel about this. This is rooted in cissexism or cisnormativity, the idea that anything that is cisgender is normal, and anything else that is not so, is abnormal and unnatural. The gendered language of the medical forms and tests is something I had not even considered with my privilege as a cisgender woman. We often don't look outside our bubbles, do we? Especially if we are the norm. Especially when it comes to sex and gender.

Even though we live in a highly information-saturated, sexualised culture, fertility concerns remain in dark corners, too unsightly to bring out in the open. We navigate the mysteries of our own bodies in the white corridors and ultrasound rooms, syringes drawing blood and eggs, needles pumping hormones into our unsuspecting veins, somehow cajoling our bodies to sputter into motion, shudder and judder into reluctant action from a state of stupor.

As we went through the tests, I found out that my AMH level is very low,§ and we were banking on the last of the reserves of

§ Anti-Mullerian Hormone (AMH) is a protein hormone produced by cells within the ovary, and is a marker of the ovarian egg reserve and used as a determinant of fertility. AMH levels are, on average, lower in older women (particularly over the age of forty) and higher in women with Polycystic Ovaries (PCO) or Polycystic Ovary Syndrome (PCOS). Levels of AMH decline over time and become undetectable at menopause, when a woman's egg supply is exhausted.

eggs that I was born with. I didn't know anything about AMH then – often talked about as a 'fertility MOT' – and I took the specialist's word as law. More recent studies have shown that the level of AMH and the amount of eggs remaining are not a good indicator of a woman's chances of becoming pregnant. Some reports even claim that it is a 'waste of money'. A study published in 2017 with 750 women showed that women with a low AMH value had an 84 per cent predicted cumulative probability of conception by twelve cycles of pregnancy attempts compared with 75 per cent in women with a normal AMH value, a non-significant difference of merely 67 women.¶[15]

I was told that I was very likely undergoing premature menopause. I hadn't even considered that menopause would arrive so soon; I had not even turned forty. Isn't menopause a sign of middle age, a signifier of decline, of it all being downhill from there? That's how it is seen and talked about. It does not happen to women my age, surely, I scream. No one answered back.

Scientists have been trying to understand menopause for a very long time, although the term was only devised by French physicians in the early 1800s. The question that has confounded them is: 'why live longer than you can reproduce?' In terms of evolutionary Darwinian theories of fitness, menopause is supposed to allow women to care for their children without any further offspring being born to them, so that they can devote their energy to supporting the next generation. This ensures survival of the species, and less competition amongst women for reproductive mates. As women age, the costs of reproduction become higher and so they spend that energy in supporting the reproductive efforts of their offspring. It is meant to

¶ Statistically this is a p-value of 0.000008 and a significance level of 0%.

avoid overlapping reproduction and co-breeding between different generations.

There is also the 'grandmother hypothesis' which suggests that menopausal women can then invest their energy in supporting their daughters and sons in passing on the healthy genes to their grandchildren, which not only allows the survival and fitness of the species as a whole, but also wider social networks which are important for acquisition of resources. It takes a village to raise a child. In the long distant past, with our ancestors, this would have been reasonable as life expectancy was much shorter, but as we live longer and longer, this post-menopause period is stretching out for human females.

Long postmenopausal lifespans separate humans from other primates. In our closest non-human genetic relatives, the chimpanzees, the rate of degradation of the follicles that females are born with accelerates much more rapidly after the age of thirty-five, and this has often been used as a basis for supporting the theory that thirty-five is the 'geriatric' age for human females, and that their reproductive facilities go downhill after that age. However, most chimpanzees die before this happens for them and while they are still in their reproductive phase, and so it is baffling to scientists why human females continue to live for so long after they are no longer able to reproduce. Some biologists have proposed that menopause was used as a 'culling mechanism', which sounds absolutely terrifying. Once women had produced offspring and could no longer reproduce, they were of no use to the society, and as they suffered debilitating symptoms associated with menopause, they were more vulnerable and therefore more attractive to predators. This natural cull would have ensured that limited resources were then available to those members of the community who were still reproducing and therefore more valuable. This is a controversial theory, but it is rooted in the belief that women's reproductive potential and capacity is what makes them valuable. If they do not have this capacity, they might as well make space for those who deserve to live more.

Menopause ought to be liberating for a woman, freeing her from the drudgery of menstruation every month, to a life filled with sex free from the fear of pregnancy. However the symptoms that come along with menopause and the months and years leading up to it – perimenopause – can be unpleasant and debilitating, and if you still want children, of course the delicious prospect of freedom also brings with it considerable fear and sadness. Additionally, while we are taught to view menopause as a dreaded day far in the future when we are in our twenties and thirties, something that happens to women when they are much older,** we do not talk about premature menopause or early ovarian insufficiency.

Medical websites still state that the reasons for premature menopause are often unknown. Scientists are still trying to figure out why and how this happens, as more women are coming forward with their stories of early menopause from as young as fifteen years old. According to the Daisy Network in the UK, one in 10,000 people under the age of twenty will experience menopause. A very recent study from Washington University School of Medicine in St. Louis found a link between mutations in a specific gene and premature menopause.[16] The researchers found that when the gene – called nuclear envelope membrane protein 1 (NEMP1), which has not

** The NHS website states that: 'Early menopause happens when a woman's periods stop before the age of forty-five. It can happen naturally, or as a side effect of some treatments. For most women, the menopause starts between the ages of forty-five and fifty-five.'

been widely studied – is missing in fruit flies, roundworms, zebrafish and mice, the animals are infertile or lose their fertility unusually early but appear otherwise healthy. The researchers were not studying fertility; this was an accidental discovery that may explain why women who are missing this particular gene ran out of eggs and suffered early menopause.

I go back to the doctor, and we are passed on from one specialist to another. I feel like there are no clear answers. I go through several rounds of tests; more blood is drawn, the eternal struggle to find the sprightly veins, the long walks through the lugubrious hospital corridors, the immodest green gowns, the cold numbing feeling of the ultrasound jelly, the pungent hospital odour becoming a part of me. The journey towards bearing another human has made me almost inhuman, where I am merely a vessel to be probed, punctured, examined. No one asks me how I am feeling, whether I am anxious, depressed, frightened.

An anonymous paper published in 2013 uses Cassandra as a mascot to describe the author's experience of age-related infertility and unintended childlessness.[17] As the story goes, Cassandra, daughter of King Priam (the ruler of Troy during the Trojan war) and Queen Hecuba, had the ability to see into the future. She was desired by Apollo who granted her the gift of prophecy in return for erotic favours, but she refused him. And in revenge, he cursed her so that her visions would never be believed. In Aeschylus's *Agamemnon*, Cassandra bemoans this fate:

> Apollo, Apollo!
> God of all ways, but only Death's to me,
> O thou Apollo, thou Destroyer named!
> What way hast led me, to what evil home?[18]

In this article, the anonymous author called 'Jane Everywoman' writes about her own experiences while reflecting on the broader challenges facing women today when planning a family. 'Jane' writes about the false myths that circulate about the miracle births from IVF, the celebrities who admit to the use of IVF treatment, but rarely disclose how many pregnancies were lost in the process, the toll taken on their own or their baby's bodies, what the total cost – both financial and emotional – was, or the number of attempts needed for a live birth. Jane continued to believe in this false prophecy that IVF would easily 'cure her'.

There is no hope, no comfort. As Cassandra says in *Agamemnon*: 'Caught in the folded web's / entanglement she pinions him and with the black horn / strikes. And he crumples in the watered bath.'[19] The fertility treatments become more of a curse than a boon, valid alarms ignored and disbelieved.

Slowly all the tests, appointments, cycles start merging into one another, as I sit there, feeling smaller and smaller, in my mind becoming nothing but the one with faults. I'm too old, too big, too small; it is the woman that is too much. My husband has tests too of course, but he is absolved of all responsibility as soon as these come back normal. It is on me now. All of it.

The cycle of infertility can have a huge effect on relationships: the hormones, the tests, the needles all take a toll. The militant schedule of timed sex, the mapping and monitoring of cycles, the regular poring over ovulation charts with a bowl of cereal can often kill the romance. While it is a very intensive intimate thing to go through, there can be so much heartbreak. The disappointments, the anxiety, the sadness all faced together alone, as couples often hide their fertility treatments from friends and family. We had. We were in this little bubble of ours, a cauldron of intense emotions, closer than ever before, but with nowhere to escape and hide from the guilt (mine) and helplessness (his). As the focus shifts so much to biology and biomedical processes, there can be little space for the mental–emotional connection to thrive.

One morning I had woken up, much like every other day and, over coffee, my husband had joked, 'What are your plans today? What are you going to do today to make powerful white men uncomfortable?' and I was reminded why I loved him. But there, as we sat in that room and I encountered yet another white middle-aged fertility specialist in the corridors of our destiny, I did not have the heart to make him uncomfortable. I wanted him to be content, to be very comfortable in our presence, even if it meant me biting my tongue and strangling the words that were dying to come out, the scream inside me growing into a roar that only I seemed to hear. A brown woman navigating white corridors, I had become used to hiding my true self, as I found over the years that people expected me to shrink myself, not be so loud, so opinionated, or even interesting. Women of colour get good at skirting, navigating these treacherous stereotypes and norms, but inevitably fall back into these boxes to avoid discomfort to people around them.

P reached out and squeezed my hand. He is normally uncomfortable with any sort of public display of affection, which I find irksome at times, and so I was grateful for that tiny gesture. I knew in that small moment that he could hear the cry of my words that were unsaid, and he knew that while I smiled, I was shaking and quivering inside.

VI.

HALF–WOMEN CREATURES

THE WORLD SEEMS TO BE in the midst of an infertility epidemic. While I had never felt more lonely, I was far from alone. The fertility rate is falling; there is a fertility crisis.★ Today, declining fertility rates are often blamed on wider changes in the way women are living and when they are choosing to have babies. The average age of first-time motherhood is rising in England and Wales and across most of Europe. The reasons behind this change are complex, but in Western Europe include increased educational and professional opportunities for women and changing models of family life. Childlessness is often perceived to be a direct result of these changes, so often infertility is seen as a modern problem.

However, this isn't true: it merely seems to be the case because

★ From Stone, L. (October 2019). Institute of Family Studies blog: 'Very low fertility rates are becoming increasingly normal across the globe, with most countries having birth rates between 1.4 and 1.9 children per woman. Countries with birth rates above 1.6 or 1.7 children per woman experienced fertility declines. Countries with birth rates below that saw more stability. Even in countries that are perceived to be overpopulated such as Pakistan and India fertility rates dropped by 25–27 per cent.'

women's experiences of infertility are missing from their recorded historical narratives.

> And when Rachel saw that she bare Jacob no children, Rachel envied her sister; and said unto Jacob, Give me children, or else I die. (Genesis 30:1)

In its earlier forms and discourses, infertility seems to be preceded by 'barrenness' and 'sterility' which Sandelowski and de Lacey describe as 'a divine curse of biblical proportions'[1] and Flemming as 'an absolutely irreversible physical condition' respectively.[2] The history of infertility is fascinating to me, because it is also the history of how women's bodies have been misunderstood and maligned, idolised and stigmatised. The propagation of the race, the continuation of genetic legacy, the survival of humankind, has always been a source of anxiety, and therefore a woman's ability to conceive and produce offspring has always been perceived to be her greatest asset. Advance the family name and lineage; carry the blood line. The symbols of fertility are the ones worshipped through ancient history. Many of these myths centre around goddesses who are fertile and produce male heirs. The earth mother, the mother goddess, was centred in the largely agricultural patriarchal society where women were equated to land, both having a passive role in (re)production. The nature of woman and earth is synonymous, and in fact the word woman and life are linked with each other, with women considered the source of life due to their childbearing abilities. The feminine power and magic lie in a woman's ability to conceive, much as the earth is considered the giver of new life.

In ancient Greek medical vocabulary, as early as the fourth or fifth century BC, where we first start seeing a discussion of infertility, the two main terms were *aphoros* and *atokos*, both negative adjectives referring to the absence of a productive bearing; both applied only to women. Rebecca Flemming, fellow of Jesus College, Cambridge, in her 2013 paper discusses how even as land and trees can be *aphoros* – barren or non-fruit bearing – and money may be *atokos* – if it does not bring forth profit – men are neither.[3] This gendering of reproductive vocabulary has continued: 'infertile' and 'sterile' can be used for both women and men, but 'barren' is never used for men.

> And, behold, thy cousin Elisabeth, she hath also conceived a son in her old age: and this is the sixth month with her, who was called barren. (Luke 1:36)

Even though semen is visible (unlike the egg), and the Aristotelian view shaping so much of classical antiquity was that men were the sole creative force and women the passive partners in conception, the predominant and widespread belief through time has been that women are responsible for fertility. Hippocrates, the Greek physician responsible for the Hippocratic oath that all doctors have to swear, blamed all sorts of things in a woman's body for her inability to conceive, such as fat compressing the mouth of the womb, and so any 'unnaturally fat' woman could not bear children. This is arguably one of the earliest incidents of body-shaming, which puts the onus on women to look after their bodies lest any fat renders them childless.

One of the most preposterous suggestions made by Hippocrates was that the menstruation blood could be sloshing around a woman's insides, rather than being released, and thereby inhibiting her ability to get pregnant. In the *Corpus Hippocraticum*, a group of around sixty anonymous Greek medical texts mostly composed in the eastern

Mediterranean over the late fifth and early fourth centuries BC, attributed to the physician, but not all written by him, it states that women absorb more moisture and become overfilled with blood as their flesh is softer and more sponge-like than men. Men can get rid of any excess moisture by hard labour, but Hippocrates and other physicians of the time believed – of course – that women did not have this opportunity, which could lead to excess blood being stored in their wombs. Although there is a mention of shared responsibility in one of these treatises, this gets a very cursory mention, leaving the rest of discussion open to lay the blame squarely on women's bodies:

> The cause of a man and woman's failure to generate, when having intercourse with each other, resides sometimes in both, sometimes in just one or the other.[4]

The author of another Hippocratic treatise, *On Infertile Women*, says this on the subject:

> These are the many and varied causes in women on account of which they do not bring forth children before they are treated, and on account of which they become completely barren. It is no wonder, therefore, that women often cannot produce children.[5]

Greek physicians were obsessed with a woman's womb, and it was central to their proposition that women were inferior to men. The womb was thought of as a mystical creature by Plato and Hippocrates, something that just slopped around inside, described by the physician Aretaeus of Cappadocia as an 'animal within an animal', an organ that 'moved of itself hither and thither in the flanks'.[6] The uterus wandered around a woman's body hungry for semen, and if it travelled the wrong way, it would cause choking, shortness of breath and chest pain. This illness was called *hysterike pnix*, or 'the suffocation of the womb', and was believed to cause erratic and unreliable behaviour in women.[7] The Greek physician Galen[†] also proposed that when a woman's 'seeds' are unfertilised, they 'rot' inside her and become toxic. Hippocrates, while believing that the 'wandering womb' was the reason for all of woman's wily ways and illnesses, also believed and proposed that unless a woman gave birth, she would be weakened, because a woman only stayed strong by creating new life. If she wasn't procreating she would lose not only her value in society, but also her own physical health and fitness. The threat of a wandering womb was also used to keep a woman in her place: it was suggested that keeping the bored womb occupied with consistent sex and continually keeping women pregnant could save them from hysteria (from the Greek *hystera* or womb), keeping the womb – and the notion of womanhood as motherhood – secure.

'Birds seem they, but with face like woman-kind; foul-flowing bellies, hands with crooked claws and ghastly lips they have, with hunger pale', Virgil says about the Harpies in *The Aeneid*.[8] A half-bird, half-woman creature of Greek mythology, portrayed sometimes as a woman with bird wings and legs, Harpies can also be seen in Shakespeare's *The Tempest*. Here the spirit Ariel tortured the antagonists Antonio, Sebastian and Alonso for their crimes by staging a banquet scene similar to that in *The Aeneid*. In the Tate Gallery in London there is a watercolour by William Blake titled *The Wood of*

† Galen, Greek 'Galenos', Latin 'Galenus', (born 129 CE, Pergamum, Mysia, Anatolia [now Bergama, Turkey], died c. 216), Greek physician, writer, and philosopher who exercised a dominant influence on medical theory and practice in Europe from the Middle Ages until the mid-17th century. https://www.britannica.com/biography/Galen

the Self-Murderers: The Harpies and the Suicides. Blake was inspired by Dante's evocation of the Harpy in his *Inferno*, a scene where the tortured woods are infested with Harpies:

> There do the hideous Harpies make their nests,
> Who chased the Trojans from the Strophades,
>   With sad announcement of impending doom;
> Broad wings have they, and necks and faces human,
>   And feet with claws, and their great bellies fledged;
>   They make laments upon the wondrous trees.[9]

There are other half-women creatures, but Harpies hold a fascination with artists and writers through the ages, with their long claws, embodying storm winds and ugliness, feasting on carcasses and human detritus. Ovid called them half-vultures. When I first saw this painting in all its almost monochromatic starkness, the twisted torturous trees, the soundless forest, I could almost hear the echoes of sadness from these bloated shapes of half-bird, half-woman creatures suspended high above, as if doomed to a life of pain. Their wounds were invisible, but gouged deep. It felt that there was a part of me that could relate: lost, trying to find my place in a state of delirium; repellent and marked with a shadowy curse. I had been feeling like a half-woman, slowly, gradually, steadily transforming into a body that repelled me, with swollen feet and belly, and silent lamentations in eerie nights, with an insatiable hunger growing every day, consuming everything that had been good in our lives so far.

•

Infertility has long been viewed with suspicion – as well as superstition – across various cultures. In ancient Egypt more than 3,000 years ago, Ramses II ruled the land. This great pharaoh is said to have had twenty wives who bore him as many as 120 sons and eighty daughters. He is still the symbol of virility and Egyptian women make journeys of hundreds of miles from towns and villages to circumambulate the colossal statue of Ramses II, hoping that the ritual will help make them mothers. The forty-foot statue of Ramses stands just outside Cairo, and women come here to perform the ritual of circling the statue seven times. These old myths about magic and powers residing in this old statue persist in Egyptian society. Even though the country is mainly Islamic now, the desire to have a child makes these women very pragmatic and prepared to violate any religion in the hopes of finding a cure for their infertility, which is really unheard of in the otherwise strongly hierarchical and dogmatic structures of Islam in that country.

I travelled to Egypt in 2002, and here I heard how paganism is still quite prevalent in smaller villages, and how Muslim men were enabled by the laws of their community to leave their wives if they could not bear them any children. The Egyptians blamed the woman if there was any problem in conceiving. A woman's womb was the centre of her being. Even a sty in her eye was linked to the problems in her womb. There is a belief that demons – or jinns – have taken hold of the woman's body, causing them to be childless. A deep-seated faith in the power of rituals exists to get rid of these evil spirits, including urinating on the grey sandstone statue, and bathing in the dirty pond outside the temple.

Ancient Egyptian mythology is filled with iconography, and the vulture features prominently. This is Nephthys, or as old Egyptians called her, Nebthwt, meaning 'the Mistress of the House'. I remember visiting the temples and the tour guide telling us all about the 'barren goddess'. While I don't know how reliable his testimony was, I am aware that she was originally conceived as the counterpart for the male god Set. He represented the desert, while she represented the air. Set was infertile (like the desert that he represented) and was frequently described as either bisexual or gay. As a goddess of the air, she could take the form of a bird, and because she was barren she was associated with the vulture – a bird which the Egyptians believed did not bear children. And, as an infertile woman, Nephthys became a symbol of death and mourning. The irony of this symbolism isn't lost on me. We also saw a wall relief at Karnak, near Luxor, which was known in ancient Egypt as Ipet-isu, 'the most select of places'. Min was the Egyptian god of fertility, invoked for animal, vegetable and human fertility. He is represented in this relief in a human form with legs placed close together like those of a mummy and an erect phallus. A flail is depicted above his raised arm with hand extended to one side. He wears a tight skull cap on his head with two lofty plumes and two streamers hanging down the back. Amongst the offerings to Min is a lettuce (pictured just above the tip of the erect phallus) which was considered an aphrodisiac and frequently associated with the god. Women still come to visit this image of Min, to seek his blessings.

The Egyptian goddess Maat is similarly akin to the mother, associated with the symbol of the ankh, which has become synonymous with fertility and good luck, and also associated intrinsically with the female gender. It is not the vulture, the carrier of death and feeding on carrion, the symbol of the barren goddess Nephthys, that represents female gender.

The Kahun Gynaecological Papyrus is the oldest known medical text in Egypt, from around 1800 BC. It is kept in the Petrie Museum of Archaeology Egyptian Library, at University College London where I taught between 2006 and 2009. Much of my memories during that time are of being a young female academic in a predominantly male environment, trying to balance single motherhood and work. My recollections from UCL are fiercely connected to my experiences as a mother, and the way motherhood was seen as an impediment to my professional career by people around me. And so, as I travelled to UCL to look at this papyrus, it felt fortuitous to go back there while exploring the idea of how female fertility and motherhood was written about in ancient times.

These papyri were brought into the modern world in April and November 1889 by Flinders Petrie. They were found on a site near the modern-day Egyptian town of Lehun. What is absolutely fascinating about this papyrus is that it is divided into thirty-four sections, each featuring a specific medical problem or complaint, the first seventeen dedicated primarily to reproductive problems. The translations by Stephen Quirke demonstrate the belief in ancient Egyptian times that much illness was generated throughout the whole body as a result of various conditions of the womb, some of which defy logic in terms of how they might be linked to one another.

SsAw [st irty.sy] mn n mAt.n.s Hr mn nHbt.s
Dd.xr.k r.s xAaw pw n idt m irty.sy
ir.xr.k r.s kAp sy Hr snTr Hr mrHt mAt
kAp kAt.s Hr.s kAp irty.sy Hr inst nt gny
rdi.xr.k wnm.s mist nt aA wADt

Examination of a woman whose eyes are aching till she
cannot see, on top of aches in her neck:
You should say of it 'it is discharges of the womb in her eyes'.
You should treat it by fumigating her with incense and fresh oil,

185

fumigating her womb with it, and fumigating her
eyes with goose leg fat.
You should have her eat a fresh ass liver.

[Column 1, Lines 1–5][10]

Much of it seems to be based in the Hippocratic tradition, and descriptions include 'wandering womb', 'womb discharge' and 'terror of the womb', all of which seem capable of causing difficulties with eyes, teeth, joints and the neck and head. A lot of interesting treatments are offered as suggestions, including fumigation.

SsAw st mr idt.s m xp
Dd.xr.k r.s ptr ssnt.t
ir Dd.s n.k iw.i Hr ssnt ASr
Dd.xr.k r.s nmsw pw n idt
ir.xr.k r.s kAp sy Hr ssnt.s nbt m ASr

Examination of a woman who is ill from her womb wandering
You should say of it 'what do you smell?'
If she tells you 'I smell roasting'
You should say of it 'it is wrappings (?) of the womb'
You should treat it by fumigating her with whatever
she smells as roast

[Column 1, Lines 5-8][11]

Is this the vaginal steaming that Goop seems to be recommending today, I wonder. While there are massages with scented oils, which sound tempting, they also recommend using asses' milk along with ass liver and urine, possibly not the easiest things to procure today. Where would I even get an ass's milk? The Egyptians also believed that putting a date in the vagina was a cure for sterility. Another cure was to rub the belly and thighs with menstrual blood. It is unclear why they thought the date would work, but menstrual blood was believed to be a particularly potent force and was used in many situations. It was always imbued with magical powers, which seems paradoxical with its perception as dirty and unsightly.

The Babylonian *Atrahasis* epic, from the mid-seventeenth century BC, describes a conflict between the gods and the overpopulated world of men, during which the gods flood the earth to destroy human life. Eventually repenting for this destruction, the gods decide that they need man, but to ensure that pre-flood problems of over-population do not arise again, Ea, the god of wisdom, instructs the goddess Nintu to create three new classes of human beings, one of which is women who are unable to bear children.

> In addition, let there be a third category among the peoples,
> Among the peoples women who bear and women who do not bear.
> Let there be among the peoples the Pagittu-demon
> to snatch the baby from the lap of her who bore it.
> Establish Ugbabtu-women, Entu-women, and Igisitu-women
> and let them be taboo and so stop childbirth. [12]

The interpretations of the myth remind us that the social phenom-enon of barrenness is in fact essential to the continuation of humankind as a means of regulating population. Various demons were invoked who infiltrated broader cultural sensibilities as gate-keepers of women's reproduction. From an analysis of a vast corpus of ancient cuniform texts, the University of Pennsylvania Museum's Erle Leichty writes that this was the lion-headed demoness Lamashtu, appearing as 'a nude, hideous woman with the head of a lion or bird, talons, and long dangling breasts',[13] barren and envious, who caused infertility, miscarriage and infant death. Ancient texts are filled with such representations of murderous women pushed into such motivations due to their own barrenness. The Hebrew Testament of Solomon, dated by various scholars from between the first to fourth century AD, describes the demon Obizuth or Abyzou, 'all head and no limbs':[14]

> Her glance was altogether bright and greeny, and her hair was tossed wildly like a dragon's; and the whole of her limbs were invisible.[15]

Abyzou was barren, and she confessed that her envy of women who could bear children motivated her murderous hauntings: 'For I have no work other than the destruction of children.' Women were not only being castigated for being infertile, but also were being represented as vengeful and bitter demonesses who would inflict the same suffering on other women by rendering them infertile or by snatching their children in the womb. If they couldn't have it, no one could. Women being pitted against others: age-old trick in the patriarchal kit.

In ancient Japanese society, having children or abstaining from doing so was linked to the specific roles that women had to play. While the women of aristocratic families dedicated their lives to becoming mothers, and bearing heirs, the non-aristocratic Buddhist women, and those ordained into the religious order, had to take a vow of abstinence and saw childlessness as a proof of their ultimate salvation and healing. In fact, the abandonment of their 'woman-hood' was recommended altogether by transforming their female bodies into male bodies in order to reach ultimate 'healing' in terms of salvation. Women's bodies were seen as inferior; mother-hood as a mortal quest. On the other hand, the same Buddhist women – once ordained – were worshipped as divinities to ensure that worldly healing could be achieved by women through successful procreation and continuation of the family line. In either role, women had to conform to one side of the looking glass, echoes of remnants left scattered either side of it, as they had to choose either to fulfil their feminine destiny or choose to reject it completely. There was no middle ground. This wasn't really a choice.

In pre-industrial English societies, especially in the early Middle Ages, patients commonly responded to medical problems by seeking aid from saints through a variety of devotional practices.[16] From the 1400s, infertility had gained a strong religious association and messages of barrenness were often preached from the pulpit. The notion of original sin dominated and women had very few rights or liberties. The historian Daphna Oren-Magidor explains that 'Reproductive matters had their own patron saints. Women prayed to the Virgin Mary when they had reproductive concerns, because she was the ultimate symbol of motherhood. Mary's mother, St. Anne, was the patron saint of barren women, because of a story that she had conceived only through divine intervention. St. Margaret the Virgin was a patron saint of pregnant women because she was swallowed by the Devil in the form of a dragon and then escaped from him unscathed, much as a child emerges from its mother's womb.'[17] Churches also loaned 'working relics' to women to aid them in pregnancy and childbirth. During this period there was a deep-rooted belief that women's bodies were governed by their womb, and that infertility was really a fault with the women. As Jennifer Evans, a historian at the University of Hertfordshire, quotes in her 2016 paper:

Hence we may gather, that Barrenness is oftner from a fault in the women then the men: for in men there is nothing required but fruitful Seed spent into a fruitful womb. But women besides the meeting of their own Seed, must receive, retain, and nourish the mans; and afford matter for the forming of the Child, in which divers accidents happen, and any of these will cause Barrennes.[18]

'Be fruitful, and multiply, and replenish the earth' was the command from God to Adam and Eve at the beginning of the Book of Genesis (1:28). Infertility was considered a divine curse. Procreation was a necessity and important to the continuation of the species, and a couple's sole reason for sexual intercourse was for procreation. If they did not perform their divine duty, it was believed that fertility would be decreased. The medical aspects of infertility were still not considered or recognised, and it was believed that infertility could also be the consequence of sins committed, such as infidelity and blasphemy. The Bible's pronouncements on barrenness and its divine connection to God was promoted in society broadly across different cultures, and infertility was used as a mechanism to control women, encouraging them to pray for a child, but at the same time to not admonish or reproach God if they could not bear one. The story of Hannah and Rachel from the Bible was used to show that while Hannah dutifully prayed to God, Rachel did not only ask for a child, but demanded it ('or else I die'). She therefore exemplifies impatience and a lack of humility, and it was because she 'pined' for a child that she was punished with death in childbirth. By instilling fear in the heart of women, the Church maintained control, and continued to reinforce the view that motherhood was central to a woman's identity, perpetuating the negative stigma associated with infertility. It was a punishment, and a curse. In doing so, they also managed to integrate religion irrevocably with the everyday fabric of the lives of the common people, extending as far into domestic intimacies as possible. Infertility therefore became a vehicle for the Church and religion to exert control and influence.

Infertility, the mark of divine punishment, was a real fear during the Middle Ages. The role of women was in constant flux, and they were considered most inferior in the social hierarchy. A woman's fertility was a precious commodity especially amongst the predominantly agricultural communities, and so the woman's value was linked to her ability to give birth. In 1582, Thomas Bentley published a compilation of prayers and religious guidance for women – *The Monument of Matrones* – and one of them, listed in the index as a prayer 'against barren-ness', is Hannah's prayer for a son, in which she agrees to offer her child to God if she is cured: 'Oh Lord of Hosts, if thou wilt looke on the trouble of thine handmaid . . . and not forget thine handmaid, but give unto thine handmaid a manchild (1 Samuel 1:11).' Many religious manuals and guidebooks during this period promoted the view that a married woman's ultimate responsibility and goal was to have a child, and proposed that infertile women were being tested for their faith, and encouraged them to engage in being humble and devout, a view that was also shared – and still is to some extent – in Indian societies where religion, penance, talismans and prayers are seen as a solution to infertility.

Much of this discourse – negative perceptions of infertile women and the stigmatisation they encountered – is of course rooted in a patriarchal society with clearly defined gender roles. Infertility was seen as a failure at something as 'natural' as parenthood, a failure to fulfil one's destiny, as Laura Gowing, professor of early modern history at King's College London, argues: '. . . for women, like men, infertility was readily related to a failure to conform to gender norms: inadequate men and dominant women might both miss their biological destiny.'[19] As older women approached menopause, they were more likely to be branded a witch and killed. The English minister John Oliver uses the term 'unfruitful wombs' and writes about reproductive responsibility in his *A Present to be given to Teeming Women*:

> . . . pregnant women have their particular duties, and their pecu-
> liar motives to diligence in them; and their number is considerable.
> They are a worthy part of the Community, then especially, when
> breeding; for much of the comfort of the present generation, and
> the honour of God, and future being of his Church in succeeding
> generations, is concerned in those Infants yet un-born.[20]

The responsibility to procreate as a social and personal responsibility shaped many of the attitudes around infertility during this period, and as religion and medical fear and ignorance weighed heavily on women's shoulders, it was assumed that all women desired children. The midwife Jane Sharp writes in 1671: 'to conceive with child is the earnest desire if not all yet of most women'.[21]

Infertile women were always viewed with suspicion, described as manly, domineering and overly sexual in early modern England. It is a common trope in many poems and plays that 'barren' women were adulterous and that they were highly sexual beings, having dalliances with various men. In a culture that does not view mothers as sexual beings, where as soon as you become a mother your sexuality is not your own, it makes sense that infertility had to be blamed on the sexual desires of a woman in some way. These tropes of adulterous infertile women being used as political satire were laying down the gender identities that have been perpetuated through the centuries. Infertile women were also hysterical. Richard Napier, the famous physician and astrologer of the early 1600s in England, described infertility as a cause of 'mental disturbance' in his female patients. But gradually, from being a moral issue and, despite advances in understanding the anatomy of the female body, it became a pathological issue. Barren women were 'broken'. Their purpose in life continued to be birthing strong children, and this applied to women of all social class.

For the colonialists during this period, reproduction had both a religious and economic dimension, as fertility and large family units pointed towards the success and survival of the colony, while infertility did the opposite. Joyce Chaplin, Professor of early American history at Harvard University, argues that infertility was how colonial English invaders established ideas of racial hierarchy and difference with the indigenous Americans.[22] They also used differences between bodies and family structure – the white 'correctly ordered' families contrasting with the perceived chaos and incivility of the local population – to attribute the smaller indigenous families to 'barrenness', to 'other' them, discredit them and assign them as inferior. Their racialised anxieties around reproduction to maintain the survival of the colonies established infertility as a curse and a crisis afflicting the weakest and the most inferior.

•

While infertility was stigmatised in ancient societies, childbirth was believed to make women powerful, and men wanted a part of it. This is why in Greek mythology we hear the story of Zeus swallowing his wife Metis so that he himself could give birth to their daughter Athena. The power to create life resided with the woman, but this also meant that women were credited with control over conception. The Greek physician Galen asserted that a woman had to enjoy sex for the 'seed' to be released, and if she did not enjoy it, she could not become pregnant. I wonder if women were permitted or empowered to say when they weren't enjoying sex? Similarly, Aristotle established the theory that female pleasure played a part in conception, and orgasm was necessary for a woman to become pregnant. This myth also persists on some infertility forums and groups where I was constantly reminded that I 'needed' to enjoy the sex in order to become pregnant. The flip side of this falsehood has been its influence on thinking around rape and pregnancy in legal and social situations, where it is sometimes believed that a pregnancy shows a woman's consent to an alleged rape. As late as the early nineteenth century, if a woman became pregnant via rape, the claim of rape was invalidated, because it was deemed that a woman could not conceive unless the intercourse was consensual, although a British legal text from 1795 dismissed the biological validity of this claim and hence its legal legitimacy. This pseudoscience is, however, still used as an argument by some pro-life groups. As recently as 2012, anti-abortion campaigner and US Republican Todd Akin said that a woman has ways of shutting down fertilisation if it is a 'legitimate rape' and that if for some reason this didn't work 'the punishment ought to be on the rapist and not attacking the child.'[23] The burden remains on the woman to prove that she has been raped, and as we see in Sharia laws in countries such as Pakistan and Sudan, if a woman cannot prove this, she becomes the perpetrator and is incriminated for zina (illicit sex).[24] And so while women can be punished and penalised for becoming pregnant under coercion and assault, they are also stigmatised for not falling pregnant when that is expected from them. The underlying assumption is the same: if they willed, they could.

•

What a glance at history shows us is that ambiguity and uncertainty around infertility is certainly not new, or unique to the modern era, but it is interesting how it has never become fully resolved or normalised. It also shows us that even as the fascination with infertility has existed for so long, seeping into many of our rituals, myths, art and literature, it has been linked largely with a fascination with women's bodies through a male gaze. While fascination with infertility has not diminished, it remains shrouded in ambiguity and abstruseness, and there has been a surprising lack of medical focus and clarity around it for too long.

Even today, infertility can be hard to explain and even tougher to talk about. Reporting on infertility and assisted technologies has followed the same old narrative, where women are either the helpless victim or the malefactor. Depictions of infertility on reality TV shows are significant as they shape public perception as well as being a potential mechanism for emancipation. I found a study from 2019 that identified four types of infertile 'monsters' through a content analysis of seven reality TV shows: the cyborg, the freak, the abject and the childless. The researchers encapsulated the primary narratives and themes as: 'women as only mothers or mothers-to-be'; 'women should (be able to) conceive (naturally)'; 'women being made responsible for in/fertility issues and choices'; 'women being blamed for in/fertility issues and choices'; 'women disciplining themselves and their bodies during infertility treatment'; 'women with perfect or perfected bodies'.[25] The image of an infertile woman has long been equated to a monster, a freak, outside the social and cultural norms, and what is considered as an ideal form of embodiment. The use of technology in helping a woman to become pregnant is still seen as 'unnatural', and in this way women redefine their own sense of identity or being as 'weird', and 'insufficient'. Most women still have an expectation that they should conceive naturally, and any external medical intervention obstructs their sense of self that they have maintained. And even as discussions around IVF have become normalised, studies or media reports emerge now and then debating whether such technologies contribute to emotional and physical problems in the children born as a result of them; so a sense of guilt and suspicion often remains.

Infertility can change a woman, and in cultural depictions of it we see women being murderous, as in the 1992 thriller *The Hand that Rocks the Cradle*, or patriarchal collaborators, as in Margaret Atwood's *The Handmaid's Tale*. Infertile women are variously seen as rejecting their womanhood, rebuking and rejecting their feminine selves, manifesting their anger and rage at society, unnatural and unruly, or literally as demons and serpentine monsters, or witches hunting children. On the other hand, they are often also written as characters who have accepted their fate and are gracious and humble in their own failings. In the Old Testament, infertile women are passive instruments of their reproductive fate: 'self-controlled, pure, working at home, kind, and submissive to their own husbands.' (Titus 2:5) This is the only way they could be acceptable as barren: pining but virtuous. Shifting forms between pious and religious to angry and promiscuous, infertile women do not belong with other women, narrowly fitting into the boxes that society prepared for them at birth.

Many representations involve mechanisms of excluding or condemning infertility in relation to what is considered normal and acceptable womanhood. Many of these popular media narratives around infertility fall back on the trope that the woman is respon- sible for a couple's childlessness (in straight couples). These popular media representations portray these women as 'desperate', so anxious

196

for a child, incomplete and unhappy without one, and then show a sense of completeness as the fertility treatment is successful. And we buy into these media narratives. On one hand, they demonise and condemn, and on the other they pity and commiserate. While representations of infertility are important, it is also concerning because such portrayals not only project the reality, but they also construct reality and reinforce existing biases against women who do not conform to the societal norms of motherhood and repro-ductive fecundity.

But even as we talk increasingly about infertility, we have to remember that it is not the same for everyone. It has so many dimensions, however much society might be intent on cutting everyone from the same cloth. Although the World Health Organization has specified reproductive health as a basic human right, anyone can see that the landscape of women's reproductive rights is not an equitable landscape.

Since then, with much more research, I have discovered that infertility in black and brown women is not diagnosed as quickly and is much more heavily stigmatised. The rate of success in assisted reproduction technologies for infertility varies considerably between white, black, Asian and Hispanic women. For instance, in the USA, analysis using data from the Society for Assisted Reproductive Technology Clinic Outcome Reporting System online database (SART CORS) has provided evidence that women from the three major minority groups (Black, Asian and Hispanic) have poorer outcomes compared to white non-Hispanic women.[26] Black women in particular have the highest rate of miscarriage and infertility along with low birth rates compared to the other groups. How much of this is biological and how much due to societal, cultural and systemic inequalities is not clear but evidence is mounting that access – both financial and physical – to assisted reproduction services is also a huge factor in these discrepancies as well as the disparity in medical care. Inequalities and bias in medical diagnosis and treatment have seen an increased focus recently, although these efforts have yet to be directed towards assisted reproduction services. Racial inequality in reproductive services has existed long before the assisted reproduction technologies but is exacerbated in this context where a higher cultural sensitivity is needed. Research has shown that when the physician and the client hold different class and racial/ethnic positions in society, 'the interaction is likely to exhibit difference in power and even attempts at social control.'[27] This can result in disparities and inequities being amplified.

Global health efforts have tended to focus on curbing the overpopulation in many areas of the global south, which compounded with how infertility is ostracised and stigmatised, can lead to these population groups being ignored in the infertility surveys and statistics. There is both an unconscious and sometimes a conscious set of beliefs about who can and should be able to reproduce – termed *reproductive imaginaries*.[28] As most of the research studies are carried out in the West, there is a definite Western bias towards infertility being perceived as a condition commonly impacting white, Western, heterosexual, middle- and upper-class women. The infertility experiences of underprivileged, non-white, non-Western and/or non-heterosexual women and men do not fit within this model of reproductive imaginary; they are marginalised and invisible and have difficulty obtaining assessment, medical treatment and social support for their infertility. So much of this certainly resonates, and speaking with many women of colour, those who are not cisgender, those who identify as LGBTQI, and hearing their stories, it becomes very clear to me that their narrative is not mainstream. The challenges these already marginalised minority groups face in diagnosis and treatment of fertility is compounded by their position in society, and the biases and stereotypes that are already assigned to them. Many of these people do not come forward openly and publicly — as I didn't — because they are afraid of the backlash, of the stigma from others but also often from within their own community, and frequently because they do not consider their stories and experiences to be of value to anyone else, or think their pain and distress to be too personal and private.

Infertility is often assessed on the basis of intent (actively trying for twelve months and not being successful) and so those women without intent — those who are not actively trying to get pregnant — often do not realise that they have fertility problems and are unlikely to seek treatment until it is too late. These are the 'hidden infertiles' that surveys and statistics do not account for either.[29] And then there is *social infertility*, a relatively recent label accorded to women who are childless because of their circumstances, choice, or because society makes it much harder for these women to be mothers. There is an argument for seeing infertility beyond just the physiological reasons, which has mainly focused on heterosexual couples, and also consider how social constraints can limit an individual's ability to conceive by including the 'invisible infertiles':[30] the single, poor or non-heterosexual people who can't have children for reasons that are only sometimes related to their bodies. The infertility statistics ignore these groups, which leads to their being left out of the infertility discourse.[31]

What historic and contemporary stories show us is that infertility has long been stigmatised and misunderstood, and perhaps it is time that we change the narrative, but it is imperative that we do not homogenise this discourse. It is critical that any discussion of infertility is intersectional.

•

A woman's identity is so strongly attached to her womb and the notion of motherhood, that the way women navigate identity – especially gender identity – when they cannot become mothers deserves more attention in popular media and scientific studies. Hilary Mantel said, 'I miss the children I never had', but it is hard to imagine the grief and pain of missing something that you never had anyway.[32] We might feel that we have progressed and are living in times where we are talking about gender equality, moving away from the sole identity of a woman as a mother. As a feminist, I say and I truly believe these things. But our hearts and minds can work in strange unpredictable ways. I am grappling with how old-fashioned this sounds, but as we navigate such primitive and innate notions of fertility, it is easy to see motherhood and feminism as binary ideals. Either you are a mother or you are a feminist, and in choosing to be a mother, trying to become a mother, there is some sense of betraying the feminist beliefs that question the societal norms that a woman's value lies only in her ability to carry and deliver a baby. And even as feminism reinforces choice in childbirth, and a woman's reproductive rights, there is a lack of consideration of the full spectrum of reproduction and access to safe and affordable infertility treatments. And so the mind keeps forming knots, spinning round and round. I have been a mother once, so I should not have this desperate need and desire to be a mother again. I should not be so greedy when there are so many who cannot conceive a child. Infinite loops; twists and hoops. I wander around my identities trying to hold on to the walls to steady myself, looking for a place to call my own. I don't know whether to grieve about it or even how. No one has taught me how to talk about being 'barren'.

Sylvia Plath writes in her poem 'The Disquieting Muses', an allegory to the painting of the same name by the metaphysical artist Giorgio de Chirico, of women whose 'arms frame a bulging stomach hollowed out by a shadowed void' and are 'mouthless, eyeless, with stitched bald head'.[33] I feel like one of these maternal effigies, these forlorn figures, collecting together in a barren landscape of maternal desire, hollow-wombed and inhumanely mutilated, stitched together into some sort of mutated notion of femininity.

In 1532 Catherine de Medici was married to Henry II, the king of France, as a young fourteen-year-old girl, and Henry not much older. For years she failed to produce any offspring. Consultations with physicians, quacks, magicians and astrologers failed to achieve the pregnancy she desired. Henry II succeeded his father and took as his mistress Diane de Poitiers who had been his father's mistress. She almost persuaded him to divorce Catherine so he could take a wife who was capable of bearing him children when, quite unexpectedly, Catherine became pregnant. Historical records show that Catherine's sterility had been a source of ridicule, with her being scoffed at and scorned throughout France at the time.

I don't think my husband will abandon me because I cannot have children. Or, at least I hope not. But many women around the world still live with this fear. In certain societies, there are huge social and personal consequences of childlessness resulting in ostracisation by their social groups, divorce and remarriage by husbands, physical and mental abuse, neglect and economic deprivation. In Nigeria, if a wife does not bear many children, the husband has a reason to seek another wife and live polygamously. In ancient Rome, a woman's inability to bear children was addressed in a fairly perplexing manner, and I cannot find the rationale around it. Perhaps there wasn't any, and it was just a way for men to blame women and assert their superior position in society. At the festival of Lupercalia on 13–15 February, goats and a dog were sacrificed, and then two priests cut out bits of skin from the dead animals and ran around the Palatine Hill in Rome, hitting any women they found. Mark Antony runs the Lupercal in Shakespeare's *Julius Caesar* (Act I, Scene 2). Caesar positions his childless wife on a street corner and pleads, 'Forget not in your speed, Antonius, to touch Calpurnia; for our elders say the barren, touched in this holy chase, shake off their sterile curse.'[34] A blow was meant to make you bear children, and if not, then it was legitimate grounds for divorce. What an enticing prospect! I should feel glad that I don't have to be whacked on the face by a bloody goatskin.

I cannot shake this huge feeling of guilt that I have failed my husband in some way, that by not being able to provide him with a child, I am not doing my duty. It sounds so odd when I say it out loud to myself. And as we talk over the next few days, months, years, I tell him that he made a mistake in marrying me. I make comments on how he must rue the day that he met me, trying to do that little laugh that I do when I pretend to be funny, but when I am in fact deadly serious. We all have these personas we inhabit, these roles that we play, the skins we put on. Mine was of a woman tap-dancing away merrily while trapped alone in a glass box, looking outside, slowly feeling suffocated.

When I say these words, he looks at me with scepticism, wondering whether I am joking, as I often am, or being dramatic, but then sees that I am sincere. He shakes his head with disbelief that I would even consider this possibility, and then gets angry that I would even consider him to be so shallow. I try and imagine what he must be feeling, but he does not say much. He has never been a big conversationalist, keeping his feelings to himself, calm and composed. Somehow, I wish he would just cry and wail, and berate me, confirming my very worst fears. But he doesn't, instead reassuring me again and again that everything will be all right. I am tired of his optimism. I cannot shake these centuries of ingrained conditioning, those implicit messages that have told me that I should be able to control my body and my conception. That I should be able to conceive when I want to, and that my ability to give birth is inherently linked to my identity as a woman.

Having grown up in a world where women are 'the Second Sex',‡ still considered the 'other' with a man still being the default, I've become accustomed to assigning my value to success. Failure has not been a part of my vocabulary, because I did not have the luxury or the freedom to fail. Every failure, even the tiniest one, is hugely personal. This failure to conceive is something I cannot share with anyone, not even my own mother. I have pretended to be strong for so long, with that unwavering sense of reliability and solidity that others fall back on, that I cannot share my hopelessness and desperation, and my crushing sense of despair with anyone, not even those closest to me. Infertility is a social curse, to be pitied, and abhorred, rarely to be empathised with. In this journey, I am alone. Not even my husband understands my acute sense of failure, and he watches, helplessly. Even though we were in this together, me and him, I have never felt lonelier. It is the grief that should bind us, but I don't know if he is grieving. He does not say. I wish he would.

‡ The 1949 book of the same name by the French existentialist Simone de Beauvoir, maps women's treatment through history, and is often regarded as the starting point for second-wave feminism.

I work.

I make lists.

I pretend everything is good.

I pretend that I am happy.

I make more lists, and I find more to do.

I keep pulling myself up, holding on tightly.

I go to work. I talk to people. I want to shut myself away.

Everyone looks happy. Why don't I?

Lists, lists, lists.

To-do, to-write, to-be-busy, to-not-think.

I don't even want a child now. I could be happy with just one, I think. But what if I am not. What if I look back and regret? What if we drift away untethered?

What if, what if, what if.

If not now, when?

If not like this, how?

A vortex of debris, a whirlwind of thoughts, splintering the mind, shattering the tough unassailable crust accumulated around me, from barbs and prejudices, years of being a woman, and trying to be one: a complete one.

I think of Elena Ferrante's *Frantumaglia*, a word she borrows from her Neapolitan mother, 'a malaise that could not be defined otherwise and that hinted at a crowded, heterogeneous mix of things in her head, like rubble floating on a brain's muddy waters.'[35]

We go through round after round of IVF, living through intense hope and intense despair, every time clinging on desperately and hopefully to success, even when the chances are less than 10 per cent, all the odds stacked up against the walls of desire and longing. Despite all our technological advances there are people who are going back to spells, magic and witchcraft to help them conceive.

According to the popular parenting website Netmums, a 2010 survey shows that of 2,000 women canvassed, 51 per cent had obeyed old wives' tales like rubbing a pregnant woman's belly or planting rosemary bushes, with more than 35 per cent spending at least £500 on alternative treatments. As many as 29 per cent of women had visited a clairvoyant, and a quarter had resorted to witches' spells and hexes.[36] The relationship between witchery and infertility is not a new one, of course. In medieval Europe, childless women were considered as witches, cursed and evil, bringing bad luck to others. The *Malleus Maleficarum*, or the *Hammer of the Witches*, was a popular witch-hunting book written in 1487 by Heinrich Kramer in Germany.§ The text argues that women are more susceptible to demonic temptations through the manifold weaknesses of their gender. It was believed that they were weaker in faith and more carnal than men. The devil and witches could not really harm the reproductive organs but could use their magical powers to render them useless, and could render a man's imagination in a way that could make a woman appear loathsome and undesirable. From the early fourteenth century to 1650, continental Europeans executed between 200,000 and 500,000 witches, 85 per cent of which were women.[37]

In India, childless women, bhanj, are still sometimes called Putana: one devoid of virtue, an infant-killer in Indian mythology, one of the few malevolent Indian goddesses, who kills little babies after breastfeeding them poisoned milk, and who was sent to kill Krishna after his birth. Ancient Indian medical texts prescribe her worship

---

§ Jacob Sprenger was also added as an author beginning in 1519, 33 years after the book's first publication. This was twenty-four years after Sprenger's death. But some historians have since contested this.

to protect children from diseases. Putana is interpreted as a bird –
reminiscent of the Harpies – symbolising danger to an infant, and
carnal desire, and consequently a bad mother. She stands for death
and darkness, forever committed to being hidden and invisible.[38]

There is not much to say about each of the IVF treatments. Bags
filled with medications, small glass vials and syringes, a schedule to
be followed closely. I don't follow schedules and calendars very well,
my brain jumping from one to another, multiple projects on the go.
To-do lists have become my saviour as I meticulously try and control
the chaos of my life to organise my scattered thoughts. I have never
followed a schedule as closely as this: there is no other choice. There
is not much to say as I learn to inject myself every day, finding an
odd sort of comfort in punching the needle inside the fleshy part
of my stomach, finding the parts where the purple burnish hasn't
spread very far, where the skin is still intact. Every day, every single
day: it becomes the rhythm of my life. The days are measured out
in injections and pessaries to cajole the dormant ovaries into
producing more eggs, as many as possible. Push, pull, push, pull, then
discard the syringe in a small yellow plastic container that they have
given us. Every night, I try and focus on the writing on the container
as I grit my teeth once again, and push the needle in. My stomach
is puffy and bruised, my mind anxious and strained, my body
misshapen, but still barren. I carry this secret inside me, one cycle
after another.

Not much stands out as days merge into one another after a while.
But there were some beautiful tender moments too, when I could
almost imagine being pregnant, when there was wistful optimism for
a new life inside me. When we went for the first embryo transfer,
I had my nails painted the day before. I never go for manicures, but
this felt special. 'I will not be able to have my nails painted for a

while,' I remember telling the manicurist, feeling butterflies in my stomach. 'It is bound to work,' P had said to me that morning of the transfer – our first cycle – keeping hope alive for both of us, and I believed him. He had bought me fluffy slippers, and I had laughed out loud when I saw those. It is the kind of thing he does, silly things that are utterly adorable. He knows that my feet get cold, and how I hate that. 'You are lucky that I am pleased with so little,' I remember saying to him, and his eyes had twinkled. I remember sitting there in the small hospital room in a green medical gown and my fluffy pink and white slippers, my feet dangling at the end of the bed, like a kid at Disney World. They had shown us the embryos being transferred on the screen above us, and I had to twist my neck to look at them, little clumps of cells, with potential to become so much more. I had taken a picture of the screen, hoping to stick it in an album one day, show it to the babies. Look, this is where you started. We had both looked at the embryos as if they were already what we were hoping for them to become, that they would stick, choose us. The heart is a strange beast. I never took photos of embryos ever again in any other cycle.

Every time we go through this, I truly feel pregnant. I test again and again in case the test is faulty. 'It is only 99 per cent accurate, isn't it?' I tell myself. And then, of course, I stop, as the synthetic hormones fade away. With that I feel hollow and empty, just flat, devoid of the high that I had so got used to, from the chemicals pumped into my body and from the delirious anticipation. Recently, I finally took a bag full of unused pregnancy tests that I had kept hidden at the back of a cupboard to a homeless shelter.

We fail, and then we try again. Let's hope, let's dream, we agree, and every time a little part of the fantasy refuses to step up. I was reminded once again of Beckett. Good old Beckett, who says in his

1983 story *Worstward Ho*: 'Ever tried. Ever failed. No matter. Try again. Fail again. Fail better.' So much despondency, so much resilience; so much hope, so much hopelessness.

Maybe I shouldn't have had my nails painted. Maybe the fumes of the nail varnish were not good for the embryos. Maybe I didn't rest enough. Maybe I was not good enough. The churning of the mind, those cogs and wheels processing through our anxieties and fears, is how we know we are alive. I felt more alive than ever now, living in the present so much more than I had ever been, every moment expanding into an eternity. These are the days we remember, the days, weeks, months when we drift between resolute courage and determination and utter hopelessness and despair.

The South Carolina aristocrat and author Mary Boykin Chesnut wrote a diary documenting social and political life between 1861 and 1865.[39] Even though filled with racialised imagery and ideology, her diary is seen as one of the best records of the time, and the edited version won the Pulitzer Prize for History. In the edited version by Catherine Clinton,[40] we see that Mary always knew from the earliest days of her marriage that her duty was to become pregnant. However, she could never carry a child to term and give her husband an heir. Consequently, Mary felt social stigma, as women were still at fault whenever a couple failed to reproduce. Her father-in-law lamented that 'with the war we will be wiped out' and told his wife in front of Mary that 'You have not been a useless woman in this world', because she had given birth to children and had twenty-seven great-grandchildren. In her diary Mary also documents how she even suffered reproach from other women because they had 'contempt for a childless wife'. Internalised misogyny, of course, means that women can be women's worst enemies, and enablers of patriarchy. In 1883, Mary's despair and disappointment is clear when she writes to Confederate First Lady Varina Davis: 'You should thank God for your young immortals – I have nothing but Polish chickens – and Jersey calves.' We also see that even as Mary achieved great societal standing and repute as a hostess and author, she could not shake off the sadness and stigma of not bearing children.

Infertility was always a woman's fault. We are at the mercy of our biology, and it has never been as clear to me as now. Each time the grief appears in solitude, when there is no one to hold my hand as I sit alone with a negative test, when it snatches at any marginal notion of peace and quietude, when the heart aches heavily with loss, when it can flail about in abandon and agony. As the silence widens, as my husband grows even quieter every day, I am increasingly quarantined with my own meditations, and the grief feels as if it is mine alone.

VII.

THE BLUE LINE

'IF YE WATER TURNS BLUE, a baby for you! If purple ye see, no baby thar be! If ye test should fail, to a doctor set sail!'

These were the words on the 'Barnacle Bill's Home Pregnancy Test' that Marge takes in episode 47 of *The Simpsons*. In the past, women – and healthcare professionals – used to rely on intuition and guesswork. And time. Time for the body to show the signs. Also, sugar. If you added one tablespoon of urine to one tablespoon of sugar, then, if the sugar started forming clumps, it was believed to be a sign of pregnancy, and if the sugar dissolved quickly, it meant that the woman was not pregnant. Also, allegedly, white vinegar or baking soda changes colour or produces bubbles. Do not try this at home!

The first mention of a pregnancy test has been found on Egyptian papyrus, where women were asked to urinate on barley or wheat seeds,★ and if the seeds sprouted then the pregnancy was confirmed; wheat sprouting meant a girl, and barley sprouts predicted a boy. Scientists speculate that the elevated levels of oestrogen in a

★ In ancient Egyptian medical texts from around 1400 BC in the Papyrus Carlsberg Collection at the University of Copenhagen in Denmark.

pregnant woman's urine might lead to additional growth.[†] Much like the Egyptians, the Greeks had a seemingly tenuous grasp on human anatomy. Ancient Greeks believed that the alimentary canal (from the mouth), the anal canal, and the uterus all opened into the belly. In a healthy person, then, all three channels were linked. A common way to measure a woman's ability to get pregnant involved placing a clove of garlic or an onion in her vagina. If the odour did not pass from the vagina to the mouth, there was a blockage and pregnancy would be impossible. She was considered fertile if the smell could be detected on her breath the following morning. Such a test has no medical basis and is unlikely to work but there was an interesting logic behind it. Another test to measure a woman's fertility involved smearing new oil on her breasts and shoulders as she lay down. If the following morning all her blood vessels hadn't collapsed and looked healthy, then she would be able to bear children. A woman's rounded hips and large firm breasts became associated with a sign of fertility. This seems almost alien to us today with increasing pressure to maintain a slim and slender image. I wonder what the ancient Egyptians would have made of a modern woman, who is not such a big fan of the well-endowed full figure that was a symbol of fertility, but still living in a society that is equally obsessed with a woman's fertility and ability to conceive and give birth. The standards to which we must conform have changed, but our value and our role as women, perhaps not so much.

•

† According to the US National Institutes of Health, a study conducted in 1963 found that this method of determining pregnancy is accurate about 70 per cent of the time.

We have moved away from sugar and baking soda. And from grandmothers looking at your palms to tell you when and how many children you would have one day.

I had stared at the little window for an eternity, until everything started spinning wildly. I felt like such a cliché, experiencing all the symptoms of a panic attack. But a part of me seemed very calm as well, and for the first time I really understood what it means to have an out of body experience, like being in a dream. Psychologists have called this depersonalisation, feeling like what you are experiencing is not reality. Except that this was real and my worst nightmare.

The chill from the cold tiled floor was rising up to my head, in the bathroom with old grey linoleum tiles and faded yellow wallpaper that we had been planning to change since we moved in but hadn't had time to do. Other things had become more important in the meantime. And I had become strangely fond of this awful-looking room, something that had become home, even if it was ugly, and decrepit. I hid here sometimes when things seemed too overwhelming, and I wanted to be alone with my thoughts. The frumpy walls seemed welcoming when the grey cloud didn't lift. It did not expect anything from me, and I didn't have to pretend to be anything. In its ugliness lay a severity that had always been comforting to me. I often wondered how I could like the raw unpretentious nature of Brutalist architecture, while also be brought to tears by ornate baroque embellishments. I would be terrible at that celebrity Q&A in magazines, with snappy responses to brisk questions such as 'favourite architectural style' or 'favourite place to visit'. How can they decide on one thing that defines them completely, when our identities are not carved in stone? Our values might be certain, even as they too shift over time and through our lives, but certainly not what kind of food I like to eat or what kind of films I like to watch, or even what my favourite city in the world is. How does one make these decisions with so much assurance and confidence, certain that one won't get up the next day and regret one's choices? The season of regret is evergreen, never disappearing, just taking a hiatus, sometimes sprouting green leaves unexpectedly, often spreading like a wildfire raging and burning, rampant, violent and uncontrolled, storming, seething, exploding and erupting, sweeping away any signs of present ease in its swell.

I had escaped here today, sitting, waiting, watching the timer, waiting for it to beep, anxious for it to be over with, but at the same time wanting the time to stop. As long as the timer was counting down, there was still hope, and while we had been tumbling through these insane periods of uncertainty, fear and loss, moments of hope were few and far between. Hope is so tenuous and yet sometimes we crave it instead of a certain truth. Truth carries away with it the dredges of our deepest desires. The mind holds on to every last glimpse of hope by creating an illusion of time moving slowly or even stopping completely.

The hormonal injections had made my stomach swell. I felt constantly bloated and my hips were rounder than ever. Earlier in the day our next-door neighbour had smiled at me over the hedge, while I ran my hands through the strawberry bushes along the fence. We had a big garden for once, and M had run down it with her arms stretched wide when we first moved here. I was trying to grow fruits and vegetables, being marginally more successful at them than growing a child. We already had an apple tree here when we first moved in, and we had planted rhubarb and strawberries, carrots and potatoes in a haphazard way. I made little notes in a notebook that I had bought about what to plant when, and even though I tried to be systematic about it, and stick to a plan, new thoughts seeded and flowered every day, enough to ambush me, and waylay me off the trajectory.

'Oh, are congratulations in order?' the neighbour had asked with a huge smile, as she stood there pruning her roses meticulously and carefully with a device I could not name. My amateur gardening knowledge fell flat at the first hurdle. I was mesmerised by her floral gardening gloves. Probably Cath Kidston, I thought. We weren't close. We had communicated only a handful of times, but I have seen strangers bond over pregnancies and children. The swollen belly was perhaps the supposed giveaway.

'Oh no,' I said, and she looked surprised and embarrassed, and slunk away. I had wondered if it was a sign, stroking my stomach gently as if I was already carrying a secret. It had to be a sign. Everything seemed like a sign these days to me, waiting for the heavens to casually tell me what the future held for me. Fear, trepidation and unease makes us believe in magic. Maybe there was a portal that would transport me there, to a time and age where all the signs would have been neatly arranged, lined up for me already.

There is a painting in the Getty Center in Los Angeles called 'A Doctor's Visit'. It is a striking painting by a Dutch artist, Frans van Mieris the Elder, from around 1667. In this intricate painting, a maid attempts to revive an elegant young woman who has fainted. A doctor, wearing ostentatious clothing, is examining a vial of the woman's urine. The suggestion is that he is a quack, with exaggerated mannerism and clothes. A crying girl is seen in the background holding a burning ribbon, which was understood at the time as a symbol of pregnancy. These self-proclaimed 'piss prophets' were most popular during the fifteenth and sixteenth century, who applied the 'swirl and taste' approach to urine to diagnose not only pregnancy but also other illnesses and continued to flourish underground up to the early nineteenth century when more sophisticated techniques came into use. Avicenna, a tenth-century Persian philosopher, would pour sulphur over women's urine, believing that the tell-tale sign was worms springing from the mixture. Similar preposterous suggestions are found in *The Distaff Gospels*,‡ a collection of women's medical lore written in the late fifteenth century, which states: 'My friends, if you want to know if a woman is pregnant, you must ask her to pee in a basin and then put a latch or a key in it, but it is better to use a latch – leave this latch in the basin with the urine for three or four hours. Then throw the urine away and remove the latch. If you see the impression of the latch on the basin, be sure that the woman is pregnant. If not, she is not pregnant.'[1] Colour of urine was also a significant indicator for any illness during the medieval period. One text dating from 1552 explains that if the woman's urine was a 'clear pale lemon colour leaning toward off-white, having a cloud on its surface',[2] then she must be pregnant. Undoubtedly, many men would have been found pregnant by a similar measure.

Such methods will always find a place in society no matter how technologically advanced we might be. There is a primitive need in humans to trust anything that is magical, even though it might defy rational explanation; there are some remnants of magical thinking

---

‡ '*The Distaff Gospels* (*Les Evangiles des Quenouilles*) is an Old French fifteenth-century collection of more than 250 popular beliefs held by late medieval women, first published in 1480. It was edited by Fouquart de Cambray, Duval Antoine and Jean d'Arras and published at Bruges by Colart Mansion. The narrative takes place within the context of a gathering of women who meet with their spindles and distaffs to spin. They discuss folk wisdom related to their domestic lives, including controlling errant husbands, predicting the gender of future offspring and curing common ailments' (Broadview Press).

that have been passed on and remain in our make-up through evolutionary history. Throughout history we know that belief in superstition is not an individualistic isolated occurrence but something that ties people across geographies of space and time. People want to believe that there is something beyond their immediate existence, something that they might not be able to explain. It is not the action itself, but rather what it symbolises that becomes important. And there is always the herd mentality – a desire to be part of a larger group, to belong and to conform – which determines the success of so many of these so called 'quack doctors' and prophets.

The obsession with trying to find signs that indicated a woman's pregnancy continued in the sixteenth century. Jacques Guillemeau, a physician and ophthalmologist, claimed that you could tell by a woman's eyes whether or not she was with child. He believed that a pregnant woman gets deep-set eyes with small pupils, drooping lids and swollen little veins in the corner of the eye.[§]

There were other strange ideas along the way. A human body changes as it accommodates a growing foetus, and with the surcharge of hormones. There are other signs that are still in use in medical parlance, such as Hegar's sign (the uterus can be easily flexed at the soft isthmus at six weeks of pregnancy), and Chadwick's or Jacquemier's sign – darkening or blue colour of vaginal mucus membranes – at eight weeks. The cervix, labia and vagina can take on a dark bluish or purple-red hue, owing to the increased blood flow to the area. This was first noticed in 1836 by a French physician, then became known as Chadwick's sign, after James Read

§   I know that a year of pandemic-related anxiety has done the same for me.

216

Chadwick, an obstetrics doctor who brought the discovery up at a meeting of the American Gynaecological Society in 1886. Much of the testing until this stage was still out of the hands of the women themselves, relying on medical intervention and midwives, doctors and quacks to confirm or disconfirm it.

Between the 1920s and 1970s, the three primary ways to confirm a pregnancy were through bioassays,¶ immunoassays★★ and home tests. Bernhard Zondek and Selmar Aschheim, gynaecologists and medical researchers at the Berlin Charité hospital, were the first to create a bioassay called the Aschheim–Zondek, or A–Z, test which relied on the peculiar effect pregnant women's urine had on female mice, the assumption being that there was some substance in women's urine that had a measurable effect on other organisms. In this test, when the urine was injected into the immature female mice, their ovaries enlarged, and they went into heat despite their age. This rather inhumane but relatively accurate test – the first 2,000 tests showed an accuracy of around 98.9 per cent[3] – involved killing and dissecting the mice to observe the presence, or not, of characteristic ovarian changes induced by the hormone. Along with the Friedman test, which used rabbits instead of mice (which gave rise to the euphemism 'rabbit died' for a positive pregnancy test), this became the common procedure to determine pregnancy in the early 1900s. Traumatic and unnecessary interventions abounded when there weren't as strict legislations against the use of live animals in the laboratory. In Britain, mice (and rabbits) were however replaced by

¶ A quantitative method in which the potency and quantity of a chemical is assessed by its effect on other living cells and organisms.
★★ A bioanalytical method in which the concentration of certain molecules can be measured by using antibodies, proteins that are part of our immune system.

reusable toads as diagnostic services ramped up in the late 1940s under the new National Health Service (NHS).

An irascible British biologist, Lancelot Hogben, developed the 'Hogben test', also popularly known as the 'toad test'.[4] Hogben had accidentally injected a *Xenopus* (an African clawed frog) with extracts from an ox's pituitary gland and, in response, the frog started laying eggs. By this time the scientists already knew that when the human egg is fertilised, it implants itself and secretes the hormone associated with modern early pregnancy detection – human chorionic gonadotropin (hCG) – that shows in the urine of pregnant women. They extrapolated that if those same hormones could trigger egg-laying in *Xenopus*, perhaps the frog could act as a living pregnancy test. The test went something like this: collect a woman's urine and inject it, fresh and untreated, under the skin of a female *Xenopus*. Then, wait. If the woman is pregnant, between five and twelve hours later the frog will produce a cluster of millimetre-sized, black-and-white spheres. The results were reliable. One researcher reported that after injecting 150 frogs, he never got any false positives and only missed three actual pregnancies.[5] Tens of thousands of frogs were injected with human urine between the 1940s and '60s. Unlike the previous tests with mice and rabbits, researchers found this much simpler to execute and as the frogs did not die in the process, they could be reused. Sounds utterly cruel to me.

In 2012, a Brooklyn gallery tried to put on an exhibition by anthropologist Eben Kirksey, inviting women to inject frogs with their urine to replicate this antiquated pregnancy test. Justifiably there were outcries and protests from the animal rights group People for the Ethical Treatment of Animals (PETA). Kirksey retorted: 'Is peeing on a stick, and routinely sending plastic trash to a landfill, more ethical than caring for a frog at home and using it as a pregnancy test?'[6] You can be the judge, but it is disheartening that pregnancy testing has to come at a cost, that it has to be either/or.

The development of pregnancy tests were shrouded in scientific misconceptions for a long time, and often came at the cost of the pregnancy and women's health itself. Primodos was a revolutionary oral hormone pregnancy test from the 1960s and was manufactured by the German company Schering. It was marketed to doctors both as a treatment for menstrual irregularities and as a convenient test for early pregnancy. Primodos functioned diagnostically by inducing menstrual-like bleeding in non-pregnant women (a negative result); no bleeding implied pregnancy. In post-war Britain, the rise of Primodos coincided with a significant increase in demand for pregnancy testing, first prescribed in 1958 as a 'hormonal pregnancy test' (HPT). Until then women had largely been self-diagnosing by missed periods or morning sickness. Interestingly, the HPTs emerged not primarily as a result of research for pregnancy diagnosis but because of the research for treatment of amenorrhoea (or the absence of menses), a condition often caused by infertility, but of course one that can also be a consequence of pregnancy. Convenient home testing had not been invented yet, and there was a widespread unreserved trust of medical professionals. Also the toad test, although accurate, could only be used two weeks after a missed period, and doctors claimed that this pill could revolutionise early testing. According to interviews conducted by the feminist sociologist Ann Oakley, one country doctor ordered pregnancy tests for only 1.3 per cent of his female patients in the late 1940s, but this had increased to 38.8 per cent by the late 1970s.[7] The HPT was made freely available on the NHS, but only for medical reasons; doctors considering healthy married women likely to have an uneventful pregnancy to be curiosity cases and rejecting their demands for a test. Most doctors disapproved of social testing, and hence kept a tight rein on women's right to test.

As this test wasn't originally designed as a means for pregnancy testing, but rather to test fertility and lack of regular periods, it was only when medical services in the UK started to crumble under huge demands and financial crises that the pharmaceutical companies began to cash in on this hugely lucrative market of pregnancy testing. There were concerns. In 1956, London physiologist Hubert Britton voiced concern in the *British Medical Journal* (*BMJ*) that such tests could potentially 'upset the delicate hormonal balance' of pregnancy and provoke miscarriage or even damage the embryo at its 'most suscep-tible' stage of development. In 1967, in a brief letter to *Nature*, Dr Isabel Gal, a Surrey-based paediatrician, and colleagues also suggested that such HPTs might lead to spina bifida and other congenital deformities in the children whose mothers who had taken this drug while pregnant.[8] *Woman* magazine warned against the unknown risks of HPTs and suggested that women go back to using the toad, a 'modern scientific achievement'. Despite this, the doctors continued to prescribe and use these oral pills primarily to avoid the very la-borious toad test and also to keep the costs down. Women's bodies sacrificed at the altar of their whims, their health becoming a business transaction. These oral pills are now suspected of causing severe damage to the children that were born to mothers who took them (the 'silent thalidomide').[9]

It gave me some pleasure to find out that while men had for so long controlled women's reproduction and healthcare – as well as determining pregnancy indicators – it was a woman who came up with the design of the first portable home pregnancy test. The Predictor test was the idea of designer Margaret Crane, who had been hired by Organon pharmaceuticals in 1967 to work on an entirely different project to develop a new line of cosmetics. After visiting the company's lab one day, she wrote: 'I noticed multiple lines of test tubes suspended over a mirrored surface. I was told that they were pregnancy tests . . . Each test tube contained reagents which when combined with a pregnant woman's urine, would display a red ring at the base of the mirror.'[10] At her home in New York, she put together a simplified kit of plastic paper-clip holder, a mirror, a test tube, and a dropper, and presented this home-grown pregnancy test to Organon who then patented the design in her name in 1967. When it hit shelves in the 1970s, the Predictor pregnancy test, a cumbersome contraption of mirrors, water and red blood cells taken from sheep, was sold for $10. In 2012, the auction house Bonham's sold the original prototype, along with the first consumer version of the test, for $11,875! Even though the Predictor test was available in many high street chemists in the UK in the late 1970s, self-administered pregnancy testing was still socially (and medically) taboo, and the consumer watchdog *Which?* advised going to one's GP in the first instance to avoid wasting 'almost £2' on the 'do-it-yourself' kit.[11] The whole industry was really revolutionised once the strip-based tests came into the market, with Unilever introducing the Clearblue in 1988, and then rapidly moving on from analogue to digital readers, promising earlier and earlier testing, even as early as 'five days before a missed period'. Although the tests have become easier and easier, and come a long distance from women peeing on barley and wheat seeds, we don't seem to have come very far as we have moved on to weeing on our hands! Today it is a huge global industry, and according to BioAMD data, 20 million pregnancy and ovulation tests are used in the US alone per year and around $1.7 billion worth of pregnancy tests are sold globally each year.[12] According to market forecasts, the size of the global pregnancy test market is set to grow around 5–10 per cent just between 2020–5. One of the reasons proposed for this exponential growth in recent years is the rise of infertility.

In measuring the level of hCG in a woman's urine, these tests enforce a perception that there is a standard way to be pregnant and feel pregnant. Urinary hCG shows a remarkable uniformity in its rise during early pregnancy, but dating the gestational age based on this is unreliable. Irregular cycles, early pregnancy bleeding, previous use of hormonal contraceptives or breastfeeding are common causes which can obscure the time of conception and the gestational age. The test measures chemical pregnancies, some of which can be molar or ectopic pregnancies that do not result in a developed foetus. One of the cutomer reviews for an early-detection pregnancy test says:

> Do not buy these early reading tests from Clear blue. They are absolutely horrendous. [They] have given me false positives because the blue dye runs on to the test line even if you are not pregnant. I've had my hopes up one [too] many times to be let down.[13]

Truly heartbreaking.

•

False negatives; false positives. Mind games; heartaches. I recall the time when I had that faint blue line, a little glimmer of hope. I knew I had tested early. I was being impatient but maybe this could be the truth. I had tested again. And again. And I had the same positive result, only a very hazy line, a muffled scream in the darkness. It is too easy to yearn, to hope, to dream. I didn't utter this potential possibility to anyone else, and tested it again a few days later. The faint odds had faded away.

Had I just dreamt it? Had I just dreamt all the uncertainties, ambiguities, ambivalence away? The doctor tells me that I must have read it wrong; maybe the test was faulty. Why would no one believe me? I had read about 'chemical pregnancy', when a home pregnancy test initially detects the presence of hCG – the 'pregnancy hormone' – but then either later tests give negative results or there are other warning signs, such as bleeding. Once upon a time this was just seen as a 'late period', but now it is well-documented as an early miscarriage or unviable pregnancy. Medical doctors in the UK are still sceptical about the reliability of chemical pregnancy. In hoping so fervently, desiring so strongly, willing for it to happen, women are perceived as over-emotional and hysterical, their testimonies (and their vision) under scrutiny. Even as my dreams were disassembled bit by bit, my heart ripped to shreds, all I had to show for it was a 'false' pregnancy test with the hazy line. It remained fixed in my mind: the event had occurred, but it is almost as if the pregnancy simply never happened. I had dreamt up an existence. A loss of a pregnancy was also a hope in some way, a sign that I could become pregnant after all. But in negating its existence, a possibility had been extinguished too. I had been left bereft on both counts, unsure of what my body, my mind, my eyes were trying to tell me. Unable to grieve; unable to rejoice.

Time does not stop even when we want it to. As I sat with the stick in my hands, squinting, conjuring, invoking all the deities that I had grown up seeing my mother worship, thoughts came tumbling one after another, spreading out and then tossed together, jostling, shoving, all pointy knees and elbows.

They really should make the text a bit bigger on these boxes.

I should really get my eyes checked.

Is the first sign of old age?

I would look so good in glasses.

Wispy words, scattered sentences kept leaping into my brain, jumping off into the water from a high cliff like those teenagers we had met down in Cornwall on our holiday the past year, but there was no sound of laughter. Or like that huge rollercoaster, Kraken, in Disney World, snaking around the park. I remembered wistfully how sick, how nauseous I had felt then. All those photos of me looking so ill, in the little shack just outside displayed large on the screen for all the world to see, and P and I had stood there pointing and screaming with laughter. I looked young in these memories. He looked brown and lean, and so young, with his eyes smiling at me. It was like a light shining on me, that blistering spark that went off inside me whenever I looked at him.

Linguistic anthropologist Uta Papen reads the use of home pregnancy tests as a 'literacy event' – that is, an occasion that is influenced and shaped by the reading and writing of text.[14] By giving detailed, structured instructions for what are relatively simple processes, an impression of sophistication, accuracy and reliability is created. There continues to be a culture where women are kept in the dark about the gendered nature of many of the diagnostic tools and tests, and the effect of their hormones on their bodies. The language used on pregnancy tests is similarly convoluted. Research has shown that in one study of twenty-seven home-use tests using standard urine samples, 230 of the 478 positive urine samples distributed were wrongly identified as negative by the women testing them.[15] The primary reason for this was considered to be the difficulty women had in comprehending the instructions on the box and, consequently, in reading the test results correctly. This conclusion was supported by an evaluation of sixteen home-pregnancy test instructions. This found that none of the instructions rated highly when ranked against criteria for compliance with plain language guidelines.

Some of the newer digital tests help overcome these barriers by displaying clear words such as 'pregnant' and 'not pregnant', as one in four women have been shown to misread line-based pregnancy tests. However these digital tests are also the most expensive ones. The cost of an inaccurate test, or not being able to use the test properly or read and interpret the result, can be catastrophic for a woman's emotional and mental health, but also have financial repercussions. This creates a privileged self-fulfilling cycle, where minority ethnic women are disadvantaged. They earn less – the ethnicity pay gap has been shown to exist – and they face bias and discrimination in medical and reproductive healthcare.

I recalled reading somewhere that, over the years, designers of the home pregnancy test had experimented with various symbols to convey to women whether they were pregnant or not. In the years before today's blue lines, a positive result sometimes came in the form of a baby's cute smiling face, a swollen pregnant belly with a growing foetus inside, or even a single jiggling sperm. I can't imagine the horror of being faced with – what seem to me – quite tacky images announcing news that for many women might not be cute or joyful. This is not the time to think about the design of the pregnancy tests and how inelegant and unfriendly they are, I reminded myself. Focus, I told myself.

Slowly the single blue line appeared, and the last bit of hope disappeared with it. It was our third IVF treatment, and in all likelihood our last one, our last chance to do it this way, the right way, as I called it for some strange reason which I cannot remember now. I tried and failed. The test was negative once again. I sat there, still looking at that single line, willing for another one to appear miraculously across it. Perhaps if I focused hard enough and waited long enough, it would appear. But it did not.

Even as a throbbing, groaning sadness gripped my body, the painful yearning and hunger ripping through my insides, my mind zipped methodically through the last few weeks, collecting data, picking up evidence, ticking through the list of reasons why this might not have worked. I wanted the world to stop moving, to go back and be a fly on the wall.

Some philosophers believe that our minds have the power to create our realities. 'Cogito, ergo sum,' Descartes said. I think, therefore I am. Descartes first wrote the phrase in French in his 1637 *Discourse on the Method*. It forms the basis of Western philosophy. We doubt, and so we think. We think, therefore we exist. The mere act of doubting our existence serves as a proof of our self as an entity. This is also the foundation of solipsism, the philosophical idea that only one's mind is sure to exist, and the knowledge of anything outside one's own mind is unsure. I could just pretend that this reality, the negative test, the fight to conceive, was not real. Would that make it all disappear?

'What did I do wrong?' I started moaning slowly and softly, growing into a louder drumbeat to drown out the sound of sorrow spreading through my veins. 'What did I do wrong?' Again, and again, as the dim bulb flickered, breathing its last few breaths, the beat growing stronger and louder every time. I couldn't stop it. My mind was already on a downhill slope, zooming down fast and furious: I just had to hold on tight before I lost sense of reality.

Women are sold a dream with pregnancy tests. All the adverts on TV and in magazines show happy endings in glossy, shiny bathrooms, good-looking couples embracing each other, always heterosexual, always young, mostly white. Not brown, exhausted, tired, sitting alone crouched on the toilet seat, eyes blinking through the mist, with their trousers crumpled down around their ankles in a room

226

with a broken light above the mirror, their sallowness matching the yellow walls, an image bathed in grey pallor as if photoshopped with the worst Instagram filter. It is not the most dignified way to find out about what could be one of the most transformational things in one's life.

There are no images of women crying in toilets, or a sense of the loneliness of the journey they have gone through, a body broken by hormones, saddled with injected drugs and the indignity of pessaries.

Maybe I didn't have enough pee. I had tested too soon again, and maybe if I left it another few days, it would change. Something. It had to be something. I felt pregnant. My mind was telling me this, and I really wanted to believe it. Our heart forms meanings that sometimes our head refuses to believe. Why wouldn't you believe me? Why? I was convinced that this must have worked. This should have worked. After weeks of injecting myself with hormones, clocking, timing, measuring, I needed some validation that all that effort was not for nothing. Dazed, I sat there for ages holding that urine-infused stick between my fingers, staring at it, until I began to feel cold, wishing that time would freeze.

Throwing away the test meant sealing the verdict, once and for all. The last vestiges of hope going into the bin, memories and dreams boxed away, of the past and the future, realities that we created for ourselves suddenly wiped away.

The disposing of a pregnancy test has always been a furtive act in itself. In popular culture, media and books abound with instances when a pregnancy test is found in the bin and leads to a big reveal and jubilation, or aspersions being cast on the character of the women concerned. Whether it is a positive or a negative result, or an unwanted or a desired pregnancy, there isn't an easy way to dispose of this oh-so-very personal piece of plastic. A pregnancy test, if found – no matter how carefully hidden and then secretly discarded under other rubbish – can also be used for coercion in abusive relationships. In an article on Vice in December 2017, Nancy Neylon, executive director of Ohio Domestic Violence Network, talks about reproductive coercion.[16] This is a form of sexual abuse where the abuser can force 'unprotected sex in order to ensure pregnancy, tampering with birth control' to control the woman. It is not a new phenomenon, of course, in any way whatsoever, but it was only very recently recognised as a distinct type of domestic abuse, and only defined as a concept in 2010, in a study in the journal *Contraception*. One of the forms of reproductive coercion is pregnancy pressure. This could take the form of pressure to become pregnant, carry a pregnancy to term, or have an abortion. The ability to discard the pregnancy test in an unobtrusive manner once and for all could literally save lives.

As we talk more about the impact of our lifestyle and our products on the environment, it is clear that for something that has such a tiny lifecycle, used and discarded in a few minutes, it also has a huge environmental impact. The discarded used pregnancy test sticks end up in landfill. Recently, a biodegradable pregnancy test has been launched that claims to address this. Called Lia, it is a flushable test that would be a huge step forward in not only making pregnancy testing more eco-friendly, but also more private. Lia uses natural fibres and no adhesives, so the test biodegrades in water.[17] Being able to flush a test away can empower women who are in controlling relationships, giving them space and time to consider their choices and options, which they otherwise might not have. It can give more agency to women and reduce some of the fears of being discovered before they are prepared to share this news. The relatively little innovation that has happened in this category in form or design in the last thirty years just shows how women's products and needs are ignored in the design industry. It also shows how the large pharmaceutical conglomerates control this market so that there is little investment and incentive available for start-ups that hope to revolutionise and modernise this technology. Somehow within the proclamations of progress made over the years, the needs of those who use this technology the most have been sidelined. Even as the test is touted as a feminist technology, empowering women, giving them choice, freedom and clarity, it remains ambiguous. There has not been as much research on home pregnancy tests as there has in technological apps for fertility. This is a classic case of 'technological somnambulism',[18] a technology that society adopts without due consideration, much like while sleepwalking. Home pregnancy tests have changed so much of how we live and how we experience the pain, grief, loss and jubilation of being pregnant – or not. We, as a society, are still deciding what the criteria for a feminist technology would look like, and we don't have very clear answers just yet. The way these tests are marketed, packaged, bought and used shows us that they are not feminist. Far from it.

A home pregnancy test was seen as feminist technology in the 1970s. Women could take control of their bodies and their reproductive choices without any external medical intervention, and it coincided with Roe v Wade making abortion legal in the USA. It could be done in their own time, in privacy; it was non-invasive, relatively cheap and available easily over the counter so that women did not need external medical frameworks that were sometimes intimidating and judgemental towards their reproductive decisions and choices.

Marcel Wanders, a product designer for a 1990 version of Organon's test, told the *New York Times* in 2012: 'The pregnancy test has a very different significance to different people. You can't put too much meaning into it.'[19] Linda Layne says that 'pregnancy tests are at once universalist and reductionist'.[20] Like many of the technologies around us, they reduce pregnancy to one thing, one symptom, one condition, and dismiss the fact that pregnancies can be different without acknowledging the social and physical diversity of the users: from those who wanted to be pregnant and those who did not, those who are thrilled to be pregnant to those who see it as a crisis. Layne also discusses how even though these tests claim to shift power from the medical professionals to women, in fact they did not create authoritative knowledge that was considered official, because through media reports and film representations where women take multiple tests to confirm their pregnancy, there remained a doubt about the accuracy of these tests. Even the manufacturers of more sophisticated tests such as Clearblue and First Response do not claim to be 100 per cent accurate, which means that women always have to get a blood test at a health centre to confirm or deny the pregnancy. By purporting that these tests are merely a diagnostic tool, and a step before the pregnancy is officially confirmed by a medical professional, they add to the pregnancy capitalist consumption that is prevalent in our society, the industry that thrives on women either not being able to conceive, or on those who are pregnant.

This is how our social media algorithms now work, tapping into our search histories, our vulnerabilities and our fears around not being able to have a baby, being pregnant when we do not desire one, or not being a good mother as soon as we find out that we are pregnant. I googled 'egg-freezing' and 'pregnancy tests' while writing this book, and immediately, rather magically, all the ads that I was being shown on Facebook were those of fertility centres and ovulation kits on one hand, and of baby clothes and nappies on the other.

There is so much more that can be done to make pregnancy tests truly 'feminist'. While on one hand pregnancy tests and the latest sophisticated technologies offer the possibility of early testing, so that women can start seeking early healthcare and be in a position to make decisions about their reproductive future, this does not benefit all women equally. Such easy-to-access technology is still prohibitively expensive for many women, and has not resulted in any distinct impact in terms of access to abortion or prenatal care. In many countries these tests are sold with up to a 2,000 per cent mark-up and are only available in English. Language barriers, non-existent sex education and lack of financial independence means that most women globally do not have access to the freedom and agency that these tests claim to offer. Access to medical healthcare is heavily divided across class and racial lines. Even if a pregnancy test allows women to seek early prenatal care, black women are four times more likely to die than other women during maternity, because of lack of easy access to care for minority women, both financially and geographically, in addition to the harsh healthcare insurance frameworks in certain countries.[21] It is unclear whether what has been created is a new hope or a new burden for women and mothers. For many, this merely adds another step of indecision, uncertainty and convoluted choices.

In one of my local chemists, a tiny one in a small town, I find fifteen choices on the shelves ranging from £3.99 for a single test of their own brand to a pack of nine test refills costing £47 which also needs another device – a fertility monitor – costing £140.[22] The choices are endless, with nothing much to separate the different brands, some claiming more early testing than others, some with a clearer display than others, some with a colour changing dipstick, and some packaged along with ovulation tests and fertility monitors in a neat little bundle for all fertility needs. Many of these tests are now being sold in packaged deals of three to nine tests, thereby implying that a person is more likely to test multiple times than once. One has to wonder who is benefiting from the pervasive invasion of these tests, and other fertility paraphernalia, and if these devices are really offering people more agency and autonomy or if they are merely profiting the pharmaceutical companies, private clinics and stores. There is no responsibility of care associated with the sale of these tests, so in none of the three brands that I examined was there any information on what a woman could do if they were inadvertently pregnant and did not wish to go through with this pregnancy, or what to do if a person had been unable to get pregnant despite numerous attempts. What then? Even as they afford privacy, the act of taking a test in solitude enhances the acute loneliness of some of these experiences.

While on one hand, these pregnancy tests have empowered women to take control of their fertility and be the first to know whether they are pregnant or not, Layne also argues that they have diminished the embodied experience of women, and the close intuitive relationship they have with their own bodies. Our culture and our upbringing influence how we trust and understand our bodies. I don't think I ever learnt to do so. There is therefore a need to educate all young people to establish a closer relationship with their own bodies, be able to read the signs and changes, and have an affinity with their own biology. But alongside this, it is absolutely crucial to carry out a thorough investigation of the intersectional social and cultural contexts in which these tests are bought, used and disposed of. And it is as critical to examine at policy and systemic level the inequalities that persist in access to reproductive healthcare.

•

I try to focus my mind on something else to ground me, but my thoughts flit around aimlessly. I want to feel something, anything. I sit there numb. I look at the brown walls and the tiled floor. I hate these walls. I look at the mirror with the tiny web of cracks across it, fingers spreading out like frozen stalactites and stalagmites. I can't recognise myself in it. I try to cry. I am all out of tears. Emotions seem too far away, stretching into the horizon, too hazy to touch. I reach out to grab onto one feeling, just one fleeting sensation, to hold it still, to somehow calcify it in a sculpture of time.

'The central heating isn't on, I am sure,' I say to myself, as if the act of speaking out loud in this empty space, with the greying wall-paper echoing the darkness of my heart, would chase away the ghosts of my despair. P does not like the central heating to be on, and he must have turned it off. The heating war in our household, back and forth, like clockwork, me from the warmer southern climes and he from the frozen icy north, had kicked off as a frivolous light-hearted flirtation, but had begun to feel combative. A storm rises to the surface, bubbling away furiously now in a cauldron of apoplectic fury. A fire-tipped arrow hurtling towards my husband for his apparent failure to consider my needs, at his apparent inability to love me in the way that I wanted him to, at my imaginary discernment of his many failures, my own disappointment detonating in my body, determined to find someone else to blame. It is a relief in some way. It is a relief to feel something different. This rage is soothing, calming, therapeutic, tearing a hole in the inert ball that I had curled myself into for so long in the depths of my melancholy, because it was warm and safe in there. This deep, aching sadness had been a lonely place to be.

Grief is not something that one ever has a template for. When Elizabeth Browning wrote that grief was '. . . silence like to death',[23] she shaped the loneliness of grieving into words. There is a thin line between knowing and not knowing, between living and not. A moment in time, an insignificant sliver can alter reality.

'I could die right here,' I think as despair boils over, but then the rational part of my brain kicks in and I can't help thinking that the dreary tiled floor would be an awfully desperate place to die. Then I remember that my daughter is due back from school very soon, there would be small tired footsteps running up the steps, and exhausted shouts calling out for me, and I have to be the mother that I am. I have to show up. I always showed up. Perhaps this is my only chance to get it right. I have to get it right. Perhaps I should just be happy with this. Because I am lucky, am I not? I am lucky. Yes, I am. The excited yelps and whiny barks of our dog outside the door remind me of our daily meanders through the corn fields high up behind the row of houses every afternoon. He was a rescue, but he had so often rescued me, just like now: from myself, and from my despair.

And just like that, slowly the ordinariness of life drags me screaming and kicking back from the brink, just as passing over had seemed so very enticing.

VIII.

FORK IN THE ROAD

'How can i keep ted wedded to a barren woman?' Plath writes in her diary as, in the summer of 1959, she realises she has stopped ovulating. Plath's journals show a deep and desperate fear of infertility, seeing it as a deformity in herself that she can never recover from. She writes: 'If I could not have children – and if I do not ovulate how can I? – how can they make me – I would be dead. Dead to my woman's body.'[1] The infertile women in Plath's poems, and imagination, are never at the centre, merely peripheral, and never able to cross over to the centre; doomed for the forever future.

I will not be able to carry a child, I am told. My womb, my ovaries, my body have failed me. There is no road ahead unless we carve one out, dig it from the vast unmarked landscape ahead of us. In moments of despair, weighed down with guilt, I tell him that we should get divorced and he should be with someone else, someone who can give him a child. Sometimes that just seems like the easy way out. He finds them depressing; I these discussions exhausting. But it is almost as if my mind is a hostage to unknown forces but entranced by them, a case of Stockholm Syndrome. I keep going

235

there again and again, navigating cul-de-sacs, because every road seems blocked. I wonder if I am trying to merely absolve myself of the deep disappointment I feel. If he left me, I could feel something else; I could blame someone else.

We agree that love for a child has nothing to do with genetics. We start looking into adoption and the hoops one has to jump through without knowing what lies at the end of it all. I am fearful of more rejection, people telling me that I cannot be a mother, judging us, measuring us against yardsticks that we don't know exist. How does one even know what kind of parent they would be? It is a lottery that we all have to play and jump into with both feet. The road through adoption is not for us, as we already have a child, which pulls us straight towards the bottom rung of the adoption ladder before we have even started. Much like the IVF lottery, secondary infertility is considered a side note in a person's journey to have a child, a luxury, an indulgence. I can't be a side note, just a number, an invisible statistic yet again, I think to myself, as we peer up towards a long waiting list for people who deserve a child in their lives. We don't deserve a child – this is the message we often get with secondary infertility. Even though M is mine, legally and biologically, P has been her parent for so much of her life. While we are investigating adoption, I am delighted that he is being acknowledged as a father for once, which even friends and family unknowingly and often knowingly fail to recognise. People get caught up in names and legalities, forgetting that parenting, nurturing, caring for a child is about the hours spent wiping their tears and grazed knees, sitting up with them at bedtime listening to their travails and silent agonies, going to the supermarket and always remembering what they like to eat and what they hate, making sense of their quirks, and tending to their passions with as much love as your own. Often people forget that anyone can give birth to a child, but not everyone can be a parent. But even though he has never adopted her, he is tied to me, and we have a child. My brain can't let go of the feeling that, yet again, I am the dead weight pulling him down.

Someone mentions surrogacy to us, and we start looking into it. 'Just looking into it,' we tell each other. Just checking it out to see what it involves, but surely it is not for us, we remind ourselves. I trawl forums, day and night, ignoring and avoiding work. I just want something to happen. The no-man's land does not feel like home. Neither here, nor there. I message a few people who've undergone surrogacy; I read their blogs; I see their happy pictures of bringing their infants home, marking their first birthdays and then the ones after that. It will never work for us, I remind myself. And then before we've had a chance to think more about it, we find ourselves hurtling down the road towards surrogacy. There is no turning back now. Looking over our shoulders, we do not see a way back. Yet all this time, and paradoxically with my concentrated commitment to becoming pregnant, I also feel a deep uncertainty about whether I really want another child or not. He really wants a child; I am not 100 per cent sure. I am too exhausted, my mind and body already worn out after the many cycles, needles prodding, hopes blooming and crashing. But I love him too much, and I don't wear my guilt well. I also have a child and have given her my all. I often wonder if I have any more of myself to give to any future children. I don't know any other kind of love, any other notion of motherhood, where the love is not all-consuming. If I don't feel such an overpowering love then is it even worth it? I keep agonising over this even as my teenager pulls away from me, desperate to break away from me. This is what teenagers do, in order to seek autonomy, and this is what every parent most desires for them. But I wonder if I am prepared for such inevitable heartbreak again, if I will have the strength to keep mothering while feeling like a terrible mother. I wonder if I have enough belief in myself as a mother, whether my conviction in my ways of tending will persist even as they get knocked by a headstrong teenager. One never knows. I don't know. But how can one be certain about being a mother again, if they don't know whether they have been a good enough mother the first time around?

Any indecision on my part, any uncertainty, would be a sign of weakness. How can I be ambivalent about wanting more children? I try and think of alternative futures where it is just the two of us, as our eldest has left home, trying to imagine ourselves walking hand in hand into the sunset together. I try and foresee alternative futures and realise that I have never been very adept at this, creating and imagining other possibilities for myself. Living the life we have is hard enough. Living life fully in the present is exhausting enough: exhilarating, gruelling, bracing. How does one have energy to live these parallel lives too, even merely in one's imaginings?

I wonder if I have sleepwalked through life, treading paths that seem like a dream, never giving enough time to any decision lest I change my mind, setting myself on a course where there is never an option to return. I wonder if we often make decisions, choose choices, because they seem the easiest, or just because we dare ourselves to risk taking a path that seems dangerous. Surely surrogacy will lead to nowhere, and I will fall back into safety soon enough. I wonder if the choices we don't make in life matter as much as the ones we do make. The act of moving towards a choice can be two things: either a deliberate choosing of one, or an active rejection of another.

As I have trundled along the fertility journey, desperately wanting to be pregnant, and dreading the thought of carrying another child, apprehensive of bringing another life into this world, I wonder if I am so determined to succeed because failure is mine alone, because I cannot bear not to be successful. The more I invest in it emotionally, physically, financially, calculating odds, statistics of success, taking chances, it seems even more difficult to contemplate and accept failure. Is this a wish to test my own resilience, my own limits, my own luck? That urge to see how far I can push my luck is like a death wish at times.

As long as I can remember, even as a child, I have imagined myself dead. But I have never wanted to die. Life has always been worth living, there has always been someone counting on me, or lists that still haven't been ticked off. How could I leave people depending on my existence, and to-do lists unattended? With this somewhat morbid fascination with death, I've often plunged myself into lives that feel precipitous, closer to death or some vision of it, even though it is only then that I feel that I am living life to the fullest, responding to the call of the siren, heralding me, daring me to the unknown lands.

P reads this over my shoulder as I write this today, in 2020, and asks me if I thought having more children was akin to death. 'No,' I assert firmly. 'Of course not,' I say with an exaggerated conviction. 'No, that's not what I mean. At least I don't think so. I must have wanted it at some level,' I say. It was easier to envision a life with children than without. I could see that it would be easier. 'So, it seemed like an easier choice?' he asks in disbelief and with a laugh, looking at the chaos of our lives around us, our exhausted lives, stretched and worn out to the limits as we, two adults, work and parent full-time during this lockdown.

'Did you imagine that this was the easier option?' he asks, his question suspended there between us, poised expectantly. Neither response – yes or no – seems accurate right now. Life would have been much easier, perhaps, but maybe it wouldn't have been. Fighting against our own expectations, and my own sense of failure, seemed so much harder then, even as I knew that I had set out on a path which would be gruelling. I knew that I wasn't young enough, in body or in mind, that I had lived so long for someone else, and I wanted to be myself for a few seconds, minutes, hours. How would that be possible with more children? 'You wouldn't have to sacrifice much,' I had wanted to say to him so many times when we were setting forward on this path. But in admitting this, I was admitting to my own frailties and limitations as a woman. How could I admit that being a woman, and a mother, or not being one, was still a choice based around our careers, our whole selves, our dreams and aspirations for ourselves? I could pretend that I could have it all, that I wouldn't be limited by motherhood, but that is – alas – not the reality. 'Of course, you wouldn't have to sacrifice anything,' he had said.

But that is not true, is it? It never is that straightforward. It is not just what society expects of us, but also what we expect from ourselves. I know I can drown myself in motherhood until I lose sight and sense of myself. I have done it before. How would I know that this would be any different? But then if I don't submerge myself, am I really giving it my all?

•

Surrogacy has been around for a very long time. The first mention is in the Bible, in the Book of Genesis with the story of Abraham and Sarah, who are married but could not conceive a child of their

240

own, so their servant Hagar has their son, Ishmael, instead. This was a traditional surrogacy where the surrogate mother has a biological link to the child using her own egg. It has a chequered past too, of course, as black women slaves were often used as surrogates for white couples. And this naturally makes the discussion emotive. But it is also controversial because it questions the very foundation of what makes a family, and what motherhood really is. It challenges the legal, emotional and ethical dimensions of parenthood and parenting; it proposes the disputable idea that a woman's reproduction is labour no matter what form it is in. It challenges the pervasive notion of a 'natural motherhood', one where maternal instinct and bond is determined by pregnancy and carrying a child in a womb for nine months.

There have been two primary perspectives on surrogacy. On the one hand there is the Western view, grounded in radical feminism, focusing on women as victims of patriarchy, propagating the view that surrogacy is an extreme exploitation of poor women. On the other hand, the Eastern perspective, which relates to liberal feminism and mainly emphasises freedom from patriarchy through women's empowerment, argues that surrogacy is simply a means through which women can have their own homes and financial resources, leading to increased independence from their husbands and other family members.[2] Once again we only see things in black and white, in binaries. It is much more nuanced than this. The legal and human elements of surrogacy remain in conflict, even as surrogacy brings joy for transgender couples, those with interminable infertility, and gay men who wish to have a biological child.

Much of the writing – especially in the media – on surrogacy is largely speculative, as there are very few research studies that document the experience of surrogates in different global contexts. Much of this is also very polemic, each side passionately attacking the other, a binary argument often seen as an uncompromising debate between radical and liberal feminists. The surrogacy industry is certainly not without its problems and we are likely to hear of the cases where things go wrong, of places and clinics where surrogates have not been treated well, of couples abandoning their babies after birth, where surrogates have refused to give up the child after birth to the intended biological parents, or where 'extra' babies have been sold on the black market. Of course, the media focuses on the negative cases, the ones where things went wrong, as they would. These are the bylines that sell newspapers, that are sensationalist. And as Professor van den Akker argues, most people never have to question or challenge their normative views around reproduction, because they don't have to, and so they persist with their uncompromising views on third party reproduction.[3] They continue to live in what Leon Festinger called a 'cognitive consonance state',[4] one where they believe that their beliefs and actions would always be in equilibrium. Many infertile couples who resort to surrogacy go through a long period of internalised (and external) debate and conflict trying to align their beliefs with their actions. This path from cognitive dissonance, where there is a disequilibrium between beliefs and actions, to one of consonance can sometimes be a long and agonising one, where not only do they finally have to reach an acceptance that they would never be able to procreate 'naturally', but also reconcile themselves to a different family model than they might have originally imagined.

Anti-surrogacy campaigners have called it anti-feminist, arguing that poverty-stricken women cede control of their bodies in exchange for money. There have also been disturbing parallels drawn between surrogacy and Margaret Atwood's dystopian world of *The Handmaid's Tale*, a world where the underclass is designed to carry children for the privileged upper-class society, a story with problematic 'eugenic feminism'* that Sophie Lewis in her book *Full Surrogacy Now* calls a 'anti-totalitarian and anti-patriarchal but not anti-racist or anti-imperial or pro-trans version of women's struggle'.[5] And I wonder if this version of surrogacy that we hear again and again serves any other purpose than to reinforce a monolithic version of womanhood and fertility. This vision is used again and again to discredit surrogacy, where commercial surrogates are used as mascots to campaign against what is perceived as 'unnatural' and exploitative. Some equate surrogacy to sex work, both industries discredited for the exploitation of human bodies. Much like sex work, which has been denigrated, stigmatised and the subject of controversial legislation, the focus swings continuously away from the rights of the workers, those providing the labour, as well as the capitalist forces that might lead to exploitation. Instead, the narrative is framed to stress that surrogacy of any form goes against the traditional reproduction model, that it is sexual and reproductive servitude. Andrea Dworkin, a radical feminist writer, argues that surrogacy is like prostitution because the surrogate has no choice, calling it a 'brothel model'; a reproductive brothel.[6] Yes, sex work is not free from exploitation, but it also is about allowing a woman the choice to use her body in a way that she wants to, and having the choice to do so. Obviously, choice is a complicated concept and doesn't exist in a vacuum outside socio-political-economic forces. But it's clear that surrogacy is a women's rights issue, at the heart of bodily autonomy and choice. And limiting choice is never equivalent to protection.

There is also a moral judgement while falling back onto the

---

* As discussed earlier in the book, many of the earlier suffrage movements overlapped with eugenic beliefs.

notion of motherhood equating solely to the womb. The focus is primarily on the two women, without due consideration of the role of the partner or their decision together as a couple to undertake surrogacy: the responsibility as well as accountability is placed heavily on the woman who is the intended mother. The surrogacy debate becomes solely a moral and ethical one. The exercising of choice by the woman who opts for surrogacy is vilified, but there is also a complete dismissal of the possibility that in choosing to be a surrogate, a woman may be exercising her own agency and choice too. It is an inherent paradox, where motherhood is demonised as well as idolised. There is a refusal to accept that motherhood and mothering are two entirely different things, the reluctance to acknowledge that motherhood and surrogacy are not the same thing either, that motherhood is ultimately a social construct, one where the notion of 'nurture' creates value and meaning, and one where parenthood can be defined by 'intent'. Margarete Sandelowski, a liberal feminist, in her book *With Child in Mind: Studies of the Personal Encounter with Infertility*, claims that much of the debate around surrogacy is emblematic of the larger discourse in Western cultures, where there is a tendency to 'view as opposite and conflicting the natural and the artificial, the biological and the technological, and to value one over the other.'[7] Helena Ragoné, an acclaimed anthropologist, was one of the first to carry out extensive surveys documenting the experiences of surrogates and intended parents, and challenge hegemonic ideas of kinship and parenthood. In her paper 'The Gift of Life' Ragoné argues that surrogacy encourages procreative freedom, and is a gift to infertile and non-normative families.[8]

There are many misconceptions around gestational surrogacy. This is a variant of surrogacy in which the surrogate conceives using in vitro fertilisation with the egg of the commissioning mother or an egg donor, which has been fertilised in a petri dish with sperm provided by the commissioning father (or, in some cases, a donor). Traditional surrogacy, on the other hand, is where the surrogate provides the eggs as well as the womb. In gestational surrogacy, the surrogate's genetic makeup becomes less relevant for the intended parent. Even though gestational surrogacy often faces heavy criticism, it has redefined what it means to be a family. For same-sex male couples or single men, it offers the option to be genetically linked to a child. For those without a uterus, for trans men, for women who are confronting infertility, it has opened up the option to have a family for so many who did not think that it would ever be possible for them.

I wonder if, in a world where all of us are selling our bodies and minds, assigning value and worth through action, words, gestures, why we are so puritanical about women taking control of their bodies, be it sex work or surrogacy? I wonder about this quite a lot. I don't have very many clear answers just yet, but I do wonder if for some the notion of consent and agency is relatively quite straightforward, while for others who are more marginalised, living on the edge of poverty, those who do not have many choices, whether for them the freedom of choice to consent is more constrained, and more easily veering towards 'yes'. I wonder about this a lot too. When we talk about reproductive agency, especially in terms of surrogacy, we have to think about how much a woman is worth. How much is a woman's body worth? I am worthy, and valuable, but by what measure? And in using another woman as a surrogate, am I exercising my own privilege and becoming part of the machine that siphons women's bodies and uses them for its own good, churning out parts as and when it deems fit, exploiting, abusing, dismantling piece by piece until what is left is only a semblance of what a woman ought to look like? In doing so, could I be an unwitting cog in the system that values women only for their power to procreate? I would like to think that my surrogate has agency, and in using the womb that has only served men until now, conforming to a patriarchal expectation of bearing children and carrying on the family line, boys that would bear the load of the parents financially as they grow older, and physically as they carry their bodies towards their final rites, she is taking her body and making a choice to use it in the way she deems fit. But in hiring out a womb, are we refusing to acknowledge the agency and choice these women have, and are resentful of it? Or are we merely unwilling to acknowledge that procreation can be used for the purposes of a woman's own advancement as well, if that is the way she wants to, and chooses to?

The expansion of surrogacy as a commercialised enterprise went hand in hand with the broader commercialisation of the fertility industry, making it into a big-bucks enterprise, a global industry which grew relatively quickly. With this rapid growth also came the dangers of unregulated, uncharted waters. The relatively low cost of living but similar levels of infrastructure and medical expertise available in India made it into a major centre for surrogacy arrangements. Prior to the 1980s, most countries in the global north allowed genetic or traditional forms of surrogacy (where the eggs of the surrogate were used), but then several cases such as that of Baby M, where the surrogate Mary Beth Whitehead refused to part with the baby and hand it over to the intended parents, occurred. This case really highlighted some of the issues of the ethical, moral and legal dilemmas around surrogacy, and how it was such a divisive and unregulated domain. A report from the Asian-Pacific Resource and Research Centre for Women (ARROW) in 2016 discusses this case and the backlash.[9] There were the more conservative feminists who advocated for the maternal bond created in pregnancy and how surrogacy disrupted the natural model of family and motherhood. Some questioned the commercial aspects of surrogacy and how it amounted to 'baby selling', and commodified women's bodies. While on one hand, the surrogate was deemed as an unfit mother and untrustworthy, the intended mother was also considered a bad mother as she had used the services of another woman to carry her child, even when she was not infertile. The fact that she had multiple sclerosis which could be severely exacerbated by pregnancy was overlooked. Amongst all this debate, which was really rooted in the notion that women could not be trusted to make their own decisions about their bodies and procreation, the intended father unsurprisingly remained untarnished, and as the biological parent, having donated the sperm, he was given custody of the child, which was deemed in the 'best interest of the child.' Following this highly public case, however, a committee was set up for Inquiry into Human Fertilisation and Embryology and on recommendations by the Warnock Report, the United Kingdom prohibited commercial surrogacy in 1990. Most other European countries such as France, Germany, the Netherlands and Spain have also since banned such surrogacy arrangements.

Today I can look through the data, stats and facts and absorb it all with a calm and rational mind. Hindsight is also such a magical thing, the rearview mirror into our lives seems so unambiguous. Of course, we knew it would be like this. Of course, it is crystal clear we should have done this, not done that. But right there, then, when we are in the midst of it all, clarity is often elusive. Those days seemed blurry, sleepwalking, like bumper cars at a fairground.

•

I am exhausted; we are both exhausted. I feel like I am rapidly zooming around in a twister, churned back and forth, like Toto in *The Wizard of Oz*. I feel like we are being dragged around with some mystical force, not knowing whether we are destined for a magical land at the end of it all. There is so much information but also very little at the same time, details and regulations ignored while heavily segregated discourse on the moral discussion around surrogacy swarms the bits and bytes of the digital world. Because even in academic social science literature, there are heated volatile debates on surrogacy as the commodification of motherhood, especially pertaining to transnational arrangements, focused primarily on the binaries of altruistic (where the surrogate accepts no monetary compensation for carrying the pregnancy to term) and commercial surrogacy (the surrogate is compensated monetarily).

I want to be in India – again – when my child is born, a natural urge to return to my mother's fold, and the first place that I ever called home. I want my unborn child to come as close to being inside my womb as possible. Sometimes we go back to a place to remind us of ourselves, and what we might have forgotten, and sometimes we go back to forget things that we remember too keenly. Sometimes we go back to places to ask questions, and sometimes to recognise that we don't have them any more. Maybe I want to tell my children who I was before they came along. I want to remind myself where I came from, even though I ran very far away from that place. We seek comfort in the familiar even though it can have hard edges.

This isn't just about me though, but I was the one who couldn't carry a child. I was the one who had failed us, and I had to put this right. It is on my shoulders to make it right. I have to.

I find that many couples of Indian origin or those that are

248

inter-racial do not share their stories publicly. They are the ones who feel the most shame. I worry about this the most, whether if as a feminist I am going against my ideals by using another woman's body to have my child. Even as a brown woman, I am exercising my privilege of being educated, and resident in a Western, wealthier country, to use a surrogate in the geographical south. I agonise over this decision and thereafter whether this was oppression, whether I was using my power and privilege to oppress another woman, especially from the same country that I came from, and where patriarchal roots have been as deep as its history and heritage. I research surrogacy obsessively. As I go down the labyrinth of online forums focused on infertility and pregnancy, a (white) woman based in the UK tells me: '3rd World women, wives and mothers, such as in India, [are] exploited and then cast aside by 1st World women who see babies as commodities one can buy'. I feel shocked, angry, humiliated. Am I a first world woman, I try to reason? But the boundaries are fuzzy as I stand with my feet in both worlds, and often in none.

It is not only the widespread media interest in India in the lives of Bollywood stars and the increasing popularity of surrogacy amongst the wealthy elite that has created a one-dimensional narrative around intended parents, but also Bollywood in general has perpetuated harmful narratives around surrogacy. In a few films that have portrayed surrogacy, such as *Doosri Dulhan* (1983) and *Chori Chori Chupke Chupke* (2001), once again sex work and surrogacy have been equated to each other, both using sex workers as surrogates, both depicted as exploitative, completely dismissing the fact that many women undertake both out of free will. The films had mixed reviews, as the subject of infertility but specifically surrogacy is taboo in broader Indian society. The media depictions vacillate between two views of surrogacy: one where the motherhood of a surrogate is commodified and bought by someone who is not deemed to be a 'good mother' because she is unwilling to give birth and face the ordeals of pregnancy, and the other a glorified version of motherhood where the surrogate is sacrificing her motherhood by giving away the child that she has given birth to, and in the process redeems herself from a sex worker, a 'bad woman'. By becoming a surrogate, a woman becomes a victim, but also a 'good woman', one who is seen as a perfect mother because she is ready to sacrifice. On the other hand, the woman who opts for surrogacy is not a good mother, as she is exploiting another woman, unable or unprepared to undertake pregnancy herself. This casts doubts on her suitability as a mother, and the idea that motherhood is inherently linked with carrying a child for nine months is reinforced. These representations also create the binary paradigm of body and morality within which all surrogacy discussions are usually framed, a falsehood that it exploits women who are financially destitute, completely discounting that many well-to-do women from the middle and upper class also choose to be surrogates in the global south, especially in India.

I don't follow Bollywood news or even news in Indian media, as I try and separate myself from the hugely divisive politics there based in dogmatic religious ideology. But as I research surrogacy obsessively, I slowly find that with the spate of celebrity surrogacy stories in India, primarily from Bollywood stars, on one hand discussions around surrogacy have become more normalised and part of the broader social and cultural consciousness, on the other this has fostered a harmful narrative. One where a very specific image has been created of the intended parent: rich, powerful, famous and able to use their power and privilege to opt for surrogacy, where the 'intended mother' has been too career-minded or lazy to have children, does not want to go through the ordeals of pregnancy or childbirth, because that would somehow interfere with her perfected idealised body, ambition or social image. This is however not always the case. It isn't for us, of course. I read these horror stories again and again, my inherent curiosity becoming my worst enemy. I cry and I ache with the feeling of despair, longing, guilt and shame. I want to be pregnant. I just can't be. I am prepared to go through the ordeals of pregnancy. My body and my hormones have other plans. I don't want to do this, I tell myself again and again, but silently, very silently.

I am acutely aware of the many reports of exploitation of Indian surrogates who primarily come from poor parts of the country. I lie awake at night, trying to reach some level of cognitive consonance that I am comfortable with. We talk and talk some more, discuss it with lawyers who have extensive experience with surrogacy arrangements across the world, and we discuss at length with the medical team in India before we finally decide to go ahead. We had selected this clinic after speaking with four other clinics across the country and speaking to parents who had already undergone surrogacy at each of these clinics, and scouring the internet for reviews of this clinic and the medical team. We had long phone conversations about their values and ethos, and the care that they provide to the surrogates before, during and after the process.

There is no sale of a baby. We are not 'buying a baby'. For me, this is extremely important, in fact one of the crucial determinants to ensure that the human rights of my future children are not violated. We hire a surrogacy lawyer here in the UK who looks through all the contracts, and does an extensive legal review, even though that is not a standard practice. We ensure that all legal documents are translated into Hindi, the local language, so that both the surrogate and her husband can read them before they enter any contractual agreement.

In 2016, the Indian government passed a draft surrogacy regulation bill soon after we had our twins by surrogacy and brought them back home to the UK. The bill proposed banning surrogacy for all foreign nationals. As someone who handed over an Indian passport for British citizenship, I would have no longer been eligible for it either. In fact, since then surrogacy has been banned in all its commercial forms, restricting it solely to an altruistic form, where the surrogate cannot expect any payment in the form of any remuneration, except for medical expenses and sixteen months' health insurance coverage. The regulation bill is a reflection of the current political agenda and nationalistic religious fervour in the country, where even though homosexuality has been finally legalised, surrogacy is not allowed for homosexual couples. The pernicious nature of the bill is evident by its prohibition of live-in partners, same-sex couples, foreigners and single parents from using surrogacy services. The homophobia of the government has never been more clear than when the then Indian Minister of External Affairs Sushma Swaraj very clearly stated that surrogacy for homosexuals is against 'Indian ethos', although homosexuality has been regularly mentioned in various Indian religious texts. Neither is it for unmarried couples (they choose to term them live-in couples) or single parents, or even for people who already have a biological child, thereby completely ignoring and dismissing secondary infertility. Once again, rather than managing and regulating a situation, a complete blanket ban has been imposed that harms more women than it benefits, removing their agency and bodily autonomy through a paternalistic enforcement of cultural norms, while also discriminating against any non-heteronormative relationship, side-

252

lining and removing access to surrogacy for all of the queer community.

Why does a woman agree to become a surrogate? Would I be prepared to carry someone else's child and then give it away nine months later? I don't know. I doubt it. My pregnancy, the first one, the one where I came home with a child, was very very tough. The thought of going through something like that again for someone else seems unimaginable to me. For many women, the idea of being able to do something good for a couple who are desperate for a child, to give them the 'greatest gift' they desire is the motivation, while for others the pleasure that a pregnancy brings is the primary driving force. Whatever the reasons might be, it fills me up with a huge amount of respect and admiration for women who do it. I wonder about the men in their lives, their husbands in the Indian context (as only married women who have their own children are allowed to be surrogates), and I find that we do not know what they think, what they feel. They remain a silent, often invisible party, even in a largely patriarchal society where men have traditionally controlled their wives' reproductive choices. In the ARROW report, we hear of the surrogate Rita who reiterates her own contribution to this process. As per her interview in 2012, her own husband had no contribution to the pregnancy, no sexual relations with her while she was away, and had to take care of the children and cook, which was her job, hence redefining the traditional masculine/feminine roles.

Amrita Pande is one of the few researchers who has carried out in-depth ethnographical academic enquiry into the experiences of surrogates contextualised by the anti-natal industry[†] and labour

---

† Anti-natalism is a philosophical movement that assigns negative value to birth.

market in India.[10] Pande also places this debate at the centre of the broader discussion[11] around 'stratified reproduction'[12] which Rayna Rapp, a professor of anthropology at New York State University describes as 'the hierarchical organisation of reproductive fecundity and birth experiences that supports and rewards the maternity of some women while despising or outlawing the mother-work of others'.[13]

Pande's research highlights how in contrast to the global north where women often struggled to get access to any form of contraception, in India it was imposed on women, and their fertility seen as a detriment to their financial prosperity by the state and medical professionals.[14] The notion of class is an important dimension in the discussion about surrogacy in India and hence it is important to consider how class has historically influenced access to contraception, as well as the perception that illiterate housewives from lower strata of society were recklessly reproductive, and hence to be blamed for their own poverty. When forced to adopt some of the modern contraceptive technology such as the pill and IUDs, these women see it as an assault on their body and their reproduction. Therefore, while we are aware of the gender asymmetry in contraceptive technologies, as most of these modern technologies are designed only for women, there is also a specific class-based asymmetry in India, where contraceptive pills were available only for upper and middle-class educated women living in urban areas.

A number of women in Pande's research admit to feeling delighted that they had 'turned the tables' where their reproduction was an asset, and they could use their bodies to empower their families. Many of the surrogates whom I spoke to in the process of writing this book, and while researching surrogacy in 2015–16, confessed they were more in control of their bodies, and had a better understanding of their mental and physical needs during the surrogate birth compared to the birth of their own children. They also valued the hyper-medicalisation of the process rather than resenting it, seeing it as a luxury. One of these women saw this as an opportunity to create a better future for her own children, pleased that her reproductive fertility was helping her family rather than hampering them, and to be making good use of her 'body and her motherhood'. While their own pregnancies had been seen as normal occurrences, with not much medical care or a break from everyday household work, during surrogacy they enjoy the 'luxury' of regular health checks, nutritious food and a break from their everyday work, and time to spend on themselves during and after the pregnancy. Of course, this is also largely due to the stratified nature of the surrogacy process where the child is undeniably considered more precious and valuable than the surrogate's body and power dynamics are at play along the intersection of class, race and gender, so that the surrogate's body is valued only because it carries the child that is cherished. This is, however, something that is not strikingly different to the experience of many women giving birth to their own children in the global north, where motherhood is valued while mothers not so much.

The whole surrogacy domain is still fraught with uncertainty for everyone involved because of the lack of regulations, and clear legal language that can determine the status and identity of the child born through this arrangement. There is so much more to consider other than the 'nature/nurture', 'reproductive oppression/procreative labour' or 'pro-ban/anti-ban' binaries. We could instead focus on dissolving the archaic notions of motherhood and narrow ideas of biology, moving towards a familiar kinship where collaboration and shared responsibility towards creating families and childcare can become the norm. The legal framework is lagging and stuck in the traditional notions of who a mother is, and who has claims to a child, even when there is no genetic link with the surrogate. The surrogate is always registered as the legal mother of the child, even if an embryo from the recipient couple is used as in gestational surrogacy. Many of the contracts are not legally enforceable, and the social support for the couple undergoing surrogacy and the surrogate, during and after this period, is sorely lacking. It feels like a lonely journey; it felt like a very lonely journey. For me personally as someone who underwent surrogacy, and as a feminist, this lack of regulation is what is most worrying, not that surrogacy exists or should be allowed to. There have to be clearer laws to protect the rights and status of children born through surrogacy arrangements, a thorough examination of power hierarchies that influence the surrogate's rights and choices regarding her own body as a resource, and a state-led commitment to care and responsibility for the well-being of everyone involved.

•

It wasn't going to be easy, but we didn't do it because it was easy. In fact, we were aware of the difficulties in bringing a child born via surrogacy in India back to the UK. We had been told that we would have to uproot ourselves and live in India for over six months. All this seems so self-regarding and mercenary as I write it, as if my concern for the woman who was to carry my embryos, my unborn children, was not our primary concern, as if our difficulties and anxieties trumped what she would have put her body through to carry the children for what turned out to be seven months. But she was never away from my mind through those very long months. I felt connected to her through an invisible thread, burdened with gratitude, drained with worry, resenting her at the same time because she could do something that I couldn't. She could carry my children, feel them moving in her womb, feel them kicking, go to scans and hear their heartbeats, and talk to them. I could not. I could not do any of those things. Resenting is really not the right word. I *envied* her. I envied her fertile, fecund body, and despised my 'inhospitable' and empty womb, disgusted with myself. During those months, I was aware of my infertility and limitations more than ever. I knew I could not be defined by my womb and my fertility. Of course I did. But emotions and rational, logical thinking are not always bedfellows.

I have been thinking more about this as I write and wonder if I found a sense of camaraderie with our surrogate in India because I felt that we were not only bonded by our mother tongue and our skin colour but also our status at the fringe. She, a woman, within the patriarchal structures, and I an immigrant, diasporic, living at the edges. Both never in the mainstream, both very much outsiders.

As far back as 1594, a translation of Lambert Daneau's *A Fruitfull Commentarie vpon the Twelue Small Prophets* talks about the Jewish diaspora, scattered abroad after the Babylonian exile: 'This scattering abrode of the Iewes, as it were an heauenly sowing, fell out after their returne from the captiuitie of Babylon . . . they are called Diaspora, that is, a scattering or sowing abrode.'[15]

Diaspora is descended from the Greek word *diaspeirein*, meaning 'to scatter, spread about', found in the Greek translations of the Hebrew Bible in the Septuagint (Deuteronomy 28:25) as the phrase 'esē diaspora en pasais basileias tēs gēs' ('thou shalt be a dispersion in all kingdoms of the earth'). An individual standing at the cusp of different cultures inevitably creates what Homi Bhabha calls the 'third space', a transition space between the different hybrid identities.

In imagining myself returning to India, I feel safe, as if there is a place to collect all my scattered selves, which had been roaming abroad for many years.

In her essay *Street Haunting*, Virginia Woolf asks:

Is the true self this which stands on the pavement in January, or that which bends over the balcony in June? Am I here, or am I there? Or is the true self neither this nor that, neither here nor there, but something so varied and wandering that it is only when we give the rein to its wishes and let it take its way unimpeded that we are indeed ourselves?[16]

We have tried to do everything as rigorously, and as above board as possible. But we worry; I worry. Guilt remains, and now this guilt has taken on a huge life of its own for me. Guilt for my infecundity; guilt for my entitlement. Fruitless. Futile.

So there we are. Heading back to the fold, the place I still think of as home, where the familiar words and phrases leave a tantalising trail on my tongue. Unspoken, unsaid, but still understood. Inured for so long by dreaming and speaking in a language that was not my own, nor that of my mother or of her mother before then. My mother tongue, the language that had been breathed into my being; a language that I yearned for my unborn future children to hear first, even if it wasn't my voice they would be listening to.

IX.

UMBILICAL CORD

THE TWINS MUST HAVE BEEN about six months old, and it was really the first time I had stepped out to a social gathering of sorts since I had brought them home.

Our neighbour was celebrating her ninetieth birthday and so P and I decided to take turns to go and mingle, something I had completely forgotten how to do. The last few months had been a whirlwind. As the birthday girl introduced me to her friend, another elderly lady as sprightly and glossy, I felt shy about how tired I looked. I must have aged about a decade in the last few months, and I tried to brush back my hair, smoothing my crumpled top, pulled out from under a pile of clothes lying on a chair next to my unmade bed.

'They have just got their twins from India,' she exclaimed to her friend.

'Oh, they are adopted, are they?' The other woman examined me closely.

Suddenly my brown skin wasn't the only fascinating thing about me in this sea of white faces. I wanted to shrink myself, curl up in a ball, and felt my voice hardening.

'No, they are not adopted,' was the only thing I could muster up, trying to smile, unsure whether I should be offended, or be afraid of offending. I made my excuses and left, wondering whether I had over-reacted. I wasn't really offended that my children were considered to have been adopted. My annoyance lived on the surface, edged with frustration and my personal failing at still not having the right vocabulary for talking about my own children.

'I am their mother, just me. That is all that matters,' I repeated to myself for the hundredth time, as I had done over the last six months, to remind myself, to reassure myself, and to refresh my mothering instincts.

You are supposed to feel love with the surge of hormones, the chemical reaction that happens when you give birth. I knew that sensation of blood intermingling through the placenta, feeling life grow. It was magical. The process of carrying my first child in my belly for eight months had made me sure of my role as a mother, more than anything else I had ever felt confident about. She had come unexpectedly but I had fallen in love with her, again and again, ever more, every time she moved inside me, or I heard her heartbeat inside me on the scan, every time I felt sad or happy.

I had sung to her, and I had talked to her, shared my innermost thoughts with her. I knew her even before she was born. Her face was familiar to me, and I had forgotten myself in loving her. She has been the love of my life. As a single parent, I felt like we were a unit, one against the world. I knew how to be a mother.

This time I don't feel my children move inside me, or kick or grow, or feel my heart and my belly expand over weeks and months. I don't feel anticipation, dread, excitement. I don't have morning sickness, or swollen ankles. I have no agony and no joy. No, I feel none of that. I stand on the sidelines, waiting, watching.

I remember that I had this recurrent dream during these months. Waking, sleeping, walking. I had swallowed a seed. My mother used to say that if we ate the seeds from the fruit in the garden, a tree would grow inside our stomach. And I had believed her, terrified, as a child. The dreams returned in those long weeks and months. It was not the nightmare that I'd had as a child, and I remember waiting for the dream, eagerly and patiently every time. I will myself to dream again. I lie awake at night, stroking my empty stomach, imagining that life grew inside me, as they did inside another.

'If you were here, I would have sung to you, and would have talked to you, and told you stories. You would have known my voice. You would have loved me,' I recite in my dreams to my children, so far away from me. The constant drum of anxiety beats away.

'Will I even love you when I see you? Would you even know me now?'

I keep wandering round and round the narrow corridors of my unresolved questions, and there are so many. I live in dread and fear of coming to the end of that time when I will see them and hold them, waiting, watching, imagining and dreaming through these long weeks which should be the happiest months of our lives. I wake up sweating every night with the surge of panic attacks hitting me like a wave.

I try to dream up the faces of my future children, but they seem murky and dark. I try and reach out to a ghost-like figure in the dark but it is always just out of reach. I try to feel the love that I should have for them, but it doesn't feel real.

I keep wondering if I have made a mistake, if we have made a mistake. But I can't take it back. We chose a door and we have to follow through, always wondering what would have been through the other sliding doors of our lives. How does it feel to see your

261

child growing inside another woman? I hadn't even thought about it before I went down this road.

'It will all be okay,' is all P ever tells me whenever I feel brave enough to mention it to him.

Maybe I jumped into it, only trying to absolve myself of my guilt at not being able to give him (us) the child he so desires. And I resent him at times for making me make this decision, even though he never forced me to.

'It will all be okay,' is all he says to me. 'You worry too much,' he tells me.

'What if I can't love her as much as I should? As much as a mother should . . .' I want to say, but I don't.

The scans come with an email every month, just a dark picture and a tangled mess, inches gained every month. And there are two. We are having twins. I see the clump of cells grow without ever feeling them grow. They are my DNA, so why don't I feel the pull, the tug at my heartstrings, the lullaby in my heart when I look at these scans? I stare at them for ages, wondering if I will ever feel the same love for them.

M is a teenager by this point, exerting her independence at university, and she is pulling away. I text her and leave voicemail messages, and she replies, annoyed, at times, and not at all at others. Of course, I keep loving her the same, and often remind her that I carried her for eight months in my belly, and she laughs that wry smile, both of us reminded of the irrefutable bond that we share.

'I know, I know,' she always says, trying not to laugh, but is betrayed by the crinkle in her nose, just like mine, cords of genes wrapped around us like the mauli or the kalava, the crimson thread, a blessing from Trideva – Brahma, Vishnu, Mahesh and Tridevis –

Saraswathi, Lakshmi, Durga, protecting her forever from evil eyes and enemies.

And then immediately I wonder, every time, what I will tell the twins. What will I say when they scream at me in their sulky teenage phase? How will I feel if they ever tell me that I hadn't ever loved them, because isn't this what all children do at some point or the other, trying to cut the umbilical cord once and for all? But we didn't have one to start off with. What if they grow up, and tell me that I wasn't their mother? Because I surely don't feel like one right now as I look at these grainy scans. And what if I love my daughter less when the babies arrive? She has been my whole life for so long.

We don't tell many people that we are pregnant, and that soon we will be bringing two babies home. Not one, two more. Only a few very close family and friends know. I remember P and I standing away from a party that we were at to celebrate his PhD supervisor's knighthood in this very long, empty corridor and sharing the news with his best friend, T, who was the best man at our wedding. 'We have to tell T,' we had agreed, and as we whispered out the words to him about the twins, saying it out loud for the first time, I had felt my heart explode. He had hugged us, grinning ear to ear. And for a few minutes, happiness had shoved away the anxiety biting at my ankles at all times, day and night.

Isolated incidents like this aside, I feel like a failure, like I want to protect them and myself – I'm not sure from what. Maybe from the judgement. Like some sort of strange masochistic routine, I regularly pore over all news items that talk about wombs for hire, and I try to imagine what she must be feeling, that woman to whom I refuse to give a name, because I feel the guilt and shame, of being so bloody grateful to her, of being indebted to her with all my life, but resenting her the same. She has what I can't have. She is feeling the little lives grow inside her, while I walk around being a mother, but not feeling like one. Resentment comes in waves. Love and hate: friends, enemies, frenemies. I am as much a mother as she is, I tell myself. Just because I cannot carry my children doesn't mean that they aren't mine. All mine. I feel competitive. She has something that I can't have. But that doesn't make her the mother, I tell myself. And then I berate myself for my privilege and my selfishness all at once. I am not proud of it. I am confused. I am ashamed. I beg my husband not to tell anyone about this. I plead, I cry. He placates. 'Why all this secrecy?' he wonders. But how can he understand? It is not his failing, not his verdict, not his trial. What would people say? 'Who cares?' he says. I do, I do. For once in my life, I really do. My emotions are scrambled, untethered from rationality, top to bottom. 'Maybe it is your hormones that are playing tricks on you,' he suggests gently as I sit in the aftermath of the last cycle, the reverberations still being felt in every pore of my body. I don't believe him.

Every day I wake up and think about the woman 4,500 miles away, shaping our destinies, and I feel grateful. Is she happy about all this, I keep wondering every day, or is she just another statistic, a data point in the patriarchy, where women are not even a body that they own themselves? I don't get any answers to this. I still don't know if I am okay with this.

'Why wouldn't she be? She wants to do this,' our gynaecologist in Delhi reassures us, again and again. This will mean a house and school for her own children, and haven't we seen the contracts, those long documents that she signed herself? She wants to do this. She is creating a life for her children.

But what about our children, that life that she is creating too? Does she feel attached to them? Does she ever sing or talk to them at night? Does she feel any love towards them? What is she eating? Are the babies getting enough nutrition? Is she being kind, gentle, calm? Does she resent my children for making her feel sick, for the morning sickness, for the swollen ankles and belly?

Motherhood always seems like a minefield. I remember worrying if my unhappiness would filter through and embed sadness in my unborn child's veins, or if my love for pizza, pakoras, dosa and idli would somehow create a recipe for an eating disorder, alter her genes in some way, and if my most unpleasant traits would be picked up in the nine months of connecting so closely across the bodily fluids. This time around, I cannot even obsess over these details; I cannot watch what I eat, or what music I listen to, what books I read, and if I laugh, smile, cry.

After keeping a tight hold over my life for so long, and the strict routine of fertility cycles, mapping, managing down to the minute detail, for the first time I have no control. I feel lost and untethered from the notion of motherhood and from my life, this in-between state of flux, where you are neither one nor the other. Mother, or other, or both.

We haven't bought any new clothes for the babies, or even decorated the nursery.

'Let us see if everything works out,' P tells me, ever the pragmatic type. It is easy this way, easier to pretend that our lives aren't going to change. But we are going to bring two babies home, and the surrogate is going to go home without one. I cry to myself in the bath that day, as the reality hits me. Will she suffer, I wonder.

'No, she is prepared for this, and is happy for you both,' I am told in the emails that bounce back and forth across continents.

•

A ten-year longitudinal study by Vasanti Jadva and colleagues from Cambridge University has shown that in the long term surrogates do not experience psychological problems.[1] The initial study,[2] based on interviews and surveys conducted one year after birth with thirty-four surrogates, some gestational carriers while others undergoing genetic surrogacy, and then the follow-up study ten years later, showed that none had any signs of depression and all had normal or above-average self-esteem. Their marital lives were positive, and none of them expressed any regrets at undertaking this role. None of them reported feeling that the child was their own and a majority had no special feelings towards the child. Even though the sample size is relatively small, the researchers conclude that 'contrary to concerns about the potentially negative long-term effect of surrogacy, the findings suggest that surrogacy can be a positive experience for some women at least.' I cling on to such studies.

'You are going to be parents. Are you excited?'

'Yes, of course. Very. This is all that I ever wanted.'

But my heart is full of so much sadness. I will be a mother, I remind myself. I don't feel like one.

'How is the mother? Have you heard from her?' a close relative asks on the phone, and I slowly go into the bathroom and sob into the towel, rubbing the blunt razor back and forth on my finger. Seeing tiny spots of blood coming up for air numbs the pain. I throw up again on the bathroom floor.

•

We get a phone call.

'You have two daughters,' a voice tells us.

I remember P coming into the room and telling me as I was pottering about, oblivious that my life, our lives were about to shift so seismically in this way so suddenly. It jolted me and the physical sensation of sand shifting under my feet left me reeling. I had imagined this moment for some time and wondered what it would be like. We had always planned to be there at the hospital when the babies were born. It had been decided and we knew that we still had about eight or so weeks to go.

In between the kaleidoscope of emotions, I distinctly remember feeling shocked and angry. The surrogate had to be rushed to the hospital and they had no time to contact us, they tell us in the phone call. When the earth has stopped quivering, my husband and I hug each other slowly, holding each other close, knowing that we are transformed in some way already.

My anger grows as time goes on. Why weren't we there? Why weren't we contacted, informed as soon as they knew, and involved in this decision? How does one respond to the news of your own children being born 4,500 miles away? I had often wondered this, and had anticipated my reaction, imagining how I would feel and react. We never know how our emotions will play out, do we? Now I know that our two daughters are here, and I slowly roll this around on my tongue, then scream it out loud in the room to myself. The echoes of my own feelings reverberate inside my head and my heart, so much so that I can feel the phantom of a child in my arms, and on my breast. Then instantly the guilt arrives, that we have abandoned our children.

They were born in the NICU, premature by eight weeks, and they are there, citizens of nowhere, aliens in no-man's land, with no one to hold their tiny fingers and tell them that they are ours, that they are loved more than they will ever know. On the flight to India, I can't sleep. I watch so many films, knowing that this is an indulgence that we won't have the time or space for very soon. This feels like the last act of freedom, and so my husband orders champagne, as I sit through the long flight with the nerves and worries of a newly minted mother, one who cannot sleep but wants so desperately to. I keep returning to the memory of the tiny face of M and the tiny fingers wrapped around mine as our eyes had met for the first time eighteen years ago. It is not the same. I wish it were. Joy and sadness are so often allies, not complete without the other.

I see them for the first time, lying in the incubators wrapped up in wires, like little alien creatures who have seen things they shouldn't have, and who have entered a world that is not yet their own. Their eyes are barely open, and they seem fragile. The fragility of a newborn always takes one by surprise. These tiny bodies, so pure, unsullied, not yet crushed or moulded by our hopes, desires, dreams. Not yet put into boxes or labelled. Not expected to be anything else but themselves. So tiny, with pipes and tubes, their hearts thumping loudly on the monitors, and their little chests heaving with the effort of staying alive on their own. While I look at them, suddenly all my worries and concerns of the past few months have dissipated.

And suddenly I am a mother again. I hug the little bundles tighter and smell their heads, a bouquet of jasmine and monsoon, and the big brown eyes gaze back at me. It is like looking in a mirror. Their tiny heartbeats on the screen, the lungs struggling to take in enough oxygen, tubes and wires cutting across any doubt that I ever had of feeling a fierce protective motherly love towards them. I am familiar with this feeling of intense protectiveness that surges through you on seeing your newborn, tiniest fingers and toes, with nails as tiny and pink as rose petals that can be squashed so easily.

Yet this is different. I try to make sense of how I feel, all sorts of emotions tumbling inside me. I don't look pregnant, my breasts aren't swollen, I don't feel the pangs and pains, or the surge of natural hormones to ride me through this new motherhood. They have half of my genes, my skin colour mixed with his, my dark hair, my brown eyes, his long limbs and nose, but is this enough for me to be a mother, I wonder.

There are two more babies in incubators in the neo-natal unit, even tinier than ours, little humans struggling to make sense of this world around them. Their eyes are still closed, and their tiny fists clenched tight. It is impossible not to have the primal urge that surges from deep within, an evolutionary response to these helpless beings. Perhaps my mothering instinct was just an evolutionary response. I stop to check, and to remind myself. I should be in love.

We are allowed into the NICU for an hour or so twice a day. We are staying in a small hotel just twenty minutes' rickshaw ride away, in a tiny room, and we huddle close, sharing our solitary moments together for the last time. It becomes a daily routine, walking the dusty path under the scorching sun along that straight road between our hotel and the hospital. The days are marked by the two hours when we can hold them. As we are handed the blue gowns and hospital masks, washing our hands many times to make sure we leave the remnants of our lives outside, I dredge away any doubts and fears, and it feels like stepping into parenthood. The nurses are keen for us to bond, their fears compounded by stories of surrogate babies who were abandoned by the intended parents. I do not know of any such stories personally, but often these circulate around like urban myths.

For the time being, relief overrules anything else, counting days until they are ready to step outside of their incubators, making sure they are growing, counting their growth in numbers and charts. Every ounce gained is cause for euphoria, every ounce of milk drunk successfully is a triumph. I will have to remember this, I think, these tiniest moments of joy and delight, celebrations over these accomplishments that come naturally to many other babies, and just pass other parents by. I will have to remember these for when they are older, and we let their minor victories go unnoticed, always pushing them to achieve more and more. I will have to remember this to remind myself to notice the little things around me that work, the signs that we are alive despite all the struggles and skirmishes.

We lose sight of these tiny joys, don't we? I know I do, and I have done. Seeing these little bodies heaving and pushing, struggling for every breath, their tiny lungs working so hard to take these big gulps of air, somehow bigger than their tiny bodies, is a sight of awe and wonder. The human spirit is so resilient. We work so hard to stay alive as little babies, and I find it miraculous that I have managed to bring up a child who is almost an adult. How did that happen with all the pitfalls and dangers around us? It gives me hope and it makes me feel so determined. It is so easy for us to give up as we grow older, ready to give up this life that we fought so hard for. I know I have come close in the past. But I can't think of those dark times right now. I can't think of anything else besides keeping these two alive. I am a mother again, I say silently, trying to remind myself, because when I step away from the hospital, in that hotel room with my husband it could just be us. It is easy to forget that we have changed, miraculously shape-shifted into parents somehow.

I take many photographs and I look at them closely for signs that I might have missed in the whirlwind of the hospital visit. I have since looked at these videos and photos millions of times, hearing their tiny hearts beeping on the machines, and their little chests going up and down with the strain of breathing unaided. My little warriors. It is surprising how much we miss in the throes of new motherhood even though when we are in the midst of it, everything stands out in neon colours, brighter than ever, sparkling and shimmering with vivacity. One would think that we would remember every single moment, every colour, every detail. But now as I look at these videos and pictures I notice that I don't really remember it all. We walk in a haze as a new mother, focused so intensely on keeping our babies alive, exhausted, sleepless, crazy with love and mayhem.

After the birth of M, when I came back from the dead, I had a grey fog for many months that didn't seem to lift. Those timeless sluggish days reminded me of childhood coming full circle. For days, months, years, I felt disconnected from my own body, as if with her, something that bound me together had also left. I felt possessive, protective, proprietorial of the tiny being with whom I was connected through blood and skin, through the days and nights spent feeling her every breath, and heartbeat. But the world seemed washed out, and the danger of things festering unknown under the layer of social niceties seemed imminent. I felt like I was constantly watching over my shoulder for an attack, but by whom I could never tell. There is research in psychology to show that a traumatic experience, such as in childbirth, can lead to anxiety and fear being lodged in our brains.

This time around, I hadn't birthed, but I was mothering, nevertheless. I still felt like an imposter as I did not deserve these unearned emotions. They belonged to someone else.

We rent an apartment in central Delhi not far from the shops and cafes and we bring the twins 'home' when they have been out in the world for almost three weeks. There is a temple just opposite.

The apartment is just one big room, really, divided into sleeping spaces and a small kitchen and bathroom next to it. I am used to being in Delhi but I have been away for too long to be familiar with its ways any more. I also have a white husband and two tiny fragile premature babies who need more comforts than I was ever used to or grew up with. It is expensive, even as we convert rupees into pounds. My husband's whiteness and apparent foreignness immediately makes the price go up.

We are supposed to be having the best time of our lives, grateful for these two children who we have been 'blessed' with after so many struggles. But it didn't always feel like this. I remember sitting on the floor of our tiny apartment, everything strange, desperately unhappy and sobbing uncontrollably. I was miserable, living out of a suitcase, without my home, without everything that I thought made me whole, without a place that I felt I truly belonged in, and I was trying to bring up these vulnerable babies in my half-human, othered state. They were stateless, and I felt so, too, completely and utterly.

Fear, loneliness, helplessness, anxiety had all surfaced again with a force that I had not anticipated. While I marvel at their tiny dainty fingers, and stroke the soft cheeks, I cannot escape the panic and anxiety I feel at the thought of yet another sleepless night spent walking around the tiny apartment, trying a rocking motion to soothe them that never seems to work except to agitate them even further, counting steps and watching the clock go forward for another twelve hours, the anguished screams growing stronger. Guilt, helplessness, fear all jumbled up together in a furious indiscernible mass. Feeling that my head would explode too if I didn't scream, but holding it in forever because that is what a mother should do.

Unlike single births to two parents, with twin or multiple births, there is no opportunity to take turns because there are at least two of them. Even as we try to follow all the advice for synching their clocks, it seems that they refuse any sort of conformity. They stand as individuals the moment they step out in this world, with their own rhythms and cadence. I understand this, and I love them more for it. They have something of me already, I remember thinking proudly just a few weeks after they had come to us.

•

New motherhood does strange things to a mother's brain. We become fearful of what can happen, imagining the worst scenarios, anticipating disasters before they occur.

I have this recurrent dream that I am driving with them in the back seat, and I crash headlong into an oncoming truck. On other nights, I see myself throwing them off a bridge into the dark cold water, as if they have just been propelled from my arms with some external mysterious force. I wake up not screaming, but paralysed with fear. I lie there with eyes wide open, my arms by my sides, frozen, entombed with my thoughts. Much like a mummy, I think, then start laughing wildly to myself, as I realise that that is exactly what I am.

I buy a picture to celebrate their birth by an artist that I have followed for a while over social media. 'It is for their nursery that they will have one day when they are back home,' I tell the artist. It is a multimedia illustration from *The Velveteen Rabbit*, which used to be one of my favourite books to read to M, a story of becoming whole with love again. It is a story of finding that one pure unadulterated love that all of us crave and look for. And no matter how broken we might be, we can always find it one day.

You become. It takes a long time. That's why it doesn't happen often to people who break easily, or have sharp edges, or who have to be carefully kept. Generally, by the time you are Real, most of your hair has been loved off, and your eyes drop out and you get loose in the joints and very shabby. But these things don't matter at all, because once you are Real you can't be ugly, except to people who don't understand.[3]

When the real seems unreal, and the fear of being seen as broken does not matter any more, then we need those people around us, close to us, who will see beyond our sharp, jagged edges.

I've always had these sharp, hard edges and often I felt that I did not do a good job of hiding them, putting them away discreetly as I had done while I mothered the first time around. I want to become a mother again. Maybe this time, these hard edges will not matter as much. I find a copy of *The Velveteen Rabbit* in a lovely basement bookshop in New Delhi and read it to the twins again and again, often whispering it silently so as to not interrupt those few precious moments of quiet lull. It fills up the space between one sleep to the next.

•

I don't deal very well with change, even though I am restless and crave it, and unchanged movements make me bored and fidgety. I feel unmoored and untethered from the flow of time, measured in hours since the last feed, minutes spent pacing the short width of the apartment burping them, keeping them upright, one after the other, back and forth, and then again; days spent since the last time we ever slept; weeks spent being homesick, months spent being away from home. These days seem hazy, languorous, anything but still, but it seems like I have come full circle. These listless animated days of new motherhood, time paradoxically standing still yet breathlessly moving fast forward at a breakneck speed, rolling rapidly with no sense of seconds, minutes, hours.

'Where is it, this present?' the American philosopher and psychologist William James wondered as he devised a 'specious present',* something that 'has melted in our grasp, fled ere we could touch it, gone in the instant of becoming.'[4]

We don't touch, hear, feel time, but we all can sense it acutely as it ebbs and flows, watching clocks, suspended, frozen, lost in time. The present that can become the past before it has even passed. The dread of losing time before we've had the chance to live it fully too. The joy of gaining time that we thought that we had lost. Even as we think of time as infinite successions of past, present, future, it shimmers with its elusive, ephemeral, chimeric quality, not so easy to grasp or hold on to, even as we get caught up in the whirlpool of time and try and find stable ground. Kierkegaard questions our temporal ordering of past, present, future, time as an 'infinite succession' where the present is infinitely contentless, and we cannot remember the future. Time constantly intersects eternity and eternity constantly pervades time. We can live an eternity in a moment, any moment of sheer intense joy or sadness.

As new mothers, we rely so much on our hormonal shifts, the release of oxytocin or the 'hormone of love' that prepares a body for nurturing and creation of familial bonds. Larry Young, a behavioural neuroscientist at Emory University in Atlanta, Georgia, has said that

* The term 'specious present' was first introduced by the psychologist E.R. Clay, but the best-known characterisation of it was due to William James, widely regarded as one of the founders of modern psychology.

'oxytocin released during pregnancy does seem to have a role in motivation and feelings of connectedness to a baby'.[5] A study by psychologist Ruth Feldman and colleagues at Bar-Ilan University in Israel, published in the journal *Psychological Science*, looked at oxytocin levels in sixty-two pregnant women during the first trimester, third trimester and first month after delivery.[6] Then they observed the mother and infant interact to measure levels of attachment. The study found that mothers with a high level of the hormone in the first trimester engaged in more of the bonding behaviours after birth, and mothers with lots of the hormone during the entire pregnancy and in the first postpartum month showed more concern and worry for the newborn, and attempted to bond with them through songs. This sample size is not big enough to make many broader generalised assumptions about how exactly bonding suffers with lack of oxytocin, but this kind of research creates a general view that a mother can only really bond properly with a child if they have given birth to them.

If maternal bonding is really hardwired, then where does that leave me? Where does that leave all the mothers who have not birthed but are mothering?

Bonding isn't attachment, and attachment – which isn't a myth – is a process and a complicated dance of maternal–infant interaction on physical, psychological and neurological levels. It's not always successful. Nor does it take place in a moment. The popular idea of bonding focuses on the mother, but attachment is a thoroughly dyadic process which requires the mother to be responsive and attuned to her infant's cues which, when successful, creates a specific kind of synchronicity. Science has shown again and again that how an infant is attached – whether securely or insecurely – is highly predictive of the emotional and relational trajectory of that individual's life.

So many of these studies are really trying to find an answer to the question: what makes a mother?

In the UK, the common law definition of mother remains attached to the notion of 'giving birth' and of conception: 'motherhood, although a legal relationship, is based on a fact, being proved demonstrably by parturition.' Mr Justice Scott Baker, hearing one of the first surrogacy cases, observed in 1991: 'Until recently, when the advance of medical science created the possibility of in-vitro fertilisation, it was not envisaged that the genetic mother and the carrying mother could be other than one and the same person. The advent of IVF presented the law with a dilemma: whom should the law regard as the mother?'[7]

This has made me think of those who are mothers but on the fringes of society, and those who give birth but are not a mother, because of their identity as a trans person, legally identifying as a man. The experience of transmasculine and non-binary people is relatively understudied and researched. Because of societal stigma and prejudice, many are reluctant to come forward and so they remain discreet. In one of the very few studies carried out with transmasculine people, in Canada, researchers interviewed twenty-two transmasculine individuals to understand their experience of pregnancy, childbirth and feeding their infant.[†8] The words and language used around them matter, as people are often misidentified, nominated as the wrong gender, and called 'mum' and 'mother', which heightens their gender dysphoria. One of the non-binary

† The study defines transmasculine individuals as 'people who were assigned as female at birth, but identify on the male side of the gender spectrum. Their anatomical birth sex does not match their inner sense of gender identity. This incongruity may be a source of gender dysphoria, the experience of distress or anxiety regarding one's gender and body.'

academics I spoke with, who chose to remain anonymous, reiterated this. They had not revealed their nonbinary identity to the health practitioners to avoid discomfort and awkwardness around any such conversation, fearful as they were of any subsequent prejudice.

This issue remains of course in the words and language we use, of how acutely mother and father are inherently gendered terms as defined by our society. Women are seen as 'mothers' merely because they have a uterus and have given birth. In countries such as Sweden and Canada, it is possible to be registered as 'father' or even a 'parent'. Surprisingly there is no clear distinction between sex and gender in UK law. When a person who identifies as a man as per the Gender Recognition Act, and in every other legal situation, is then labelled as a mother on the child's birth certificate, this creates an incongruity, an absurd misalliance between the mental constructs, the outside and inside worldviews, of how a person perceives themselves and how society views them. For a man to have to declare himself as 'mother' can be a deeply distressing, and subjectively traumatic requirement. And it once again questions and casts a patriarchal view on the inherent notion of what and who a mother is, and who has a right to be one.

In September 2019, the UK's High Court ruled that Freddy McConnell, a transgender man who gave birth to his child, does not have the right to be registered as a 'father' on his child's birth certificate. The court also ruled out the possibility of registering him simply as the 'parent'. McConnell is legally a man, with his passport and NHS documents confirming so. The law will continue to require that people who give birth to a child in the UK are always registered as the 'mother' – even if they are legally men. This ruling by Sir Andrew McFarlane, while stating that 'mother' isn't a gendered term, and does not equate to someone who identifies as a woman, raised a huge number of concerns around the notion of what a parent is, and how motherhood is defined and understood. As per this judgement, the question raised is whether being 'female' is the essential or determining attribute of motherhood even as it is undoubtedly the case that throughout history the role of being a gestational mother has been undertaken by females.

> There is a strong case to be made for the role of 'mother' being ascribed to the person, irrespective of gender, who undertakes the carrying of a pregnancy and who gives birth to a child. In that regard, being a 'mother' is to describe a person's role in the biological process of conception, pregnancy and birth; no matter what else a mother may do, this role is surely at the essence of what a 'mother' undertakes with respect to a child to whom they give birth. It is a matter of the role taken in the biological process, rather the person's particular sex or gender.[9]

In saying this, the judgement immediately dismisses the motherhood of all those who have not given birth or carried a pregnancy. While seemingly trying to break out of gendered norms, at the same time, it traps women, mothers, transgender men back in the roles and boxes that they are so desperate to break out of, reaffirming the same gendered notions of what motherhood is, and that it is determined by biology alone. It alienates those who seek validation as a mother when the law doesn't see them as such, as well as those who are labelled as a mother because of having carried a child even as it casts reservations on their own gender identity. Registering as 'mother' means that a trans man's transition is no longer confidential, and although the chance of unwanted disclosure is not huge, it is possible, which will inevitably be a deterrent to anyone considering starting a family after transition. This was not the first case of its kind although it received unprecedented media attention. According to the Trans Pregnancy project at the University of Leeds, more than 4,500 people worldwide are members of a private, secret social media group for trans people who give birth. In Australia, which at the time of writing was the only country known to collect statistics on male birth parents, 205 men are recorded as having given birth between 2013 and 2018. What Freddy's case and the documentary *Seahorse* he made about his experience also sensitively showed was that while motherhood is almost always accompanied by a complete loss of a sense of self, it can become even more acute when it conflicts with the gender identity of a person, with their morphing body not seeming like their own any more.

A case was reported in *The New England Journal of Medicine* in May 2019, where a thirty-two-year-old man was brought to the emergency room with severe abdominal pain. Despite a positive home pregnancy test that morning, with high blood pressure and discomfort, and with the knowledge that he was a transgender man, the nurse triaged him to non-urgent assessment, concluding that his condition was stable. His condition deteriorated rapidly and with an emergency caesarean section, a stillborn baby was delivered. Despite acute dysphoria, the man discontinued testosterone treatments to ensure that he continued with menstruation and avoided any similar future medical crisis.[10] In this case, the nurse, with all their honourable intentions, failed to recognise that the patient fell outside the binary mutually exclusive male and female categories. The nurse deployed implicit assumptions about who can be pregnant, attributed his high blood pressure to untreated chronic hypertension, and classified his case as non-urgent. These classifications can assist medical professionals in making diagnoses and prescribing treatment. But these rigid classifications, and assignations of who and what a woman is, based on appearances, and who can give birth, who should be called a mother, are all traps that do not consider multiple experiences, especially of those who are on the fringes.

Is there a colour of motherhood?

Is it all pink and blue? Or is there room for grey?

Is there a colour of womanhood?

Is it all red, ripe, or green, so fertile? Or shades of pink and grey around the edges, and brown?

Is there a colour of home, of belonging?

Is it all a shifting purkinje, dark when it should be light?

I see in colours, in hues, in shades.

But sometimes there just aren't enough colours, enough names, enough words.

Have we been looking at the black and white for too long?

•

In a 2010 study, researchers looked at brain-scan images of nineteen women before and after they gave birth and found that the size of mothers' brains increased shortly after childbirth.[11] The study co-author Pilyoung Kim, a developmental psychologist at Yale University, found small but significant increases in the volume of grey matter in the brain after childbirth. What this study also shows is that the act of childbirth prepares a woman for mothering, by increasing brain matter in areas associated with emotion, sensitivity and reward and motivation. If a woman's emotions are so strongly linked with her hormones, and the miniscule shifts in these, then for those women who become a mother without giving birth, would there always be doubt of their ability to form those crucial bonds with their children, the surge of emotion and love, the desire to protect them at any cost?

Is motherhood only shaped by our hormones and our biology or is it shaped by love? I keep coming back to this question several times in the next few days and months, as hours tick by when they don't sleep, when my eyelids go heavy sagging with the weight of their illnesses and screams, and my love for myself and for this world crumbles. I hold on steadfastly to my utter and absolute belief in the power of love, love that does not rely on the initial surge of the cuddling hormone, that does not need these shifts in our biology and our brains.

Matrescence is the word which describes a transition into motherhood, the deliberate resonance with adolescence to signify the transitions that happen in a body: emotional, physical and mental. The term was coined by anthropologist Dana Raphael in the mid-1970s and brought into common use in psychology by clinical psychologist Aurelie Athan, head of the maternal psychology lab at Columbia University. It is the slow unravelling of the consciousness to acknowledge the journey that lies ahead, not an 'aha' moment, or the hormonal shift, but a series of moments that slowly shifts the person towards acceptance of their own motherhood.[12] Often motherly love is talked about in terms of a hormone-fuelled, pumped-up love, the sense of overwhelming emotions that accompany a birth of a child. Love at first sight. But with matrescence, we can begin to acknowledge the slow metamorphosis, the steady, measured, gradual process of getting to know each other, the comfort and discomfort experienced together, and through this process, becoming sublimated and individuated as a mother and child at the same time.

I take on the role of a mother suddenly, without the transitional space between not being a mother and being one, those seven or eight months, that time to step inside the role, to expand my own expectations of myself, and limit that of others. There is no alchemic love flowing through my veins, because my uterus has not expanded and contracted, my body is still the same, no stretch marks, no swollen breasts this time around.

Brenda Shaughnessy writes in her poem 'Liquid Flesh':

> I know I am his mother, but I can't
> quite click on the word's essential aspects,
> can't denude the flora
>
> or disrobe the kind of housecoat
> 'mother' always is.[13]

Here is a mother, much like other mothers, who has to nurture despite the pain, loneliness, exhaustion. I have to do the same. No kinks in my armour are allowed as I take on this role. It feels like a role at first, a thespian on a vast stage, a gladiator striding into a huge arena. 'You have done it before for so long,' you hear the imaginary flashbulbs call out, 'surely you are a natural at doing this.' But imposter syndrome kicks in. What if I am not as good as they think I am? What if I completely mess this up, in my eagerness to be a mother, what if I smother them with my love, what if I can't love them enough, what if I don't want to play this role any more? I am living in what ifs.

As someone who did not ever want to be a mother, my preoccupation with mothering and motherhood seems paradoxical and allochronic. Asynchronous layers shifting and sliding over time, not sitting comfortably, all part of me but not quite so, oddly comforting and bewildering.

•

It is around forty degrees outside, everything seems strange, discomfort clinging closely to my clammy skin, even though I can speak the language, and I have the same skin colour as everyone else.

It is strange how language shapes our identity. Am I a different person when I speak in different languages, and are my thoughts mapped by the language that I use to think and to speak in? M has often told me that I resort to Hindi when I am angry. Even though I switch between Hindi and English fluidly without a flicker of a thought or hesitation, no doubt there are things I cannot think or feel in either. Do I take on a different persona, another shift of identity as English becomes my way of communicating in writing and in speech? And in dreams, which are never in Hindi any more? The rhythm of each language works on different meters, and I slow down when I speak Hindi. There isn't that rush to get the words out before I forget, the precariousness exacerbated by the ever-present awareness that my accent will always belie my notion of being at home in this English language. But does the core of my self change with these shifts too? Do I become less funny, more opinionated, more at ease in one than the other?

I went to a school run by Irish Catholic nuns, all through my primary and secondary education, where we were penalised for speaking in Hindi, the deeply ingrained colonial hangover persisting, where we were better if we spoke in a language that wasn't our own, that marked the gentile from the ordinary. English was the only language that could help us make our way in a world where we were never the desirables. I realise the irony of this as I write now in English. My parents wanted me to be good at English because that was how I would make a place for myself in this world. My mother wanted me to be good at English because she didn't think she was, and she wanted me to spread my wings in a world that wasn't designed for women. My father would take me to the only bookshop in the town, where they had a tiny selection of books in English: some Enid Blytons, and Stephen Kings, occasionally classics such as *Gone with the Wind*. It was our ritual every month. I wanted to be good at English so that I could read all the books that showed me a world far beyond my own, those books with green pastures and *Little Women* who were fierce, independent and strong-willed, the female protagonists of their own life. I wanted to drink elder-flower juice and have afternoon tea, not knowing what it tasted like. I loved this window into a new world even as I felt my face flush with embarrassment when my father would proclaim with fatherly pride that 'she only reads English books'. This felt like betrayal at times as I read about the imperial rule, the Jallianwala Bagh massacre and the centuries of British oppression in India. The marks left by colonial rule and partition had seared into our consciousness and there was no escaping it.

This push and pull persisted as this language of our oppressors slowly became my home, even as Hindi was still the language that bridged the gap between my parents and me.

I still find it fascinating that we studied Hindi as a second language, even though it was our first: it was the language of the first word that I heard, the language of my ancestors, the one that our stories were written in. I keep wondering what the world would have looked like if it hadn't been like this, if we did not grow up with this shame. And I wonder when I started dreaming and thinking in shapes and patterns that were alien and uncomfortable to my own mother.

My ma felt ashamed all her life that her spoken English wasn't that good, an inferiority that she carried because my father could speak better English than she could. I have never thought about this deeply: how this shame marred her view of herself, and her own place in society; of those times that she would stay quiet, only smiling shyly when she thought that she didn't know how to talk in public, or anxious that she would say the wrong thing, come across as ignorant and uncouth. So much of that anxiety shaped her mothering, her lack of recognition of her talents that she just took for granted. And perhaps that is why it took me so long to acknowledge all that is so luminous about her, as she hid her resplendence from everyone including herself.

Choosing the language we speak is also linked to our autonomy, our view of our body is shaped by the words we speak, and thoughts we think, the space we occupy, and the way our mind inhabits our body.

Growing up with this discomfort around a language that is your own mother's tongue, hiding it as a dirty secret at home, while only speaking in English at school, creates a split personality, where one has to keep shifting between two worlds of thoughts, words and dreams, at home in one, in both, and sometimes in neither. Most people I know speak in Hinglish, an amalgamation of both, stepping inside both worlds at the same time, equally comfortable with Premchand and Amrita Kaur as with Hilary Mantel or Margaret Atwood. But people carry this unconscious bias that those who can write or speak better English are better, just better people, this halo spilling over their other attributes, giving them opportunity and privilege, while making others tongue-tied and even more inhibited in their thoughts.

Would our stories be different if this comfort around our own language had not been seeded and planted from a young age, and would the stories we write and tell our children be any different too? These switches have become part of my identity, and it is how I belong in both worlds, but sometimes I can feel like an alien in both, with my accented English, never escaping the roots that I come from, and becoming stronger when I have been immersed in that world for a while, and the tinges of my nondescript British accent speckled around the spectrum of my spoken Hindi.

I remember when M came back irate from school one day saying that she had pronounced geography incorrectly because that is how she had always heard me say it: 'jaw-gruphy'. I had laughed but she hadn't found it amusing at all, though now she has outgrown that adolescent shame of a mother who has accented English, compounded by her classmates giggling at her quirky pronunciation of words that she had grown up with. I still catch myself worrying about how to pronounce words, and whether the way I speak marks me out as other, often searching for the right expression to say what I feel. It takes a while to shift this persona when I am in India, a few days to overthrow this worry about speaking the wrong word or the wrong accent. Instead, I find myself searching for the right word in Hindi, which has been buried deep inside the mists of my time away from this place. I find myself stuttering over expressions, feverishly searching quickly for the word that would stop me from being marked as a 'foreigner', and slowly it all comes back. I worry less about switching between languages, and it becomes second nature once again, jolting me into a recognition of myself that I keep abandoning as soon as I leave India and fly back to the UK, reminding me how much I miss these words, this language, the poetic sensibilities of expressions that say so much.

How do we give words to our children when we ourselves feel wobbly around the edges of our languages?

As well as the removal from my mother tongue, I had also removed myself from this city, from a life that I no longer wanted to inhabit, a place that I didn't feel I belonged in; a life that was a lie that I didn't want for my daughter. And yet I had chosen to return here to be a mother once again. Life comes full circle, although this didn't seem like that: it felt like I had stopped running from a life that was never mine, and like I was running back towards the past.

Painful memories of a life once lived come rushing back as I go past the streets, shops, signs, smells and sounds that I had inhabited. I had also been happy here. I had also been in love. I had also become a mother here once. There was so much that was still the same. Our memories are so intrinsically tied with places, and the shock of remembering too much jarred with my desire to just focus on the now, on my two newborn babies, my wish to nurture and bond. The oxytocin that I so needed for forging that maternal bond was already in short supply as I felt uprooted from my home.

Many days and nights have become one. There is no escape from this tiny third-floor apartment in a six-storey building in the centre of Delhi. The sweltering heat of the Indian summer rising through the walls slowly takes up room in every pore of my body. Claustrophobia swamps my mind, the sense of entrapment engulfing, consuming, noisily overwhelming me. The heat and humidity outside is comforting to my dark skin, but the intense blaze of the sun is making me feel nostalgic for the cool, misty days in the north-west of England, the rain that I complained about so habitually. The cannibalistic cacophony of the grey concrete wilderness with its harsh urban sweep has swallowed up most of the trees and green spaces. I miss the greenery. I miss my things around me, my clothes, my bed with the messy bedspread and the fragrance of our everyday lives, the chair in the corner of our bedroom with my clothes peppered around it, the large window through which I could see the seasons changing, the sunlight and the rain pattering against it, beating to match with the rhythm of my life. I miss myself, who I was when I was at home, along with all my cookbooks, my studio, my desk, and the ease of knowing where everything was, even in the disordered chaos that I was so used to. I could make sense of it all so easily and effortlessly.

Here I am trying to make a home, build a nest in this sparse apartment, the minimalism providing very little comfort. An alien in a sea of faces that look like me, reminding me of the unfamiliar comforts of home where for a long time I had felt like an outsider, regarded as an outsider, and a perpetual foreigner. Here I was one of them, but still not, with a white husband, and my accented Hindi.

The babies cry. I sit and weep; I bang my head against the wall. I wail. And I scream, silently.

I sometimes curl up in a corner and weep inconsolably, exhausted and deprived of sleep for more than forty-eight hours.

'What did I do? I did not want this,' I whisper to myself silently, screams resonating like echoes inside my head. My head is filled only with the anguished screams of the babies, taking turns, one after the other in an asynchronous relay race. I am swimming against it all, wanting to be the best mother I can be, noting down their feeding times diligently in a notepad, my life, my day, my nights only marked by their sleep and the ritual of feeding, walking, rocking them.

Sylvia Plath's words from her poem 'Morning Song' echo in my head:

> One cry, and I stumble from bed, cow-heavy and floral
> In my Victorian nightgown.
> Your mouth opens clean as a cat's. The window square

Whitens and swallows its dull stars. And now you try
Your handful of notes;
The clear vowels rise like balloons.[14]

'Morning Song' was composed when Frieda Hughes, Plath's first child, was eight months old, and records the intimate moments between mother and daughter as the child wakes in the middle of the night. Most analyses of the poem consider this a testimony to the love and awe in the presence of her child, but I have always seen it as an ode to her motherhood anxiety, both fascinating and frightening, joyous and anxious, as she confronts the assimilation and diminishing of her own voice as the child's voice becomes stronger and louder, and finally she loses autonomy in favour of the child's demand.

I feel restless, craving motion even as most of my nights, and days, are spent rocking the babies back and forth, their anguished cries borne out of severe colic, the silent reflux revealed in screams so raucous that my head reverberates with noise even when they are quiet. The stillness of these days, hours, minutes, seconds – in and out – the monotony of repetition would usually give me comfort but not now. Days blur. Time melts. It cannot calm my twitchy nerves as the old familiarity of the places around me feel cloying and claustrophobic. Even as I sing lullabies to soothe the newborns, yearning, praying, imploring for them to sleep, stillness evades me. And the memories pull me away, taking me to dark places that I had put in the deepest corners of my heart, shutting the door tightly behind me.

As we grow older, we tend to be at peace with who we have become, more at ease in our skin, less anxious and less self-conscious of our eccentricities and quirks. Now, I am here, back here not just as a tourist passing through for a few hours, but being back here, living here, putting down roots, being a mother. Waking through sleepless nights, speaking in the language that I had grown up with, feeling the sun that I had so craved and missed, getting takeaways of all the food and flavours that I could never get back in the UK, means also shedding parts of me that had grown accustomed to my life back there.

There is the food, the tastes and flavours that I have missed so much. 'We are living like locals,' P says. 'I am a local,' I want to remind him and then stop. *Am I any more?*

Dosas, biryanis, kulfi, the flavours tantalising on my tongue, growing accustomed to my mother tongue again. It is mango season, and fruit stalls are overflowing with the bright yellow Dasheri and Langra aam, blinding with their yellow skins. I can't leave the apartment much because of the heat and dust and the twins, but we have a young man who does all the shopping for us, and as soon as he returns with a bag full of mangoes every day, I stand at the kitchen sink and suck the flesh straight out of the skin hungrily and greedily, my eyes closed, remembering the days when we used to sit around the table at noon, eating mangoes until our sides hurt, our faces and hands sticky and our hearts so content.

Mango season in India is a ritual amongst families, no fruit so versatile and loved by all. Little things, seemingly unimportant things can bind us together, our oversights dismissed, our slip-ups forgiven. In my family, time was often marked by the season of mangoes. 'Remember that summer when I made the mango pickle that we are still eating?' my mum would say.

Milestones are marked by that summer when the Dasheras were particularly delicious (it had been a very hot summer), or when we had a lot of green aams to make panna every day, the sweet and sour drink with jeera in it, or that summer when the mangoes had been disappointing because of the rains, and the news had come that my grandfather was dead. How will we remember this summer, the summer of being home, and being away from home? Nostalgia, homesickness, melancholy. Love, joy, contentment. Uprooted, and rooted again after so long. Maybe I will bring back the twins one day to taste these mangoes, and then suddenly love, joy, hope bubbles up and packs my heart up to my sleepless eyes. Days stay sweet and sour, tenderness mixed with stringy streaks. Tired state, tired metaphors.

I don't go out often, punishing myself for even regretting the twins for a mere one second of weakness, my mental space shattered into shards that obtrude into my psyche from all sides. But whenever I do go out, whenever P can convince me to have a shower, get dressed, to trust him to be able to look after the twins on his own, not to feel guilty for abandoning them, I step outside hesitantly and tentatively into spaces that immediately feel my own. When I do leave the apartment, I relish the opportunity of haggling in the market. P is often embarrassed but now understands that it is a dance we are supposed to play, this to-and-fro a ritual, showing more than ever that I belong here, that I understand what it means to be home back in India. At ease with haggling, speaking the language that I grew up with, reminding myself of words and expressions that can say so much in so few words, animated nostalgia and languid elation bubbling up from every part of my fractured being, the seams closing up very slowly.

It also means reminding myself who I once was, and how I was here in a life in India, a life that I had run away from. This was an alienation of my current self, while I had lived so much of my life for the last decade alienating that past self. I had to now confront this alien self. We move through life, reconciling, rejecting and accepting different versions of ourselves, in the hope that these different selves will all come together one day to be our most authentic selves, the one that we truly are, the crux of our being.

We dream of a world where internal and external conflicts do not exist, one where peace outside and inside flows like a seamless thread, a river taking away all worries and anxieties, and where we feel completely at home. But does such a utopia ever exist? Thomas More in 1516 coined the word 'utopia' from the Greek 'ou-topos'. This means 'no place' or 'nowhere'. How can a place we most search for be no place, or nowhere? There seems to be a paradox inherent in the idea of an idealised notion of a place that we are constantly looking for. But the almost identical Greek word 'eu-topos' means a good place. The pull and push between a place that is perfect in every way, and the vital question of whether such a place ever exists lies at the heart of my constant search for home, the never shifting battle for rootedness, as if lying inside a dark cave looking at shadows of life playing out on its walls. As Plato says in his treatise *Republic*:

> Behold! Human beings living in an underground den, which has a mouth open towards the light and reaching all along the den; here they have been from their childhood, and have their legs and necks chained so that they cannot move, and can only see before them, being prevented by the chains from turning round their heads. Above and behind them a fire is blazing at a distance, and between the fire and the prisoners there is a raised way; and you will see, if you look, a low wall built along the way, like the screen which marionette players have in front of them, over which they show the puppets.[15]

In these days and nights of dissolving boundaries, punctuated by screams, sleep assembling behind crusted eyelids, and the senseless sense of time, my grasp on the world is becoming looser and I find myself drifting in and out of myself. The universe is losing its meaning, and therefore the possibility of true joy, peace, happiness seems elusive. Not that I have the time or might to gather memories or to run and chase slippery feelings.

Sometimes the heart craves an intangible feeling, a melancholic longing for something that we might have never had before, but it just seems within reach, its ephemeral shapes flowing continually in and out of focus. The Portuguese word *Saudade*, with no direct translation in English, is the deep emotional longing for the past, an indescribable yearning. While also looking towards the future with hope and optimism, it is a repressed desire for something that brings back joy but sadness, something we know would never be the same ever again. The Portuguese call this a way of life, a constant feeling of absence but an ever-present simultaneous desire for presence. A.F.G. Bell's *In Portugal* describes it as 'an active discontent or poignant sadness but an indolent dreaming wistfulness'.[16] Portuguese writer Manuel de Melo calls it 'a pleasure you suffer, an ailment you enjoy'.[17]

Being in Delhi, in India, epitomises this for me, a plaintive dreamy longing for what had once been, a forlorn desire to be what I once was, a deep ache within my whole self for what had been lost. The overpowering senseless, disconsolate homesickness while I am in my homeland, so close to everything that I had always longed for while back in the UK. I must like these indeterminate longings, the *Sehnsucht*: an unsatisfied desire which becomes embedded into our code itself, one that is itself more desirable than any satisfaction.

Saudades

Serei eu alguma hora tão ditoso,
Que os cabelos, que amor laços fazia,
Por prémio de o esperar, veja algum dia
Soltos ao brando vento buliçoso?
Verei os olhos, donde o sol formoso
As portas da manhã mais cedo abria,
Mas, em chegando a vê-los, se partia
Ou cego, ou lisonjeiro, ou temeroso?
Verei a limpa testa, a quem a Aurora
Graça sempre pediu? E os brancos dentes,
por quem trocara as pérolas que chora?
Mas que espero de ver dias contentes,
Se para se pagar de gosto uma hora,
Não bastam mil idades diferentes?

(Francisco Manuel de Melo, in *Antologia Poética*)

Is a thousand ages of waiting not enough?
Would I ever be blissful again?

Every morning the gongs in the temple start at five a.m., right across
the narrow street from us, accompanied by chanting from a group
of women. I have never been particularly religious, but for some
reason, in moments of despair, we seek hope, and we cling on to
any thread of hope we can find. Religious rituals, chants, fragments
of Sanskrit shlokas that I remember from my childhood come back
to me when I am most distressed. I might not believe in a divine
entity, a god, but visiting a temple, stepping over that threshold
repositions and realigns my defences, and as I supplicate before an
idol who is merely aesthetically pleasing to me, I feel stripped off
any layers of skin that I have donned for this world, down to my

most authentic bare self. In moments of hope, despair, joy and sadness, some of the extreme emotions, we turn to things that we cannot always explain. My scientific mind has always clashed with religion ever since I was a child. I would question the rituals, I disliked the patriarchal structures that religion imposed, and I rebelled against the strife and conflict that religion evokes. I had grown up with Hindu–Muslim conflicts in India, religion being used as bait, as a classifier, to segregate and carve us all up even further. I rebelled against the notion of belonging in a box and having these rigid walls around me.

But as I feel homesick while also feeling like I couldn't be home anywhere else, the unvarying rhythm of these gongs and chants root me for a few minutes every day. Even as I resent these inter-ruptions, dreading the babies waking up from their momentary repose, I look forward to them every morning. Within the humdrum of my life, and the unpredictable inconsistencies of present and future, turning to a spiritual hearkening, with its unvarying dependability, did not seem like a bad plan.

My mother calls me on FaceTime from a city about 500 kilo-metres away. Within the vast expanse of a country such as India, these distances are insignificant. But she does not seem any closer than when I was 5,000 miles away in the UK. That is the strange absurdity of our digital divide: that miles and kilometres sometimes disappear, yet simultaneously exaggerate the distances between us. She calls most days, or I do, just to check on the babies. I resent her for not being there with me, and I do not tell her about the temple and how that is a source of joy and relief. She had spent most of my teenage years hoping that I would seek spiritual guidance and turn to her gods, and she had stood silently and resolutely holding on to her beliefs while I protested and proclaimed that religion was the source of all evil. I cannot bring myself to tell her that our distances are not as huge as she had always thought they were, that my rejection of her beliefs is not insurmountable.

I remember people telling me that you can forget doing anything once the children are born and I adamantly refuse to accept that anything will change at all. So I order a lot of art materials, and in any of those pauses and lulls, I spread out on our one table in the small room with all my paints, pens and sketchbooks, and I draw. I paint the poppy fields and the rolling hills covered with heather, and I paint rickshaws, scooters, trucks crisscrossing the roads around me. I paint images of what I think is home, and of my homeland. In drawing these images from my recent and past travels, painting landscapes that exist in my imagination, and in the urban melee around me, I stubbornly hold on to a semblance of my old self. I try desperately to carry on with my business, my research, my consultancy, working late and little. Perhaps this release of oxytocin while curling and unfurling through these scribbles is what my mother's brain needs.

•

Stateless: roofless, homeless, dispossessed.

They are neither of these, but the babies are termed stateless, belonging nowhere. How freeing that must be, I wonder, and then hold back that thought.

Governments decide who can belong to a nation. Often we do not really belong where we ought to, and long to where we never can. There are times when we feel we have arrived, without a sound, without a fuss, somewhere that feels completely like home. 'You're here! You belong here!' the heart calls out, as if a last missing piece of jigsaw has suddenly found its place. Sometimes we search for it all our lives, this feeling of being one with the place, the space around us, and it escapes us, just out of reach. Sometimes it is not a place that feels like home, but just a person. Nook of an elbow, a shoulder, a breast. A whiff of their smell left behind on the pillow, shadowy vapours roaming around in the air long after they have gone. Perhaps we equate longing and nostalgia with the sense of belonging, because all that is familiar feels like such a soft, cosy, comforting place and time to retreat to.

Most nations recognise children as citizens of the country where they are born. But in this case, issues with surrogacy laws between India and the UK mean that our children do not naturally get Indian citizenship because although they are born here, to a woman of Indian nationality, she has legally given up her rights to them, and named us as legal parents. We are not Indian nationals, and while we have custody, we do not have legal parentage until the British legal system affords us that privilege. We don't know all the rules in these early days; we do not understand much of it. Our days are spent reading up long documents, talking to and emailing numerous people: lawyers, immigration officials, government personnel, embassy officials, the medical team.

We are in a state of limbo until we can apply for them to leave India and be given British citizenship. For this, there are numerous bureaucratic hurdles to cross. Many documents arrive at our doorstep every day, with calls from lawyers. Forms completed, signed, photos taken.

There are moments of absurdity, as my husband, so cautious and careful, has to ride a scooter, on the back seat, holding on for dear life, amongst the hyper-agitated Delhi traffic, with no helmet. He has to get a passport photo taken urgently, before we send off one of the forms to get the twins tested for DNA analysis back in a lab in the UK. This can only be done in the UK even though there ares very well-qualified labs in India, as the UK authorities only endorse the tests carried out in their country. We continue to navigate the bewildering and needlessly rigid rules, these absurdities of bureaucratic transnational stumbling blocks.

There are also moments of comfort and familiarity as P takes the same trip every day, his one respite from that tiny flat, taking an auto rickshaw to the nearest market, finding a Starbucks and having a coffee in its air-conditioned comfort, just for a few minutes remembering what it can be like to sit down without the noise and anxiety around him. The café baristas get to know him, and he strikes up an easy familiarity with the barbers, with the shopkeepers and with the rickshaw-wallas.

There is also a short period of time when M visits us from the UK to see and meet the babies for the first time. We have sent her many videos and photos, but she was deep in her first-year exams at Cambridge, stressed beyond comprehension, and in those moments my stress meant nothing to me. Even as children grow older, become more 'grown up', mothering does not stop. Not really. As Toni Morrison says in *Beloved*:

Grown don't mean nothing to a mother. A child is a child. They get bigger, older, but grown? What's that supposed to mean? In my heart it don't mean a thing.[18]

In my heart, she is still my little girl. I had spent many nights when I should have been snatching sleep as the twins settled down, calling her to make sure she was eating during her exams, ordering food for her online so that she had some sustenance, sitting with her virtually while she revised. Even as she insisted on independence, she craved support. And now she is here. 'They look like little aliens,' she says with a laugh, looking at the babies, a little resentful of sharing her mother with someone else. An only child who has grown accustomed to undivided attention and solitude, is getting used to being a 'big sister'. But for the first time, she is also seeing reflections of herself: the crinkle in her nose when she laughs, the way she stretches out her arms when she sleeps. And through her eyes, I am also seeing how we have created a family – an untraditional one – through a 'prism of delight and pain' and that it is all going to be okay. I also see how, as our family has suddenly expanded, my heart has swelled too, love stretching out beyond any confines.

Louis MacNeice says in the poem 'Entirely':

> We might be surer where we wished to go
> Or again we might be merely
> Bored but in brute reality there is no
> Road that is right entirely.[19]

It might not be the road that is right entirely. But it is a road that we were meant to follow, through anguish and heartbreak, joy and ecstasy. It is our reality.

It is a strange way of living and being, my own children stateless for now, and me stepping carefully across the two worlds, constantly a life of two halves. I am not quite British, and not enough Indian. I wonder if it would be as bad as it seems not to lay a stake on any one land, those ghostly boundaries laid down by war, strife, conflict, and still the cause of all the discordant clashes between people and nations. These are the boundaries that become our invisible branding, emblazoned into our skins and our souls as our identity, our most visceral mark of ownership, of belonging to a nation and a tribe, and it belonging to us in return.

What if we could all be stateless, belonging everywhere and

nowhere at the same time? Would that close down our gaps and distances, and minimise our prejudices against those who do not belong within the boundaries that we scratch so protectively around us? These are the dreams that I am living with often, thinking of how my children are purest, most unblemished right now, with no tainted sense of ownership, no smudges of legacy, past, present and future, just existing as themselves for the only time ever in their lives, belonging to no one but themselves.

But we live in a world of boundaries and limits, even if only visible to the gatekeepers. The genetic link has to reassure the authorities that we can take them back home. One of the results comes back as negative. The state of shock and disbelief isn't because we doubt or care if she is genetically linked to us but because we know that a simple error in the lab will set us back by another few weeks, and more cash. 'There may be an error,' they tell us. There has to be.

Here is home, the country of my birth, yet I am seen as an outsider, with a white husband, taunted and tainted by my use of surrogacy, my children seen as biological nomads. After years of living in a country which is now my home, but where I do not completely belong, it tears me up to be seen as an outsider and an oppressor in my own country of birth, merely because of my accent or the white husband who creates distance between me and others instantly, while also according me privileges that other women of my skin colour do not have. This is my homeland, my mother's home and her mother's before that, and I had longed to be back here so often when home didn't feel like the one back in the UK. In coming to India I thought that I would find the sense of home that I had been so desperately aching for all these years away from here, that a part of me that was always restless, rummaging through memories, would finally be put to rest. There is a question that lies at the core of human identity: where is home, and how do I get there? I haven't found the answer to this yet, even as I jump through hoops and hurdles to take the twins home.

Each of these steps delays us, sets us back by weeks and months, before we can apply for a passport for them, before we can even consider applying for an exit visa for the twins, before we can fly back home, before we can all be finally home as a family. They belong to us, and the mere thought that they are deemed not ours, lost with no sense of place or home, that their connection to us is even questioned makes me livid, anxious, guilty. The tests are repeated, tested against grandparents based in the UK to make sure. It seems so clinical, proving our ties and the thread that runs from us to them through the strands of genetic code.

Sometimes home and homeland are not the same thing. In the UK, I have felt like a racial outsider, but always an insider in many other ways, fitting comfortably in so many other social norms, finding it easier to navigate social and cultural structures, linguistic patterns and templates, and having the freedom of being able to be mostly myself. It was the country that had afforded me for the first time the space to breathe freely, sucking in air hungrily as if starved of it from birth. Even as I had spread my wings in India, they had always been clipped back, and the space to roam free always came at a cost, inches given to me in return for my complicity with other norms. The bars had been set by others, not me. And so arriving in the UK had felt like stepping outside for the very first time, and even though I did not fit in, something had clicked, all the broken fragments suddenly falling into place. Back in India, I was a racial insider, the colour of my skin didn't make me stand out, but I was an outsider in so many other ways. I struggled to fit back into the suffocating spaces I had fought so hard to escape, squeezing myself into the tiny boundaries while also being grateful for the freedom that women now had since the years had passed. Can I be my children's home, a place of safety they can retreat to when all else seems thorny? Their refuge, shelter, safe haven. But how can I be their home when I am still looking for mine?

According to UNHCR, 10 million people in the world have no nationality. This is a really sobering experience for me, for us, to consider the notion of statelessness. Children most affected by statelessness are generally those belonging to already vulnerable groups, such as ethnic, religious or linguistic minorities. For once I feel that my husband's privileged white framework of the world has been really truly tested. And even as the terror of losing them and being in India in a suspended state of limbo is real, it brings into sharper focus the multiple discriminations that many children face in this world, inheriting their statelessness from their parents. In our case, children born out of surrogacy are also of a minority community, those who have been stigmatised already from birth. These worries keep me awake even when for once the screams have paused, and the car horns on the road outside, the persistent reminder of the rush and the flurry trying to get somewhere at all times, and the deep whirring of the air conditioner inside the apartment, sheltering us from the sweltering heat outside, are the only things that we can hear.

The marbled floor of the serviced apartment is cool to bare feet, and I often find it comforting to just lie down on the floor with my forehead to the cold tiles. Marble is such a fascinating material – comfort and brutality existing alongside. This is the paradoxical world of Indian cities, subsisting in two halves: one that grows up with the comfort, and the other that only sees the brutality. I grew up in tiny one- or two-room rented apartments, often with no running water or electricity. Here is where I learnt to dream, and realised that one does not need a large space to spread your wings. The previous life that I lived in Delhi, in a large house similar to this, moving from air-conditioned rooms to luxurious cars, throttled and trapped, stifled and just surviving, was only a few miles from here. There I had stood alone in that large house feeling desolate and abandoned, where I had somehow hailed a taxi late at night and got myself to the hospital all alone, where I had almost died and come back to life. Not far from here at all, but a million miles away, in another dimension. I do not recognise myself in that alternative world. But I feel stuck between then and now. I want the comforts, but it makes me very uncomfortable. Ill at ease, I move between these two halves, not belonging anywhere. Yet again.

While the babies suffer colic and silent reflux, we struggle with the medical system in India, even with some of the best doctors in the world. 'Oh, foreign parents always over-react about allergies,' one of the many prominent South Delhi paediatricians that we visit tells us, and I look blankly at him, wondering whether he considers me 'foreign' or does not understand that I am one of the parents too. I feel it in my gut that one of the twins has a milk allergy, and I keep telling the doctors this. 'It is always best to breastfeed,' everyone reminds me, as if I did not know, understand, feel guilty that I could not provide my children with the nourishment they needed to thrive, my breasts dry with inspissated secretions. 'Oh, I can't breastfeed them,' is the feeble, sheepish response that I can muster, feeling sorry for them and for myself, ashamed and apologetic, afraid of being judged. Much of what people think and believe lives in our inner selves, we create these judgements and personas, remnants of past

304

experience learnt and immortalised into templates that we use forever, our shortcuts for assuming what others make of us. We live in fear of being judged, our own views of ourselves mediated by these arbitrary judgements we believe people make of us.

In July, M has to move out of her university accommodation at the end of her first year, and we have to get a letter from our local MP to support our application here for the twins' British passports, to expedite this tedious process of getting them back home. P decides to head back to the UK for a week while I stay in India with the twins, once again assuming the role that I always believe I have to play. I need space, and time apart as well, I think. We have spent those last two and half months, almost seventy-five days, in the apartment together all the time tending to these babies, who are just about reaching the age where they would be ready to face the world. We have never spent so much time together alone, just the two of us, never mind the intensity of emotions and the height-ened anxiety and stress, joy and love, of the rollercoaster that we are on together. I need some time to figure out who I could be without him, without leaning on his shoulders, without feeling like a liability. I want the space to cry without feeling like he is looking over his weary shoulders to see what kind of mother I am.

'It is only a week,' he reminds me. 'It is only a week,' I tell myself. Two days after he leaves, I have to rush the babies to the local hospital, one of the best in the country, and the nightmare begins.

I stay awake for five days and nights, not blinking an eye, lest something happens while I am asleep. I guard them with a fervour bordering on insanity, my mind and body exhausted from staying alert at all times. I remember the time when I was in the hospital in India eighteen years ago very distinctly, and what had happened. They had mistakenly given me contaminated blood and exiled me to a life with a deadly illness searing in my veins forever, slowly decimating me from the inside. Wariness and weariness prop me up, and prod me on.

I watch the nurses' every move, and walk with each of the twins in my arms every night until they settle down. We are in the children's intensive care ward but there is nothing cosy or comforting about it. Brightly lit, with a hum of activity at all times, the noise drumming inside my head and keeping the babies awake until their screams resonate inside my heart even when they are quiet. I am alone. So alone. P calls from the UK and we agree that he needs to finish what he has to finish back home. My father becomes very ill, and my mother cannot travel to be with me from 500 kilometres away. I feel alone in this place that I thought was home, the loneliness crushing any sense of belonging that I had felt into pieces so small they are wiped away along with any fond memories that I have. The food is good, though. The staff bring in home-cooked food for the parents, and I devour it greedily. I haven't had a shower for five days, and I refuse to step away from their bedside. Teams of doctors come every morning and are unable to tell me what is wrong. The children pick up a viral infection in the hospital, the nurses give them milk in an unsterilised bottle while I nod off unknowingly just for a very few minutes, and the house that I so carefully built is in danger of falling apart all around me. I am so desperate to get them back to the UK now, even more than before. I spend any spare minutes trying to get through to the British Embassy, sending them emails and requesting an urgent interview. Other surrogacy couples from the UK tell us that this process can take up to nine months. I don't think I will be able to survive for so long, I think. Immediately I feel terribly guilty, as if I am abandoning my home country once again after sixteen years.

Guilt takes on a life of its own. I also feel guilty for having abandoned M as she struggles to get all her things back home to the north of the country after her exams at Cambridge. She has relied on me for so long. 'Maybe it will be good for her,' P tells me. 'I am sure I can do this, Mama,' M says, annoyed, but also accuses me of not thinking of her, of not being there for her at other times when she is stressed and anxious. I miss her. I am failing at being the mother that I was while I try and be the mother that I am here, right now.

I call P one morning, and finally allow myself to collapse. For minutes I do not speak and he fears the worst. 'I thought one of them had died,' he later tells me. And I realise that this is the fear that I have been carrying with me for so long. What if something happens to one of them, or both, while I am here alone, responsible for them? A haunting dread has punctured any sense of calm.

•

Odyssey: a quest, an epic journey.

We often do not realise what drives us on. For me, anxiety and panicked urgency make me act; while my insides might be shaky and jittery, the outside gives the impression of a perfectly oiled machine, calm, cool and collected, performing optimally. These half-selves we contain, and exist in.

Odysseus spent ten years getting home in the face of hostility from Poseidon, god of the sea. It has only been four months for us. I will miss the ease with which I walk around, the feel of Hindi on my tongue, the food and the sun both warming up my homesick soul. I like that life isn't that easy and I can still remember where I come from, and the bubble of my comfortable privileged life is still not so tough to not show cracks.

Because I am at an advantage in being able to speak Hindi, and in knowing how to navigate the multiple opaque bureaucratic hurdles, it becomes natural for me to take on this role while P tries to take on the more nurturing role with the babies back in the apartment. Gender boundaries blur, and I feel grateful for this release from the stasis, relieved to be doing something, even though it is like painstakingly sifting through sluggish mud. I sit for hours in a large room, begging for a chance to have an interview for an exit visa. Without food and water, it seems like a protest, but not a silent one. The officers snigger and shame the parents who have gone through the surrogacy process. 'Oh yeh to bacche khareednay aaye they yahan,'‡ they tell each other while knowing full well that I can understand and speak Hindi. Once again I am both visible and invisible at the same time.

Those days and nights now are fading already in my memory. What remains is the intense heat, the smell, the sweat intermingled with the cool blast from the air-conditioner. The difference between inside and outside, between have and have-nots, the fierce love and despair, the ease with which I could flow between people and fit in, and the sense of otherness I felt in the midst of it all. Every day I just wanted to get back home, while also drowning in sorrow of leaving it all behind. All the love and sadness I felt for the land of my birth, the keen aching desire to stay close to it, plus the cloying claustrophobia of so many bodies around me. I have never been more aware of my privileges or of how my body shapes the way I am seen and heard.

I spend hours and days on the phone to the embassy, to the consulate, to our local MP back home, to the lawyers, to the hospital.

‡ 'Oh, they came here to buy children.'

Just telephone calls, one after another, beseeching, navigating the many barriers, finding out ways that we can get a foot in the door. These doors are never fixed. You have to grow up in a place like India to know that these doors are propped open for some, those who are stacked up in the hierarchy of power and privilege. We don't have either right now. But in the end, after weeks and months, we are given a temporary passport, and we get an exit visa. We book the next flight back to the UK after five months here. It is bitter-sweet.

•

'Would you like to meet her?' they had asked us, as we waited in the air-conditioned waiting room at the hospital in Delhi, filled with pictures of laughing, giggling babies and happy families, and thank you notes from around the world. I had sat there waiting anxiously to sign the final few papers, cuddling the twins in my arms, still just getting used to feeling like a mother. P had put a protective arm around us and looked at me quizzically, with a slightly panic-stricken, worried look on his face. I had felt sorry for him, and so much love. 'She is not the mother,' I had told him again and again, while crying uncontrollably in my dreams.

'Do we want to meet her?' he asked.

I felt like I had already met her. The umbilical cord stretched between us, intertwining our histories and futures together.

I passed by her in the corridor and averted my gaze. I sneaked a peek at this short stocky woman, not much shorter than me, dressed traditionally in an Indian salwar suit with her head covered, and a large bindi on her forehead, walking a few steps behind a man. Possibly her husband. He walked with a swagger, she with tiny apprehensive steps. As she sat in front of me, I looked down at her feet, caked in dust in sparkly slippers, shiny with tiny gems. Her toenails were painted in bright pink. I was wearing trainers, and my slouchy trousers that I couldn't remember taking off for the last week. I wanted to stare, but at the same time I didn't want to look.

'We are so grateful to you,' she told me in her language, in our shared language, with a shy smile on her face, the language of my ancestors, the one that I speak rarely but still sounds like coming back home. She sat there with a smile, her hands folded in gratitude, her two children and her husband, dressed in smart new clothes.

My overwhelming sense of gratitude had no words. Even as I tried to say it out loud, it sounded hollow. My voice was muffled and insincere, reverberating back at me.

'Your babies are beautiful,' she said to me with such tenderness, and I burst into tears.

I had spent the last year troubled with the guilt and confusion around her status and my privilege, so much so that enjoying any moment of the impending pregnancy had felt sacrilegious and immoral. I had spent the five months since the children's birth worrying whether I had any right to be their mother, whether motherhood had to come at a huge cost, and how to prove my love for these children to whom I hadn't given birth. I had tried again and again, and tried harder than ever to be a good mother, as if there was a predetermined way to be one, and above all, I desperately wanted to deserve to be called a mother. I know it all sounds so clear and transparent in hindsight, but it isn't when we are immersed in it, living the life we live. Then moments merge into one another, and we are carried through with the flow, the suncatcher of our dreams casting a shadow on our reality.

In that instance, suddenly, it all felt right for the first time. I

310

didn't have to try any more. The quiet contentment I felt for the first time in the company of this woman measured up against all the chaos and turmoil of the past few months. For the first time, I felt like I didn't have to explain anything to anyone, be anything that anyone expected me to be. I was a mother. I didn't have to try and be one. There was no guilt, no obligation, no judgement. Only serenity in a curious alliance, an unusual sense of belonging.

•

Although we could get a British passport for the children, and an exit order to be allowed to fly them home, in the UK we had to go through the legal process of applying for a parental order to finally be acknowledged as their legal parents. The UK law does not acknowledge or accept any legal arrangements made in India. Under the Surrogacy Arrangements Act 1985 surrogate mothers maintain legal and financial responsibility for the child until parental rights are transferred in the family court. While the parental order is being processed, the 'intended' parents do not have any authority to even make any major medical decisions about the children. This is hugely worrying in the case of a transnational surrogacy where the surrogate and her partner are not based in the UK. This was especially worrying for us as our twins were premature and faced regular healthcare difficulties. One of them was especially vulnerable. There was a time when we were calling an ambulance most nights as her temperature would spike up dangerously. Numerous nighttime visits to the out-of-hours emergency; numerous daytime visits to the local courts. This process can take up to two years because of complicated bureaucracy and long waiting lists. We were fortunate that the whole process took around a year for us.

A parental order reporter was assigned. We had numerous visits from the court official, assessing us and our home for any red flags. Both the surrogate and genetic parents must undergo a strict assessment by the Children and Family Court Advisory and Support Service (CAFCASS) after the baby is born before parental responsibility can be transferred. This is to check whether the surrogate is happy to change their legal status, and that the genetic parents are in a long-term relationship and are not going to move abroad. It added an extra layer of complexity as our surrogate was overseas, and especially as she had very clearly communicated to us and the medical team that she did not wish to continue any association with us or the children. She needed a clean break, and I respected her for it.

These visits to the family courts were painful. Each visit from the social worker, each conversation with the parental order representative, would dig through my insecurities around my identity as a mother to these babies, hard nails scraping silently through my tender heart, anxiety digging into eyes already drooping with heavy lids, sleep sitting mercilessly on them. But each visit to the family courts also revealed the many lost families, parents fighting custody battles, children looking for home. Women and children fleeing domestic abuse, beaten into submission, their will and sense of self broken and shattered. So many vulnerable children: those without parents, those without a safe home, those waiting to be placed in foster care, those whose sense of faith and trust in this world had already been abused and damaged at a young age. I saw more closely a system that was crumbling under pressure, bursting at the seams, failing to hold these little lives together.§ Each time I hugged my children a

§ As per publicly available government data, 262,399 new cases started in family courts during 2018, up 3 per cent compared to 2017. In 2018,

little bit closer, while weeping for those invisible children who did not have someone to hug them close, to wipe their tears, to kiss their scraped knees. How do we – our society – fail our children in this way? The same society that makes women have children often against their will. The same society that makes having children the ultimate goalpost to which every woman should aspire.

One of my memories of that last court hearing was the twins, now almost one year old, laughing and giggling in the waiting area, waddling through a small ball pit filled with colourful yellow, blue and red plastic balls. I saw their unbridled joy, the way they would fall into my arms fearlessly, trusting that I would always save them from falling. I knew then that no matter what happened I was their home, and their safe place. Holding, smelling, touching: we had already fitted in with each other. Sleeping, cuddling, snuggling: they were already a part of me.

I don't remember much else of the court process, paying witness and testimony in front of a judge, narrating how much these children meant to us. I was always unsure of what we were being judged on:

_____

there were 25,135 domestic violence remedy order applications, up 1 per cent on 2017, the highest figure since the peak in 2009. The number of orders made also increased, by 4 per cent over the same period. Even as the number of children in care increased, the adoption orders went down. In 2018, there were 5,104 adoption order applications, down 6 per cent on 2017. The number of adoption orders issued also decreased in 2018, by 9 per cent compared to 2017, reaching the lowest annual total since 2011. In the final quarter of the year, the number of adoption orders was down 10 per cent compared to the equivalent quarter in 2017. This makes me wonder, and despair, why the whole process around adoption is so rigid, so difficult, with so many barriers making it impossible for couples to give many of these children a home. But that is a conversation for another day, of course.

our capacity to love and parent, or our capacity to remember all the facts seamlessly without any errors.

Then, just like that, after the hearing the parental order was finally approved. The day the parental order decree arrived, with our names as parents, my name on it in black and white, I was a mother again in the name of law, though I had been mothering for almost a year. The twins were officially ours; unquestionably ours.

·

As I look at them today, photos on my phone from the first time in the NICU show me and P looking a little starstruck, emotional, and also so young. I now look as if these last few sleepless years have created furrows and lines in the sand of time, and on my face where none existed. Looking through old photographs on a small window of a phone, without the tactility of those old-school photographs from a camera, creates this sensation that no time has passed at all.

We see ourselves and our children in the past, in time long gone by, but time has stood still. These images create an immediacy where you can reach out and almost touch these old selves, a parallax of lives merging and colliding in the past and present. My children giggle around me, looking at these old videos of themselves attached to ventilators, their heartbeats thumping on the screen loudly, and I see their little faces, bright shining eyes. For me, they are as they are now, and we are us as we are, cuddling their soft faces squished against mine, as I breathe in the perfume of their heads, their grubby fingers and hands leaving their soft imprints on my arms. But at the same time, I see them as they were, as we were. I stand stunned, bright-eyed, a younger, sparkier version of me. And I stand there, looking at these tiny beings, figuring out how I became a mother again, trying to convince myself that I was one.

In fact, our old memories aren't reliable. I don't know exactly how I felt, except that I wanted to let them know that they had a family, that they hadn't been forsaken. It is impossible to remember what one experienced exactly, especially as so much has followed since. I cannot imagine not being absolutely and utterly in love with them now, or ever, but I don't know whether then it was real love I was feeling for itself, or because I thought that it was how I should feel. I cannot say with confidence which it was. I know that there were times in the next few days, months, when desperate with exhaustion I had questioned my love for them, and I had questioned my own sanity. I had sat in a Waitrose car park at midnight, crying desperately, wishing to disappear. I had driven around trying to get them to sleep somehow and had driven on the wrong side of the road. My brain couldn't fathom where I was and what I was doing in that car. I was petrified, angry and seething, and I had seen the very foundations of my marriage tremble with great force as we attacked each other bitterly; as we stood alone and apart while we parented; as we tried to hold the fort while crumbling inside; as we kept score in hours, minutes, seconds of who had slept less and done more. In parenting the children, who were a testimony to our intimacy, our shared desire to grow our family, we had become stranded, alone on the shores of many wakeful nights and worn-out days.

And then I remember the guilt. Guilt is always there as a parent, because we are not supposed to feel despondent, feel utterly defeated, feel like running away. Somehow there are no words in our armoury for maternal anger and ambivalence; words that can stand side by side with our love.

In *The Argonauts* Maggie Nelson says to her newborn son, born from donor sperm:

I want you to know, you were thought of as possible – never as certain, but always as possible – [because] two human animals . . . deeply, doggedly, wildly wanted you to be.[20]

Today, as I look at them, our family of five that has expanded – and along with it my heart – I realise that they have brought their heartbeat into the rhythm of this family. And although there have been times when, in those restless days and nights that stretched forever, I had wondered whether I had made a mistake, I have learnt to forgive myself for those. Because every new mother has certainly felt that utter desperation and the voice on her shoulder urging her to escape the chaos at some point in the early years.

And even as I felt like I was swimming against the tide, holding on somehow to a semblance of my own self, a ball of incandescent thunder, there wasn't a single day that I didn't want to hold my twins tight and tell them that they are exactly this: a long-held wish finally granted, a deliberate act, a conscious decision, a choice.

•

Lockdown, 2020

We are living in close quarters, five of us, and the dog, and the cat, all squashed together twenty-four hours every day, the same routines being repeated daily. I mother, and I work. I try to snatch every single moment through countless flustered days and sleepless nights to finish my book. I carry the guilt with me every day of neglecting my three-year-old twins, and of relying heavily on my husband's already weary shoulders. Juggling furiously the demands of running a home and business, dealing with a chronically painful body having just gone through some intensive medical treatment, lost in words, all hundred thousand of them, and working against a tight deadline,

I feel the very foundations of our family life trembling. Used to keeping tight control on my life and its course for the most part, I have tried to be a rock. Suddenly, the sand trickles through a clenched fist, me watching helplessly, trying to grasp on to the grains with trembling hands. Once again old habits return, where P and I are counting seconds, minutes, hours of childcare, negotiating and nagging, stretched and stressed. We take walks, but deep in thought, and think of everything we still have to do. Bone-tired weariness slowly reaches out its fingers into dark gloomy clouds. Overhead in the grey and pink sky, skeins of pink-footed geese with their loud honks are inking their way in V-shaped formations, coming home for the winter. Our little family of five, and the dog, stand there in the clearing watching, listening, thinking. I feel an affinity with these geese, and I understand the pain of having to travel thousands of miles in search of better climes, living here and there, equally but never completely, looking for a place to belong. As I see my three girls standing, huddled together, hand in hand without a word, I feel the heaviness in my limbs leaving me for the first time in a long time. My husband reaches out and puts his arm around me, and I know that no matter what else happens in my life, I am home, and this is where I completely belong. I have found my true north.

CODA

TICK-TOCK, TICK-TOCK.

Time runs past. It is neither the end nor the start.

Memories keep mounting up.

Words collected, language amassed, labels assigned. Symbols, signs, meanings.

Childless, barren, infertile, geriatric mothers: traps, trappings, tropes.

We get so caught up in norms and the normality of reproduction and family that the spaces outside and around seem claustrophobic.

Maybe this book is my story. Maybe not. But it is most certainly a story of how little we know of our own bodies as women, and the way we are kept in the dark about them, shamed, admonished and chastised, and how much of womanhood is signified by rigid parameters that put us right back into the boxes where patriarchy wants to keep us. How much we demand from our bodies, and how much we allow others to demand of them.

On my office wall, in front of my desk, right here as I sit typing this, I have a print of one of Louise Bourgeois's paintings that I bought from MOMA in New York, from a series called *Femme*

Maison done in oils and inks around 1946. In this a woman is depicted with a house instead of her head and upper part of the body but exposing her genitals to all. Much like most of Bourgeois's work, it is sensuous and provocative, as well as gruesome. I often sit quietly and stare at this image of a woman who seems trapped within her body, which can be both a refuge from the outside world and a trap that is difficult to escape from. It is admittedly a bizarre choice of art to look at every day. It evokes such an intense feeling of suffocation and claustrophobia in this seemingly simple and naïve image: the rage, fear and frustration associated with being a woman so palpable in these lines and formless forms; the dehumanising facelessness that makes individuation impossible. There is a feeling of entrapment from the assumptions imposed on women, the balance of societal expectations and roles abusing and patronising women at the same time. While they become a faceless mass, their sexuality (or the lack of it), their fecundity (or the lack of it) become their – our – only identifying and redeeming features. It is a curious conundrum we inhabit. Perhaps this is why I like the painting so much. Because within such debasement, there is a sort of dignity in this image. A reminder of the humiliation, but also the possibility of opening up these conversations when we bring women's own voices into the narrative, when we step away from the male gaze.

Motherhood, or the choice to be a mother, is a vast landscape. Barren, fertile; blooming, fecund. Crisscrossed with mazes, teeming with opinions. It can be a lonely journey, while we are paradoxically never alone at any step; our bodies held accountable with every choice, pushed into crevices and nooks left vacant by women gone before us. Motherhood is constructed from a patriarchal idealisation of women's selfhood. Andrea O'Reilly, professor of women's studies, describes motherhood as a 'medium for isolating, regulating, and judging women'[1] and in its current form as it is perceived and practised in patriarchal society as deeply disempowering. And, as we know and have seen again and again, when women become stranded on the shores of motherhood, they can also participate in patriarchy. The cycle continues. Mothering, on the other hand, is the act of being a mother, of raising a child. Through acknowledging the separation of mothering and motherhood, the cultural tyranny that forces the morass of motherhood and womanhood can be untangled, leaving women free to shun the social oppressiveness that shackles them into these ambiguous liminal roles.

The philosopher Julia Kristeva says in her 2005 essay that 'motherhood is not an instinct',[2] but we still believe in the myth of a maternal instinct, a desire to bear children as a biologically pre-determined reality. Bonding and attachment are not synonymous. Attachment takes time. It does not merely focus on the mother, but is a dance between the infant and the mother, a give and take, beset by trials and triumphs, joy and despair, devotion and ambivalence. Rather than the notion of a maternal bond, we need to make attachment a part of our broader cultural dialogue, because it shows the commitment and effort it takes to be a mother, and shifts the focus away from biology. When we start focusing on attachment, then perhaps it will also become easier to talk about the decision to become a mother simply in terms of preparedness – emotional and physical – and an honest reflection on the potential pitfalls and possibilities. When there is an honest conversation about this, then perhaps motherhood can be reimagined as a woman's choice rather than their destiny.

The maternal myth suffuses every human culture, from Catholicism's Virgin Mary to Hinduism's Durga or Shakti. Being a mother is considered the most natural state of womanhood. A woman who does not desire motherhood is pitied or denigrated, considered unwomanly, a traitor to her biological destiny. They are often told that no matter how they feel now, their 'maternal instincts' will take over once they become a mother. The ideas of motherhood – the imagery, the smells – are all shaped by belief in an idealistic notion of love.

Motherhood should come naturally to all women. That is the message we are fed, at least. The urge to be a mother, to mother, to nurture and selflessly raise a child is considered as *ultimum verum*: the ultimate, non-negotiable truth. And to give birth is the only way to be a complete woman. The supposedly unqualified and instant nature of the motherhood bond reinforces this myth. When the singer Katy Perry proclaims on Twitter 'Mothers are the most powerful beings on the planet',[3] I worry that this kind of trope hurts everyone: those who are mothers and those who are not. Perhaps she is compelled to say this in a haze of new first-time motherhood, but if we hear something again and again, our brain tells us that it has to be true. That is what we remember; that is what we easily recall due to availability heuristics. When we hear the same narrative, anything that does not reconcile with it then becomes a deviance, and has prejudices and discrimination associated with it. Shame and stigma cause people to shy away from sharing stories that do not conform to the narrative that society has laid out for them. Once this happens, it becomes a self-fulfilling prophecy. The less we hear diverse stories and impressions of motherhood, and more broadly of families, the less likely we are to believe that they exist.

The dominant discourse prescribes mothers to be the main ones responsible for taking care of the children and to be fully devoted to this task, putting the children's needs before their own: a 'self-sac-rificing mother', a 'good mother'. Flip the coin and there on the other side is the 'bad mother'. Dualistic designations. We know women do this to each other. We know that Instagram and other social media fuels it, this 'interpersonal surveillance' that mothers impose on each other, and that women internalise it and believe it too. No motherhood is the same. To mother, to be a mother, is layered, variegated, diverse. But we still seem to believe in the same-ness of the motherhood experience.

What about the intersection of 'other' and 'mother'? What about those who fall squarely in this Venn diagram of divergence, those outside the boxes of conformity? The 'Other Mother', the beldam in Neil Gaiman's *Coraline*, is a shape-shifting entity, a pretend mother. For so long, I felt like one too.

'When I grow up, I will have a baby in my tummy.'

'Not everyone has to have a baby in their tummy, darling.'

'But I came from your tummy.'

'You know that you didn't come from Mummy's tummy. You came from my heart [they are only four after all!]. And I love you a million trillion times. Not everyone comes from their mummy's tummies.'

My young children and I repeat this ritual several times. Mostly they ignore me and run away, unfazed by any of this. I want to keep reminding them of this though. And myself.

As they grow older, we will talk about this more. I want to be honest with them. Shame can only live in secrets. And I love my children too much to hold any secrets from them, any walls between us. I realise that the more openly we speak about this, the less there can be fear, anxiety about stigma, disgrace to make us uncomfortable.

I read Jackie Kay's poem 'The Mother Poem (Two)', which is

about an adoptive mother, but I feel echoes of it reverberating long
after the words have moved away.

> So I watched my child grow
> Always the first to hear her in the night
> All this umbilical knot business is
> Nonsense
>
> [. . .]
> I listened to hear her talk
> And when she did I heard my voice under hers
> And now some of her mannerisms
> Crack me up
>
> All them stories could have really had me
> Believing unless you are breast fed
> You'll never be close and the rest
> My daughter's warmth spills over me [. . .][4]

The questions that people ask us, and we ask ourselves. The fears
that we hold, and the lies we are told. The ways women become
mothers, and some mothers are othered.

There is this notion of 'unnatural' parenthood that still persists
in popular culture and the subconscious as if there is one correct
way to be a parent, a mother. As Rachel Bowlby, author of *A Child
of One's Own*, points out, with the changing landscape of reproductive technologies 'we cannot now assume that a child has been
born of two parents, of different sex, who've had sex'.[5] We cannot
assume this but, nevertheless, our society is slow to accept these
new forms of family, born out of active choice. We seem stuck in
an antediluvian notion of what a family constitutes, and what a
complete family looks like. It seems absurd that the intentional,

deliberate action of becoming a mother through surrogacy, donor eggs or adoption is seen as aberrant. It seems ludicrous that even as assisted reproductive technologies are becoming more normalised, infertility still carries shame, stigma, silence; the blame is still placed squarely on the woman's shoulders. And even though we perhaps know and understand that all bodies are different, society still believes in some normative template that all the diverse female bodies have to adhere to, some mythical pattern that all women are shaped from. These narrow margins within which we have to live our lives trap us, and those falling outside are othered.

Sex and gender have become hotly debated and contested themes, and much of this has seen a resurgence of biological determinism in the media. Natasha Walter in her book *Living Dolls* back in 2010 had expressed similar dismay that rather than investigating how gender stereotypes are constructed by and shape power in return, they are often seen as a fact in society: 'I am very uneasy about the way that the media has sort of pounced on biological determinism as the scientific consensus, when it isn't.' Rather than seeing any differences as a social construction, we tend to accept them as a touchstone for casting judgements and aspersions. Motherhood, maternity, motherliness are all grounded in these patriarchal constructs. Amongst feminists, and within society more broadly, motherhood continues to hold a strangely ambivalent position, which Rosi Braidotti positions as: '. . . both one of the pillars of patriarchal domination of women and one of the strongholds of female identity.'[6] In some ways, the same narrative is used by gender-critical feminists who while claiming to oppose the boxes that trap us, also want to keep them shut very tight. In trying to separate women from men, some feminists resort to reducing women to their reproductive function and their role as mothers: a woman is a woman only if she can give birth, only if she is the sum of her biological parts. This also creates the non-inclusive model of womanhood where trans women are feared and seen as outsiders. Therein lies the dilemma of separating womanhood from motherhood, and seeking emancipation of women without reducing them to a monolithic mass, while also considering the whole spectrum of experiences of mothering (or not), of choice and autonomy. Infertility, womanhood, motherhood all can mean different things to different people.

•

Women search for the perfect time to be pregnant, delaying pregnancy decisions. This might seem like autonomy, but it is often a consequence of the vast gender inequality still existing in our society. No matter what we want to believe, women do not have the same status as men. They carry more mental and emotional labour at home, working longer hours than men who are fathers. And although we are seeing a rise in single mothers, going solo is still not widely acceptable within the largely heteronormative and familial constraints of our society. White picket fences, two plus two, the glossy version of adulthood and family that so many of us grow up with, aspire to, fail at, despair of and then we sink in shame. Women who decide not to have children are marked as outsiders within the deterministic frameworks of our social and cultural norms. Mothers and non-mothers. Our language creates the falsehood that being with a child is a norm. Childless or childfree, voluntarily or involuntarily, firmly places the one without a child as the one lacking, imperfect, inadequate. Limiting labels. Many women make this decision voluntarily, while for some this happens because of biology or timing. There is no room for those that are ambivalent, those that need assistance, those that are sick of these treatments and impositions

325

on their bodies, those that decide to stop the treatments, to stop living in the land of 'maybe one day'. Either way the idealisation of motherhood undermines all women, irrespective of choices. As Adrienne Rich wrote in 1976: 'the "childless woman" and the "mother" are a false polarity, which has served the institutions both of motherhood and heterosexuality.'[7]

We stay trapped in binaries: mother and non-mother, men and women, good and bad, black and white.

•

Infertility is also colour-blind. Not a great place to be.

Much of the feminist discourse around motherhood, whether natural or assisted (in the form of ART or surrogacy), is framed around a middle-class white approach, a broad brush that dismisses the intersectional aspects of power, privilege and oppression. Inequalities of class, race, gender, culture and education all play a role in the stratification of reproduction. All forms of reproduction are racialised and due to structural inequalities and varying levels of privilege, some people have more access to fertility treatments, adoption and surrogacy, while others are excluded. Some are encouraged to reproduce, while others are stigmatised for being too prolific. This hypocrisy is founded in the racialised stereotype of women of colour, especially black women, as profligate and irresponsible, sexually promiscuous, but also with weak family structures.

As we see throughout history, images of infertility are really one or the other: either angry and bitter, or passive and hopeful. We need to flip this narrative away from these binaries. We need to cross the racial divides and reduce disparities in treatment. Not every woman who is infertile would seek treatment, not everyone has access to treatment, not everyone is allowed to have treatment. The word 'infertile' crosses cultural and racial divides and a broad spectrum of meanings are constructed: from those who haven't conceived after having unprotected sex for twelve months or more, to those who have not produced a male heir, or those who do not fall within these hegemonic ideals of sexual behaviours. My mother tells me that in India 'everyone is doing IVF now. If there is no child within six months, they go for IVF.' By 'everyone' I know she means the middle-class people who have disposable incomes, who value the social standing a child provides in Indian families. But it is the notion of how quickly fertility and infertility are determined now in a society that traditionally stigmatised any forms of 'unnatural motherhood', that is most fascinating to me. Slippery slopes. Where does one stop, and does this mean that for some this is now an even more unattainable goal?

Fertility and infertility are also slippery concepts across the temporal dimension. I was fertile (very) and then less so, and not so much after that. But then when jolted into action with hormones and chemicals, body prodded and pushed, I was fertile once again for a little while, only temporarily, but just adequately. The line between fertile and infertile is not as sharp as it is usually perceived to be. These slippery identities can be confusing and troubling. Infertile women are seen to be unfulfilled, empty, devoid of meaning. But it is society that creates meaning, and we forget that. Women have to be nurturers, givers of life, or they seem to lose value. A curiosity, presumed unfulfilled, pitied. Motherhood therefore is a labour in all its forms, even as the more disembodied forms of pregnancy via surrogates have been heavily critiqued. But rather than weighing up the morality of altruistic surrogacy as opposed to commercial surrogacy, the focus should remain on regulating the systems and structures so that the rights of the surrogate to choose and consent is upheld. And as Sophie Lewis proposes in her revolutionary *Full Surrogacy Now*, how about rather than banning commercial surrogacy and expecting women to carry children (whether genetic or gestational) for others out of the goodness of their heart and for free, we treat all motherhood as a consequence of capitalist forces, commodified and worthy of adequate remuneration?[8] That would be a level playing field, and then we can truly create a more autonomous model of reproduction.

•

When I think of the word 'mother' I am often reminded of the sculpture by Louise Bourgeois, a nine-metre-tall spider, titled 'Maman'. The spider carries a sack containing thirty-two grey and white marble eggs, protected within a steel cage-like body balancing on long and slender legs. When I first saw this, I felt awe and fear but also an immediate sense of connection. Even in its colossal scale, there is a sense of poignant vulnerability to it. I have often wondered why Bourgeois returned to this motif of a spider as a mother. Perhaps there is something about softness and strength, and the fragility and power, the irreconcilable differences somehow reconciled.

I am a mother to three girls now. And, yes, I love them. My life has revolved around them, often literally, and at times I have lost myself, submerged deep underwater in mothering, choking, spluttering, pushing myself through against the tide. At times, they are the only ones who have kept me alive, and at times they are the ones who have made me question my existence. At times I've tried to live up to the fairy-tale ideal of a 'perfect mother' but never ever been able to touch the mythical beast. Sometimes we are a cacophony of discordant notes singing to our own tune. Other times we have trundled along together hand in hand, a joyful harmonious symphony, a homogenous unicellular organism that I've struggled to separate myself from. Yes, I love them with all my heart and I feel emotional just writing this. But that does not mean that I do not now and again reflect on other choices that would have led me along vastly different paths. In these images – these alternate versions of myself – I look different. They are alternative realities, worlds where I didn't have to make any decisions about having children or not, where it wasn't considered a default that women had to bear children and be mothers. I love my children with a fierce passion that I throw into any project that I undertake. They are not a project, but I carry this huge responsibility for bringing them into this world, for ensuring they always know that they are loved, for helping them to grow into people who matter. But is this what I would have chosen if I had given space to my ambivalence?

If I hadn't gone through with things to make others happy, or lived through some of these decisions like a dream, of letting life just happen to me, and seeing where it took me? I don't know the answer to this.

Does this mean that I love my children any less, less fiercely, less passionately, less devotedly? I know the answer to this. No.

My adolescence was marked by a furious rejection of any role that seemed 'traditional', that was deemed natural for women, rooted as I was in a radical notion of feminism that rejected even a sliver of a gendered concept or belief. *Women become mothers. Women are supposed to be good mothers. All women would make good mothers. All women are nurturing.* It felt predetermined and cloying. Claustrophobic in these roles that I was supposed to play, I believed in Shulamith Firestone's stark argument that women would never truly be free of patriarchy until they were freed from the yoke of reproduction. It seems that in saying 'fuck you' to patriarchy, women have to leave their 'femaleness', their bodies behind or else they will always be determined by this, while men are free to take possession of the mind.

I never wanted to become a mother when I was younger. I thought that it had to be a choice between being a mother, and being myself, my complete self. Then I became one, twice over, and I realised that as I have spent more than half of my life mothering, it has shaped me and my identity hugely.

Dying, living, back from the brink.

Fading, vanishing, perishing.

Love, joy, bliss.

All in a lifetime. Pauses filled with uncertainties, indecisions, hesitations. Then forging ahead quietly, confidently, assertively. But it is not my complete 'self'. I love being a mother, most of the time. Not always. And I am okay with it. But I want to feel and believe that I can design my motherhood the way I want to. My motherhood does not have to prove anything to anyone. Not being a mother or being one does not shape my femininity or my value to society.

I used to feel embarrassed talking about my children in my professional arena, as if it diminished me, that people would see me differently, view me just as a mother, one who is defined and limited by it. Much of this need to separate the personal and the professional comes from the bias that women still face in workplaces. Many of our workplaces are patriarchal structures, where women – especially women of colour – are discriminated against. Research shows that it is still assumed that women will choose motherhood and will not be as serious about their careers.[9] And if they do become mothers, it is often assumed that their loyalties lie more with their family and their children rather than with their employers.[10] It seems a peculiar assumption to make, an extraordinary dichotomy, forcing women to choose one, to hide away the personal in order to demonstrate commitment to the professional. But I have a growing realisation and acknowledgement that motherhood has shaped my life, my career, my choices, my body and my mind in many ways. I have gained ownership of this label, not needing to conform to any view or model of motherhood I have seen around me.

Whether or not to create life is a huge question. It has to be. Then why do we treat it so lightly, filled with shame no matter what we decide? Why do women put themselves through this, the constant worry and anxiety, this sense of dread and fear over something happening to your child, this paranoia and agitation that you are not a 'good enough' mother? I don't have any answers to this. I am a mother all the time, even if I don't love being one ceaselessly. There are no pauses, no intermissions, no sporadic hiatuses from being a mother. The relentless, unbroken, incessant nature of being and feeling responsible for another human being can be so draining. But we are not allowed to talk about it or mention this ambivalence: this sapping, tiring, all-consuming nature of motherhood. When women are making these choices, does one ever tell them 'be prepared. It is going to be very tough'. I don't think so.

In some ways, motherhood is a transformative experience. We don't know how it will transform us. We cannot anticipate it beforehand. All we need to know is that we probably won't be the same people once we have gone through it. Whether we seek this transformation and unpredictability or not has to be entirely our choice.

Rather than dismissing the notion of autonomy within the context of fertility, reproduction, abortion and surrogacy, with a view that it is never independently situated, there can be a more equitable and transparent framework for women to make these decisions in. As an example, creating fairer workplaces where there is no bias against mothers, no fear that motherhood would impact on a woman's career progression, and a fair, equal parental leave policy for both parents, can support women in making a more autonomous decision about becoming a mother, or not.

•

I write this book while under lockdown due to coronavirus. It has been impossible to ignore the effect this is having on women across the world, and how their access to basic reproductive health services is being compromised. The limiting of choices during the lockdown intensifies everything. The sense of time standing still, days merging into each other, weeks seeming indistinguishable . . . as we get caught into Groundhog Day, and boredom becomes our significant emotion, many women have had time to consider their choices more carefully away from societal scrutiny. While for some, this time has evoked nostalgia and craving for a family, either alone or with a partner, either to start a family or extend one, on the other hand, some women have realised more strongly than ever that they would always choose to not have children, no matter what. In either case, stress and uncertainty heightens feelings of nostalgia, fear and hyper-aware-ness of one's body.

Motherhood is idealised during a global pandemic, especially during lockdown as the role of mothers as primary childcarers and the toll it takes – with the accompanying emotional, mental and physical labour – becomes visible. But as attention is justifiably focused on the vulnerable population, those with underlying health conditions and those over the age of sixty-five, it has not been clear whether pregnant women or new mothers fall under any of the high-risk categories. As lockdown measures were relieved, and people

332

were able to go to the pub – in fact encouraged to do so – women still had to give birth alone. They were not allowed a birth partner with them in hospital. The pandemic has highlighted the stratified layers of privilege and inequities in our society and their effect on women's reproductive health and agency. As people started panic-buying and stocking up on essential items, shelves were wiped clean of feminine hygiene items such as tampons and sanitary pads. But while those with more disposable income could stockpile, those who were already living from paycheck to paycheck, or those who relied on food banks, schools and shelters could not, as many of these were closed down, or ran out of supplies themselves as demands surged. As some families struggle to make ends meet with jobs being lost, compromises have been made between food and sanitary products. These are basic items needed by women to survive in a dignified manner.

Clare Wenham, assistant professor in global health policy at the LSE, who along with her colleagues researched the impacts of the Zika and Ebola outbreaks on men and women, had been looking at Covid-19, and found that in states of emergency when all resources go towards managing the crisis, often the first thing to go is maternal healthcare. Women's autonomy and agency, and access to reproductive health services, also come under attack during times of crisis and emergency. As other health aspects are prioritised, we have seen again and again that women's reproductive health is undercut, destabilised and disregarded. In the USA, the Republicans have tried to capitalise on the pandemic to sneak anti-abortion language into law. A number of states categorised abortion as a non-essential service that can be put on pause and banned during the pandemic. After a number of lawsuits, federal judges in states such as Texas, Ohio and Alabama prevented these bans, acknowledging that they could imperil the health of women. But in early April 2020, the US Court of Appeals for the Fifth Circuit allowed the ban in Texas to take effect, letting the state prohibit nearly all abortions during this health crisis. Anti-abortionists have been attempting to disempower women from making their own health and reproductive decisions since the Supreme Court granted women the constitutional right to an abortion in the landmark 1973 case Roe v Wade. The Title X funding regulations demanded in March 2020 that any centre and organisation funded has to physically and financially separate abortion from other services that they provide. They cannot refer patients to other abortion providers. This has been justified by the reasoning that abortion care must be suspended to divert resources to treating coronavirus patients.

In the UK, the government's reluctance to prioritise women's health also came under fire. In March 2020 the government declared that due to dangers associated with contact during the pandemic, women could have safe abortions at home and would not need to go to a clinic for an abortion, thereby preventing any non-essential travel. Shortly afterwards, the Department of Health stated that the reported changes to the abortion law had been 'published in error' and that 'there will be no changes to abortion regulations'. While almost a quarter of abortion clinics run by the British Pregnancy Advisory Service (BPAS), which look after 100,000 women every year, were closed due to isolation and staff sickness, this meant that either women had to travel across the country to access abortion services, putting their own and their family's health at risk, which would also put more pressure on the NHS staff and resources, or that many women would choose to continue with an unwanted or medically dangerous pregnancy. After facing severe criticisms, the government introduced a 'pills by post' system that saw women able to self-nominate for an abortion, rather than be referred by a clinician or doctor, and get in contact with BPAS for a phone consultation with a trained nurse or midwife. While this does not address the problem of women in coercive and abusive relationships, and those who are not in a position to choose for themselves, it enables and empowers many women to make their own reproductive choice.

As movement was banned across borders, and fertility clinics were closed as infertility treatment was not considered an essential medical procedure, I dread to think of the impact on the mental health of individuals undergoing fertility treatments in the UK and especially those moving across borders in Europe and elsewhere, with their embryos lying frozen waiting for the lockdown regulations to be lifted. Dr Geeta Nargund, Director of Create Fertility clinic, wrote in April 2020 that this had a huge impact on the mental health of women, increasing severe anxiety and suicidal thoughts.[11] While the World Health Organization classifies infertility as a disease, it has still not been accepted that IVF is an essential medical treatment for many women. Infertility treatments continue to be seen as a luxury and a privilege. In actively choosing to have children using artificial medical treatments, women are seen as stepping outside the acceptable social norms. In not being able to reproduce naturally, these women's bodies are not normal, and therefore seen as either privileged or deviant. In either case, these do not fulfil the societal definition of essential medical treatment, because even in trying to become a mother, a role that society idolises and expects of all women, they are perceived as outliers because of their reproductive inadequacy. These women are neither here nor there, a no man's land not deemed essential.

There is a lack of equal representation of women in decision-making around the outbreak. According to the latest report by United Nations Population Fund, this power imbalance can be reflected in the response to the crisis at a national and global level, and whether women's autonomy over their sexual and reproductive decisions is made a priority.[12]

This is just the tip of the iceberg but what it shows is that across the world, women's bodies are increasingly coming under state control. The crisis is being used to control and regulate women, and impose restrictions on their freedom and autonomy.

•

I think of the losses and gains through the years. My choices, my decisions.

I still think of the woman who gave birth to my children. I think of her often. I wonder how she is doing, and whether she is okay, happy and healthy. I wonder if her own children are thriving and giving her as much pleasure as mine are giving to us. She made a choice to not be in our lives, but she will be in my life forever.

I often wonder why I persisted with the fertility treatments and with surrogacy. Maybe I love P too much; maybe if I didn't love him as much, I would have let all this go sooner. I don't know. I am overthinking it all. Yes, throughout this process, and since then, I have been acutely aware of how privileged we are – I am. I could decide to terminate a pregnancy, and could afford to get private healthcare for it to avoid the queues and discomfort, to seek anonymity. We could afford the different cycles of the treatment and the cost of transnational surrogacy, putting our lives and jobs here in the UK on hold while we lived in India for almost five months. We live in the UK, where the healthcare system, however flawed, is still better than those in so many other parts of the world. We have a car; we have relatively easy access to clinics. And we have come through it, still somehow together, now a family unit of five. Even though as a brown woman, I have faced medical and healthcare bias, I am a cisgendered woman, educated and likely to demand and achieve better care for myself than many others.

I am angry for the trans people who are regularly dehumanised by the healthcare system, treated like pariahs, misgendered and shamed. I feel livid for black women, who have one of the highest maternal mortality rates. I am distraught for the many women who have been sterilised without their consent, or who have their reproductive cycles monitored, or who cannot seek abortion due to religious or legal barriers. I ache for those women who are forced into childbirth, who have no access to reproductive health, to basic menstrual products, to contraception, to fertility treatments. I am indignant on behalf of women who have to internalise all the shame and stigma, never daring to share their pain and suffering of infertility because of societal taboo. I am angry about so much, and grateful for considerably more. But the fact that I am grateful makes me angry too. Because women should not be grateful. Because autonomy should be – and is – a fundamental human right.

Today, 65 per cent of women worldwide have access to some form of contraception and deaths during pregnancy and childbirth have dropped 45 per cent since 1990.[13] But as we look at the broader global picture, we realise that these gains are not distributed equally. All the choices are presented to women as a shiny assortment, attractive and plentiful, but in the end, they are all just pale possibilities.

Access to reproductive health is shaped by an interplay of multiple factors: economic status, sex, gender identity, sexuality, education, social status and age – adolescents have less access compared with older age groups. Fear of discrimination by doctors, and lack of confidentiality, can act as major barriers to accessing reproductive health services. The notion of self, identity as a woman in a specific context, and collective responsibility also affect agency.[14] Even when we talk about agency we forget that women experience reproduction differently along race and class lines. If we centre the discourse around reproductive 'choice', it does not explain all women's experiences, particularly those who may be denied sex education, subjected to racialised sexual stigma, have their fertility surveilled and controlled by the state.

Any reproductive oppression is not experienced symmetrically; rather it is intersectional, a factor of a person's multiple identities. While such oppression can be explicit such as illegal abortions, forced sterilisation, abuse, reproductive coercion, policies that cap childbearing in families, it can also manifest in the form of implicit coercion with bias and prejudice from healthcare providers where women of colour are more likely to be pressured by medical professionals to follow a rigorous contraception plan and monitor their childbearing. There is also the fear of racism against our children and how that affects our choices and decisions about becoming a mother. As we talk about reproductive rights – the rights of individuals to decide whether or not to have children – we need to remind ourselves how much of this movement has been rooted in white supremacy. Reproductive justice is a more inclusive and intersectional approach to take, a framework that asserts the human right to maintain personal bodily autonomy, have children, not have children, and parent the children we have in safe communities. It brings focus to marginalised communities, those who are most harmed due to the barriers in reproductive health, and those who are also most at risk of sexual and reproductive violence. And even as we talk about how so much reproductive injustice is based in patriarchy and operates on male supremacy, benefiting cis men, it is still limited by an outdated understanding of the gender binary. Reproductive inequalities affect those whose lives are outside the binary framework and we cannot discuss autonomy without considering the intersectional aspects of its effects on trans, non-binary, agender and gender non-conforming people.

While writing this book, as the Black Lives Matter debate flares up around me with the murders of George Floyd and Breonna Taylor in the USA, and we are able to talk about racism in a more honest way for the first time, I regularly re-examine my own position on the fringes as a brown woman, and the feeling of being the 'other': a feeling that we – persons of colour – often carry around with us as a heavy backpack. Women of colour will always stand as an 'other' when it comes to mothering: disadvantaged in access to healthcare, contraception and abortion; limited in their autonomy and agency; more likely to face complications and death during childbirth and pregnancy; subject to the systemic and structural racism that permeates society; and judged more severely in their mothering than their white counterparts. Women of colour also often face increased pressure from the community to conceive and become a mother, while silence and shame around any failure to conceive naturally or the termination of a pregnancy act as coercive mechanisms, pilfering any reproductive agency.

In the positioning of pregnancy in celebrity culture and now enveloping most pregnancies on social media, a singular notion of femininity is framed. Whiteness is still a norm. While celebrities such as Beyoncé are disrupting the ideals of womanhood by bringing black and 'non-white' bodies to the forefront, in all their messiness and supposed unruliness, but by conflating sexiness and maternity, they are still to a large extent – even in their transgression –

conforming to the dominant narrative of air-brushed maternal imagery. Much of the motherhood representations that we continue to see are beatific images, of honey-hued, idealised lives: white, beautiful, slim, straight and middle-class.

With the rise of momfluencers on Instagram, we have also seen how motherhood is becoming a brand identity and part of the global capitalist culture, while also misleading women that they can really 'have it all'. We have seen 'mommy wars', the toxic school-gate rivalries, and motherhood becoming a competition. There is a trend towards women giving up their jobs to home-school their children, give them a 'natural' lifestyle, cook all meals from scratch with organic ingredients. And there is a return to domestic femininity as an idealised form of womanhood and motherhood. Guilt, and invisibility of other forms of motherhood, of women of colour and of trans-gressive bodies, flourish in this culture of 'mom-shaming'. Women – and mothers – continue to be judged by a very specific yardstick. The narrative women are being fed is not just about how they 'need' to be a mother, but also on the performance of being a mother, and a very specific way of 'doing' motherhood. It is exhausting.

Yes, it has recently become more acceptable to say that you are struggling with childcare, that mothering is often very mundane, that it is stress- and anxiety-inducing, and that often one does not enjoy it. We are also, thankfully, having broader conversations around post-natal depression and anxiety, and about post-partum psychosis. And women are, against societal expectations and norms, attempting to shatter the myth of a perfect mother.

Nevertheless, any gains for reproductive rights seem reversible and very slow to come by. We are still fighting for inches gained one day and lost the next. We are very far from having true autonomy and agency. So far. But as M decides not to have any children, tells me very resolutely that she,* never will, that her choices are not shaped by the constraints placed on mothers, and that she does not feel forced to choose one or the other 'self', I hope that she believes, truly, that her choice to be a mother or not can be exercised independently of any choices that society – and her biology – impose on women. I hope that, if she exercises her choice to not be a mother, she is not rebelling against gender-conforming identities that she feels boxed into by forces beyond her control. And I very sincerely hope that along the way, she does not succumb to the pressures to be a mother because of a sense of urgency from her body-clock or the messages she gets from media, friends, family.

I hope that it remains her conscious choice, and her free will.

•

I have been looking for belonging, a sense of place, my complete self throughout my life, not feeling like I fit in anywhere, uncomfortable in my body and my being, straddling worlds and words, language and emotions at all times, being many different versions of myself. I resisted motherhood, avoided it, capitulated to it. But in the end, it was being a mother that has been my saving grace, allowing me to reconcile all my different selves.

And suddenly, just like that, I don't need to search for a place to belong. I belong to myself as much as these children belong to themselves. I see my whole history stretching out behind me holding me close and safe. And in some ways that is a relief.

While I was trying so hard to make sure my children belonged to me, it became apparent that they will always only ever belong to

---

* As I'm completing this book, M is exploring non-binary identity.

themselves. And, of course, even though we are used to seeing them as one unit: the twins, the babies, they, them, the girls, my children, they are each unique: so intertwined but so specific. So exquisite, tender, fierce: shaped perfectly in their distinctiveness.

Although I have worried about my right to be their mother, all that truly matters is their right to be their own person.

Their bodies; their privilege. No external gaze; no scrutiny. No shame imposed; no transformation wrested. No elegies to lives unlived, and life unfulfilled. No one carving out a life for them; they carve themselves.

Only a world unzipped for them to expand their selves, claiming infinity.

They claim themselves. I claim myself. You claim yourself.

An incantation, a prayer, a charm. An ultimatum; urgent demand. For today and aeons to come.

AUTHOR'S NOTE

THIS BOOK SITS SOMEWHERE BETWEEN a memoir and a scientific and historical disquisition of women's reproductive choices and infertility. This has potentially triggering themes of abortion, miscarriage and infertility. But I write about them because we need to. We need to normalise these conversations, outside our comfort zone. If we do not sit with our discomfort, we cannot change things. We cannot question and challenge conventions. And so here I am. And here you are. Thank you.

As I was completing this book, I saw a campaign on Twitter by an app to encourage people to have cervical smears. You might have seen it too. It used the analogy of a 'pussy', featuring cats in their graphics, asking people to 'share an image of the cat that best reflects your undercarriage/flower/bits,'(technical term vulva!) current look'. Infantilising and body-shaming language, awkwardness around using the correct scientific terms, ignorance of how pain and trauma can often be the reason why people do not go for cervical smears. I hope we can move past this. There is a long way to go, but hopefully this book starts (and continues) this much-needed conversation around women's bodies, what makes a family (and home), and how

343

we allow women the space to make their own choices about their own bodies and fertility. And hopefully the intersectional discussion in this book helps challenge the norms around words and language that can be a barrier in achieving reproductive justice for all.

Memories can never be reliable, but I have tried my best to represent my story as I remember it over the last thirty years or so. Other people sharing this journey with me might have experienced it differently and remember it some other way. That is not to say that they are correct, or I am. We all create snapshots of the world, this mental model, a databank of experiences and memories, specific and unique to us. I can only tell this story as I remember it.

Some names, places and identifying details have been changed to protect my family and other individuals.

ACKNOWLEDGEMENTS

I READ SOMEWHERE THAT THE ACKNOWLEDGEMENTS section in a book is a statement of the privileges that an author has: the team that makes a book possible, the luxury of time and space, the peace and quiet that is impossible for some, tools and equipment, networks and peer group, mentors and allies. A book might be my words, but I could not have done this alone. So, here I want to recognise and acknowledge my privileges. All of them.

My agent. Robert, who has held my hand through this whole process, and who always has my back.

My team at Canongate. My wonderful editor Hannah, who is really the very best; Anna, who championed the book tirelessly; Vicki, who patiently went through numerous rounds of proofs with me; and, to Vicki (W), Leila, Aa'Ishah.

My family, our DNA tangled together with love, who are my dil, jaan, jigar. My husband first and foremost for taking this path with me, for sticking by me, for not giving up on me even when I gave up on myself.

The women in my family: my mother, my two sisters, my three daughters — the strongest people I know.

Our surrogate, to whom we will be eternally indebted.

And, finally my father. A man amongst four women in our house, he was unlike any man I have known. Imperfect, and so loved. I miss him every single day.

RESOURCES

Note: I have not used all these services personally. However, I have tried to include those that appear to be most inclusive.

Abortion Rights IE Qouted in: https://www.abortionrightscampaign.ie, @freesafelegal

Abortion Support Network: https://www.asn.org.uk

At Your Cervix: @AtYourCervix_x

Brilliant Beginnings: https://www.brilliantbeginnings.co.uk

British Fertility Society: https://www.britishfertilitysociety.org.uk

British Pregnancy Advisory Service: https://www.bpas.org

Brook Young People's Information Service: https://www.brook.org.uk

CARE Fertility: https://www.carefertility.com

Children and Family Court Advisory and Support Service: https://www.cafcass.gov.uk

CliniQ: https://www.cliniq.org.uk

Endometriosis UK: https://www.endometriosis-uk.org

Engender Scotland: https://www.engender.org.uk

The Eve Appeal: https://www.eveappeal.org.uk

Fertility Network UK: https://www.fertilitynetworkuk.org

Growing Families: https://www.growingfamilies.org

International Council on Infertility Information Dissemination (INCIID): https://www.inciid.org

International Planned Parenthood Federation: https://www.ippf.org

Natalie Gamble, NGA Law: https://www.ngalaw.co.uk/meet-our-team/natalie-gamble

National Center for Transgender Equality: https://www.transequality.org

National Institute for Health and Care Excellence: https://www.cks.nice.org.uk/topics/infertility

National Network of Abortion Funds: https://www.abortionfunds.org

National Women's Health Network: https://www.nwhn.org

Outspoken Sex Ed: https://www.outspokeneducation.com

Professor Geeta Nargund, Create Fertility: https://www.createfertility.co.uk/about/meet-our-team/members/professor-geeta-nargund

See Her Thrive: https://www.seeherthrive.com

Split Banana: https://www.splitbanana.co.uk

Surrogacy UK: https://www.surrogacyuk.org

Trans Fertility Co.: https://www.transfertility.co

Trans Student Educational Resources: https://www.transstudent.org

Terrence Higgins Trust: https://www.tht.org.uk

United States Surrogacy: https://www.creativefamilyconnections.com

ENDNOTES

INTRODUCTION

1 Swir, A. (1996). *Talking to my Body*. Washington: Copper Canyon Press.

2 Definitions from the Oxford English Dictionary.

3 Swir, *Talking to my Body*. Washington: Copper Canyon Press.

4 Cusk, R. (2001). *A Life's Work*. Faber & Faber.

5 Friedmann, J. (10 May 2019). 'Motherhood Is a Political Category'. *Medium*. https://humanparts.medium.com/motherhood-is-a-political-category-5b5be72b5531

6 Rich, A. (1977). *Of Woman Born: Motherhood as Experience and Institution*. W.W. Norton & Company.

7 Weil, S. (2001). *The Need for Roots: Prelude to a Declaration of Duties Towards Mankind*, Routledge 2nd Edn.

8 Shaughnessy, B. (2010). *Our Andromeda*. Washington: Copper Canyon Press.

9 O'Brien, M. (1981). *The Politics of Reproduction*. London, Boston and Henley: Routledge & Kegan Paul.

10 Schmidt, S. (16 August 2019). 'A Mother, but not a Woman'. *Washington Post.*

11 Foucault, M. (1978). *The History of Sexuality: Volume 1, An Introduction.* Translated by R. Hurley. New York: Pantheon Books.

CHAPTER I

1 Brown Sherborn, F. (1925). 'Preparing the Girl for Motherhood'. *The Iowa Homemaker.* 5 (7), Article 9.

2 Martin, E. (1991). 'The Egg and the Sperm: How science has constructed a romance based on stereotypical male–female roles. *Signs: Journal of Women in Culture and Society.* 16 (31), 485–501.

3 Campo-Engelstein, L. & Johnson, N.L. (2014). 'Revisiting "The fertilization fairytale": an analysis of gendered language used to describe fertilization in science textbooks from middle school to medical school'. *Cultural Studies of Science Education.* 9, 201–220.

4 Wassarman, P.M. (1999). 'Mammalian fertilization: Molecular aspects of gamete adhesion, exocytosis, and fusion'. *Cell.* 96, 175–183.

5 de Beauvoir, S. (1989). *The Second Sex.* Translated by H.M. Parshley. New York: Vintage.

6 Metoyer, A.B. & Rust, R. (2011). 'The egg, sperm, and beyond: gendered assumptions in gynecology textbooks'. *Women's Studies.* 40 (2), 177–205.

7 Pabst, K., Cépeda, P. et al. (2018). 'Gender bias in linguistics textbooks: Has anything changed since Macaulay & Brice (1997)?' Annual Meeting of the Linguistic Society of America. Salt Lake City, UT.

8 Lawrence, S.C., & Bendixen, K. (1992). 'His and Hers: Male and female anatomy in anatomy texts for US medical students, 1890–1989'. *Social Science and Medicine.* 35 (7), 925–934.

9 Moore, L.J. & Clarke, A.E. (1995). 'Clitorial conventions and

transgressions: Graphic representations in anatomy texts, c. 1900–1991'. *Feminist Studies.* 21 (2), 255–301.

10 Braun, V. & Kitzinger, C. (2001). 'The perfectible vagina: Size matters', *Culture, Health & Sexuality.* 3:3, 263–277.

11 Lloyd, E.A. (2005). *The Case of the Female Orgasm: Bias in the science of evolution.* Cambridge, MA: Harvard University Press.

12 Doan, A.E. & Williams, J.C. (2008). *The Politics of Virginity: Abstinence in sex education.* Westport, CT: Praeger.

13 Bergvall, V.L., Bing, J.M. & Freed, A.F. (eds). (1996). *Rethinking Language and Gender Research: Theory and Practice.* London and New York: Longman.

14 *Menstrual Health in India, Country Landscape Analysis.* Report sponsored by the Bill and Melinda Gates Foundation, 2016. National Family Health Survey 2015–16 available from the World Bank.

15 Dasra is one of many new NGOs in India challenging taboos associated with menstruation and working with local government and international partners through grassroot and media campaigns.

16 Pruthi, S. (2012). 'The Case of Goonj'. *Contemporary Issues in Entrepreneurship Research.* Volume 2, 1–24. See also: Goonj Blog, 24 August 2020. https://goonj.org/not-just-a-piece-of-cloth/

17 Doniger, W. & Smith, B.K. (1991). *The Laws of Manu.* London: Penguin Books.

18 Oudshoorn, Merel. (18 April 2019). 'Indian Temples, Pollution and Menstruating Women', Leiden Arts in Society blog, https://leidenarts-insocietyblog.nl/articles/indian-temples-pollution-and-menstruating-women.

19 Jones, I.H. (6 March 1980). 'Menstruation: the Curse of Eve'. *Nursing Times.* 76 (10), 404–6.

20 Green, M. (2000). 'From "Diseases of Women" to "Secrets of Women": The Transformation of Gynecological Literature in the

Later Middle Ages'. *Journal of Medieval and Early Modern Studies*. 30 (1), 5–39.

21 Clancy, K. (2011). 'Menstruation is just blood and tissue you ended up not using'. *Scientific American* blog.

22 McCracken, P. (2003). *The Curse of Eve, the Wound of the Hero Blood, Gender, and Medieval Literature*. Pennsylvania: University of Pennsylvania Press.

23 Quoted in Webster, S. (2017). 'The History of the Curse: A Comparative Look at the Religious and Social Taboos of Menstruation and the Influence They Have on American Society Today', Charlotte: University of North Carolina.

24 Clancy, K. (2011). 'Menstruation Is Just Blood and Tissue You Ended Up Not Using'. *Scientific American* blog.

25 Macht, D.I. & Lubin, D.S. (1923). 'A Phyto-Pharmacological Study of Menstrual Toxin'. *Journal of Pharmacology and Experimental Therapeutics*. 22 (5) 413–466.

26 Rozin, P., Haidt, J. et al. (1999). 'Individual Differences in Disgust Sensitivity: Comparisons and Evaluations of Paper-and-Pencil versus Behavioral Measures'. *Journal of Research in Personality*. 33 (3).

27 Roberts, T.A., Goldenberg, J.L. et al. (2002). '"Feminine Protection": The Effects of Menstruation on Attitudes Towards Women'. *Psychology of Women Quarterly*. 26 (2), 131–139.

28 The research, which was commissioned by THINX, an innovative period solutions company and makers of period-proof underwear, was reported in the *New York Post* on 3 January 2018 by Valerie Siebert.

29 Freidenfelds, L. (2009). *The Modern Period: Menstruation in Twentieth-Century America*. Maryland: Johns Hopkins University Press.

30 Commons, J. (13 September 2018). '"I felt my body was wrong": the women who don't have periods'. Refinery29, www.refinery29.com/en-gb/absence-of-menstruation.

31 Atkins, C. (11 January 2020). 'For transgender men, pain of menstruation is more than just physical', NBC News, https://www.nbcnews.com/feature/nbc-out/transgender-men-pain-menstruation-more-just-physical-n1113961.

32 Steinem, G. (2019). 'If Men Could Menstruate', *Women's Reproductive Health*, 6: 3, 151–2.

33 Chrisler, J.C. (2011). 'Leaks, Lumps, and Lines: Stigma and Women's Bodies'. *Psychology of Women Quarterly*. 35 (2): 202–14.

CHAPTER II

1 *The Hymns of the Rigveda*. (1892). Translated with a Popular Commentary by R.T.H. Griffith, E.J. Benares, India: Lazarus & Co.

2 Aiken, A.R.A., Dillaway, C. & Mevs-Korff, N. (2015). 'A blessing I can't afford: Factors underlying the paradox of happiness about unintended pregnancy'. *Social Science & Medicine*, 132, 149–55.

3 The series of questions used to measure intention status in the National Survey of Family Growth (NSFG) grew out of earlier knowledge, attitude and practice surveys that had been systematically refined in the period just after World War II.

4 Trussell, J., Vaughan, B., & Stanford, J. (1999). 'Are all contraceptive failures unintended pregnancies? Evidence from the 1995 National Survey of Family Growth'. *Family Planning Perspectives*. 31 (5): 246–60.

5 Rich, A. (1995). *Of Woman Born: Motherhood as Experience and Institution*. Norton.

6 Enright, Anne. (2005). *Making Babies*. London: Vintage.

7 Baldi, P. (1983). An *Introduction to the Indo-European Languages*. Illinois: Southern Illinois University Press.

8 Hyde, Lewis. (2019). *A Primer for Forgetting: Getting Past the Past*. Edinburgh: Canongate.

9 Plath, S. 'Medusa'.

10 O'Brien Hallstein, L. (2015). *Bikini-ready Moms: Celebrity profiles, motherhood and the body*. Albany: State University of New York Press.

11 Barr, S. (2019) 'Megan Markle admits feeling vulnerable.' *The Independent*, 18 October 2019.

12 Hearn, K. (2020). *Portraying Pregnancy: From Holbein to Social Media*. London: Paul Holberton Publishing. Published to accompany an exhibition of the same name.

13 Quoted in: Allara, P. (1994). '"Mater" of Fact: Alice Neel's Pregnant Nudes'. *American Art*, 8 (2), 7–31.

14 Tyler, I. (2011). 'Pregnant Beauty: Maternal Femininities under Neoliberalism', in R. Gill and C. Scharff (eds), *New Femininities: Postfeminism, Neoliberalism and Subjectivity*. Basingstoke: Palgrave MacMillan, 21–36.

15 Musial, J. (2014). 'From "Madonna" to "Whore": Sexuality, pregnancy, and popular culture'. *Sexualities*. 17 (4), 394–411.

16 hooks, b. (1992). Quoted in *Black Looks: Race and Representation*. Boston: South End Press, 115–31. https://theconversation.com/how-beyonce-pregnancy-pics-challenge-racist-religious-and-sexual-stereotypes-72429

17 McNish, H. (2016). *Nobody Told Me: Poetry and Parenthood*. London: Fleet.

18 Kohli, A. (2016). 'Examining middle-class women's reproductive agency in collective and patriarchal settings of urban northern India'. *Women's Studies Journal*, 30 (2), 23–37.

19 Young, I.M. (2003). 'The logic of masculinist protection: Reflections on the current security state'. *Signs*, 29 (1), 1–25.

20 Agarwal, B. (1994). *A Field of One's Own: Gender and land rights in South Asia*. Cambridge, England: Cambridge University Press.

21 Michaels, Paula (2014). *Lamaze: An International History*. New York: Oxford University Press.

22 Saleeby, C. (1909). *Parenthood and Race Culture: An outline of eugenics.* London: Cassell & Co (as quoted in Moscucci, O. (2002). 'Holistic obstetrics: the origins of "natural childbirth" in Britain', *Postgrad Med J* 2003;79:168–173).

23 Quoted in Eliane Glaser's review (4 June 2015) 'Tell her the truth', *London Review of Books*, 37 (11).

24 Chaplin, J.E. (2003). *Subject Matter: Technology, the Body, and Science on the Anglo-American Frontier, 1500–1676.* Cambridge, MA: Harvard University Press.

25 Dick-Read, G. (1933). *Natural Childbirth.* London: Heinemann.

26 Hrešanová, E. (2016). 'The Psychoprophylactic Method of Painless Childbirth in Socialist Czechoslovakia: from State Propaganda to Activism of Enthusiasts'. *Medical History.* 60 (4), 534–56.

27 Gurol-Urganci, I., Bou-Antoun, S. et al. (July 2013). 'Impact of Caesarean section on subsequent fertility: a systematic review and meta-analysis'. *Human Reproduction.* 28(7), 1943–52.

28 Kjerulff, K.H., Paul I.M. et al. (2020). 'Association Between Mode of First Delivery and Subsequent Fecundity and Fertility'. *JAMA Network Open.* 3 (4).

29 Swain, J.E., Tasgin, E. et al. (2008). 'Maternal Brain Response to Own Baby Cry Is Affected by Caesarean Section Delivery'. *The Journal of Child Psychology and Psychiatry.* 49 (10).

30 Spinner, M.R. (1978). 'Maternal–infant bonding'. *Canadian Family Physician / Medecin de Famille Canadien.* 24, 1151–3.

31 Loy, M. 'Parturition'. In *The Lost Lunar Baedeker*, edited by Conover, Roger. New York: Farrar Strauss and Giroux.

32 From 'I Wandered Lonely as a Cloud' by William Wordsworth.

33 George, A. (2002). *The Epic of Gilgamesh: A New Translation.* London: Penguin Classics.

34 Thomas, P. (25 April 2018). 'Calculating the Value of Human Life:

Safety Decisions that Can Be Trusted'. University of Bristol, Policy Report.

35 Appelbaum, B. (16 February 2011). 'As US Agencies Put More Value on a Life, Businesses Fret', *The New York Times*.

36 Partnoy, F. (2012). *Wait: The Useful Art of Procrastination*. London: Profile Books.

37 Viscusi, W.K. (2009). 'The Heterogeneity of the Value of Statistical Life: Introduction and Overview'. *Journal of Risk and Uncertainty*. 40, 1, 1–13.

38 World Health Organization. (19 September 2019). 'Maternal Mortality'. https://www.who.int/news-room/fact-sheets/detail/maternal-mortality.

CHAPTER III

1 Steinbeck, J. *East of Eden*. London: Penguin

2 Mullin, A. (2015). 'Early Pregnancy Losses: Multiple Meanings and Moral Considerations'. *Journal of Social Philosophy*, 46: 1.

3 Rocca, C.H., Kimport, K. et al. (2015). 'Decision Rightness and Emotional Responses to Abortion in the United States: A Longitudinal Study'. *PLOS ONE*. 10 (7).

4 Rocca, C.H., Samari, G. et al. (2020). 'Emotions and decision rightness over five years following an abortion: An examination of decision difficulty and abortion stigma', *Social Science & Medicine*, 248.

5 Biggs, M.A., Upadhyay, U.D. et al. (2017). 'Women's Mental Health and Well-being Five Years After Receiving or Being Denied an Abortion: A Prospective, Longitudinal Cohort Study'. *JAMA Psychiatry*. 74 (2), 169–78.

6 Mackenzie, D. (16 April 2019). 'Sex-selective abortions may have stopped the birth of 23 million girls'. *New Scientist*.

7 United Nations Populations Fund. (August 2012). 'Sex Imbalances at Birth: Current Trends and Policy Implications'.

8 Rich, A. (1996). *Of Woman Born: Motherhood as Experience and Institution*. London: W.W. Norton & Co.

9 From an interview in the *Guardian* with Emma Brockes, 17 October 2015.

10 Dannenfelser, M. (4 November 2015). 'The Suffragettes Would Not Agree With Feminists Today on Abortion', *TIME Magazine*.

11 From the Elizabeth Cady Stanton letters in the archives of the Library of Congress.

12 'Like Sarah Palin, Early Feminists Were Pro-Life'. (10 December 2010). US News online.

13 Blackwell, E. (1895). *Pioneer Work in Opening the Medical Profession to Women: Autobiographical Sketches*. London and New York: Longmans, Green and Co.

14 Borchelt, G. (1 August 2018). 'The Impact Poverty Has on Women's Health', *Human Rights Magazine*. American Bar Association, 43 (3).

15 From the Ministry of Justice 'Statistics on Women and the Criminal Justice System 2019', A Ministry of Justice publication under Section 95 of the Criminal Justice Act 1991. Accessed on 26 November 2020.

16 Abbott, L., Scott, T et al. (2020). 'Pregnancy and Childbirth in English Prisons: Institutional Ignominy and the Pains of Imprisonment'. *Sociology of Health & Illness*. 42 (3), 660–75.

17 Guttmacher Institute. (January 2020). 'Medicaid Funding of Abortion, State Policies in Brief'. https://www.guttmacher.org/evidence-you-can-use/medicaid-funding-abortion.

18 Kendi, Ibram X. (2019). *How to be an antiracist*. New York: One World.

19 Quoted in Douthat, R. (25 July 2020). 'The Ghost of Margaret Sanger: Planned Parenthood and the complexities of anti-racism'. *New York Times*.

20 Stewart, N. (21 July 2020). 'Planned Parenthood in N.Y. Disavows Margaret Sanger Over Eugenics', *New York Times*.

21 Dr Paul Fine, an ob-gyn and medical director of a Planned Parenthood affiliate serving Texas and Louisiana is quoted in his testimony in a trial over the 2013 law which required doctors performing abortions to have admitting privileges at local hospitals, quoted in Lyman, B. (21 May 2014). 'Doctor: Abortion safer than getting shot of penicillin'. *Montgomery Advertiser*.

22 Norris, S. (28 August 2020). 'Undercover in the anti-abortion movement: How abortion became a tool of white supremacists'. *Byline Times*.

23 Norris, S. (29 October 2019). 'Satanic conspiracies and Brexiteers: inside a bizarre "academy" for anti-abortion activists'. OpenDemocracy.

24 Glick, P. & Fiske, S.T. (1996). 'The Ambivalent Sexism Inventory: Differentiating hostile and benevolent sexism'. *Journal of Personality and Social Psychology*. 70, 491–512.

25 Duerksen, K.N. & Lawson, K.L. (December 2017). '"Not Brainwashed, but Heart-washed": A Qualitative Analysis of Benevolent Sexism in the Anti-Choice Stance'. *International Journal of Behavioural Medicine*. 24 (6), 864–70.

26 Osamor, P. & Grady, C. (January 2018). 'Factors Associated With Women's Health Care Decision-Making Autonomy: Empirical Evidence From Nigeria'. *Journal of Biosocial Science*. 50 (1), 70–85.

27 Reported by Debbie Sharnak, Argentina–Paraguay country specialist for Amnesty International, 14 May 2015.

28 Nick T. (4 March 2020). 'Why the Supreme Court Case on Abortion Access is a Queer Issue'. *Out*.

29 Penny, L. (17 May 2019). 'The Criminalisation of Women's Bodies Is All About Male Power'. *The New Republic*.

30 Bendavid, E., Avila, P. & Miller, G. (2011). 'United States aid policy

and induced abortion in sub-Saharan Africa'. World Health Organization.

31 Kirschen, M. (26 January 2017). 'Meet the French feminists behind a viral meme about a male ejaculation ban'. BuzzFeed News.

32 Ward, T. (1845). *England's Reformation: A Poem in Four Cantos*. London: D & J Sadler.

CHAPTER IV

1 Hurston, Z.N. (2006). *Their Eyes Were Watching God*. New York: Amistad.

2 Haas, N. (28 April 2011). 'Time to Chill? Egg-freezing Technology Offers Women a Chance to Extend Their Fertility'. *Vogue*.

3 Fertility Health Summit Survey: https://www.britishfertilitysociety. org.uk/2016/04/15/fertility-health-submit-survey-results/, 2016. Fertility Health Summit is a partnership between the British Fertility Society, Royal College of Obstetricians and Gynaecologists and the Faculty of Sexual and Reproductive Healthcare.

4 Sennott, C. & Yeatman, S. (2018). 'Conceptualizing Childbearing Ambivalence: A Social and Dynamic Perspective'. *Journal of Marriage and the Family*, 80 (4), 888–901.

5 Tornello, S.L. & Bos, H. (2017). 'Parenting Intentions Among Transgender Individuals'. *LGBT Health*. 4 (2), 115–20.

6 Chen, D., Matson, M., et al. (2018). 'Attitudes Toward Fertility and Reproductive Health Among Transgender and Gender-Nonconforming Adolescents'. *Journal of Adolescent Health*. 63 (1), 62–8.

7 Cheng, P.J., Pastuszak, A.W. et al. (2019). 'Fertility concerns of the transgender patient'. *Translational Andrology and Urology*. 8 (3), 209–18.

8 Koert, E., Harrison, C. et al. (2018). 'Causal explanations for lack of pregnancy applying the common-sense model of illness representation to the fertility context'. *Psychology & Health*. 33 (10), 1284–1301.

9   Jensen, A.M. (2016). 'Ideas about childbearing among childless men'. *Families, Relationships and Societies*. 5 (2), 193–207.

10 Mayo Clinic Staff, (20 June 2020). 'Male Menopause: Myth or Reality'.

11 Soules, M.R. (1 August 2003). 'The Story Behind the American Society for Reproductive Medicine's Prevention of Infertility Campaign', *Fertility and Sterility*. 80 (2), 295–9.

12 Ivens, S. (2015). 'Woman who delayed having children until her 30s reveals heartbreak of trying for a family . . . and urges other women NOT to leave motherhood so late', *Daily Mail* Online.

13 Hope, J. (11 December 2013). 'Dangers of delaying motherhood until 30: Don't think the risks begin at 35, say researchers'. *Daily Mail* Online.

14 Waldenström, U., Aasheim, V. et al. (January 2014). 'Adverse pregnancy outcomes related to advanced maternal age compared with smoking and being overweight'. *Obstetrics and Gynecology*. 123 (1), 104–12.

15 Aasheim, V., Waldenström, U. et al. (27 February 2013). 'Experience of childbirth in first-time mothers of advanced age – a Norwegian population-based study'. *BMC Pregnancy Childbirth*. 13, 53.

16 David B. Dunson, Bernardo Colombo, Donna D. Baird. (May 2002). 'Changes with age in the level and duration of fertility in the menstrual cycle.' *Human Reproduction*, 17 (5), 1399–1403.

17 Sun, F., Sebastiani, P. et al. (2015). 'Extended maternal age at birth of last child and women's longevity in the Long Life Family Study'. *Menopause*. 22 (1), 26–31.

18 Rothman, K.J., Wise, L.A. et al. (2013). 'Volitional determinants and age-related decline in fecundability: a general population prospective cohort study in Denmark'. *Fertility and Sterility*. 99 (7), 1958–64.

19 Steiner, A.Z. & Jukic, A.M. (2016). 'Impact of female age and nulligra-

vidity on fecundity in an older reproductive age cohort'. *Fertility and Sterility*. 105 (6), 1584–8.

20 Mahey, R., Gupta, M. et al. (2018). 'Fertility awareness and knowledge among Indian women attending an infertility clinic: a cross-sectional study'. *BMC Women's Health*. 18 (1), 177.

21 Ojanuga, D. (1993). 'The medical ethics of the "Father of Gynaecology", Dr J. Marion Sims'. *Journal of Medical Ethics*. 19, 28–31.

22 Manson, J.M., Sammel, M.D. et al. (2001). 'Racial differences in sex hormone levels in women approaching the transition to menopause'. *Fertility and Sterility*. 75 (2), 297–304.

23 Hewlett, Sylvia A. (2002). *Creating a Life: Professional Women and the Quest for Children*. New York: Miramax Books.

24 From an article by Sherman J. Silber for The Infertility Centre of St Louis. Last accessed 30 August 2020.

25 Quoted in Canavan, C. (January 28, 2019). 'What a Reproductive Expert Wants You to Know about Getting Pregnant in Your 30s'. *Women's Health Magazine*.

26 Phillips, N., Taylor, L. & Bachmann, G. (2019). 'Maternal, infant and childhood risks associated with advanced paternal age: The need for comprehensive counseling for men'. *Maturitas*. 125, 81–4.

27 Zhu, J.L., Madsen, K.M. et al. (November 2005). 'Paternal age and congenital malformations'. *Human Reproduction*. 20 (11), 3173–7.

28 From BioNews (7 July 2008). Dr Stephanie Belloc presented the work to the European Society of Human Reproduction and Embryology (ESHRE) conference in Barcelona.

29 Accessed on 1 September 2020.

30 Jamie Grifo, Program Director, New York University (NYU) Langone Fertility Center, as quoted in a course on Fertility IQ: https://www.fertilityiq.com/egg-freezing/the-costs-of-egg-freezing.

CHAPTER V

1 Paterson, B.L., Backmund, M. et al. (2007). 'The depiction of stig-matization in research about hepatitis C'. *International Journal of Drug Policy*. 18, 364–73.

2 Fast Facts About Infertility. Available at: http://www.resolve.org/about/fast-facts-about-fertility.html. Resolve: The National Fertility Association. Accessed 26 July 2020.

3 Wischmann, T.H. (2003). 'Psychogenic Infertility – Myths and Facts'. *Journal of Assisted Reproduction and Genetics*. 20 (12).

4 Lynch, C.D., Sundaram, R. et al. (2014). 'Pre-conception stress increases the risk of infertility: results from a couple-based prospective cohort study – the LIFE study'. *Human Reproduction*. 29 (5), 1067–75.

5 Chen T.H., Chang S.P. et al. (2004). 'Prevalence of depressive and anxiety disorders in an assisted reproductive technique clinic'. *Human Reproduction*. 19 (10), 2313–18.

6 Sejbaek, C.S., Hageman I. et al. (2013). 'Incidence of depression and influence of depression on the number of treatment cycles and births in a national cohort of 42,880 women treated with ART'. *Human Reproduction*. 28 (4), 1100–09.

7 Pasch, L.A., Holley, S.R. et al. (2016). 'Addressing the needs of fertility treatment patients and their partners: are they informed of and do they receive mental health services?' *Fertility and Sterility*. 106 (1), 209–15.

8 Shani, C., Yelena, S. et al. (2016). 'Suicidal risk among infertile women undergoing in-vitro fertilization: Incidence and risk factors'. *Psychiatry Research*. 240, 53–9.

9 Stone, L. (16 May 2018). 'Baby Bust: Fertility Is Declining the Most Among Minority Women'. Institute for Family Studies.

10 Sweeney, M.M. & Raley, R.K. (2014). 'Race, Ethnicity, and the

Changing Context of Childbearing in the United States'. *Annual Review of Sociology*. 40, 539–58.

11 Chandra, A., Copen, C.E. & Stephen, E.H. (22 January 2014). 'Infertility Service Use in the United States: Data From the National Survey of Family Growth, 1982–2010'. National Health Statistics Reports, No. 73.

12 Ethics Committee of the American Society for Reproductive Medicine. (2013). 'Access to fertility treatment by gays, lesbians, and unmarried persons: a committee opinion'. *Fertility and Sterility.* 100, 1524–7.

13 From the Arden Shakespeare edition, 2019.

14 Michas, F. (5 January 2021). 'Registered doctors in the United Kingdom in 2020, by gender and specialty'. Statista.com.

15 Steiner, A.Z., Pritchard, D. et al. (2017). 'Association Between Biomarkers of Ovarian Reserve and Infertility Among Older Women of Reproductive Age'. *JAMA.* 318 (14), 1367–76.

16 Tsatskis, Y., Rosenfeld, R. et al. (2020). 'The NEMP family supports metazoan fertility and nuclear envelope stiffness'. *Science Advances.* 6 (35).

17 Everywoman, J. (2013). 'Cassandra's prophecy: why we need to tell the women of the future about age-related fertility decline and "delayed" childbearing'. *Reproductive Biomedicine Online.* 27 (1), 4–10.

18 From Aeschylus, *Agamemnon*, the Harvard Classics. (1909–14), lines 1242–5. Accessed online at https://www.bartleby.com/8/1/3.html on 4 December 2020.

19 From Aeschylus, *Agamemnon*, the Harvard Classics. (1909–14), lines 1126–8. Accessed online on 28 August 2020.

CHAPTER VI

1 Sandelowski, M. & de Lacey, S. (2002). 'The Uses of a "Disease": Infertility as Rhetorical Vehicle'. In *Infertility around the Globe: New*

Thinking on Childlessness, Gender, and Reproductive Technologies, ed. Marcia C. Inhorn and Frank van Balen (Berkeley: University of California Press, 2002), 33–51.

2 Flemming, R. (2013). 'The invention of infertility in the classical Greek world: medicine, divinity, and gender'. *Bulletin of the History of Medicine*. 87 (4), 565–90.

3 Ibid.

4 Smith, W.D. (1979). *The Hippocratic Tradition*. Ithaca, NY: Cornell University Press.

5 Quoted in Flemming, R. (2013).

6 Lee, R. (1871). *A Treatise on Hysteria*. London: Churchill.

7 Gilman, S.L., King, H. et al. (1993). *Hysteria Beyond Freud*. Berkeley: University of California Press.

8 Virgil. *Aeneid*, 3.216. (1910). Translated by Theodore C. Williams. Boston: Houghton Mifflin Co.

9 From Henry Wadsworth Longfellow's translation of Dante's *Inferno*, Project Gutenberg.

10 The 'Kahun Medical Papyrus' or 'Gynaecological Papyrus'. Translation by Stephen Quirke. Petrie Museum of Egyptian Archaeology. UC 32057, page 1–2, 2002. Retrieved from online archives, June 15, 2020.

11 Ibid.

12 Frymer-Kensky, T. (1977). 'The Atrahasis Epic and Its Significance for Our Understanding of Genesis 1–9'. *The Biblical Archaeologist*. 40 (4), 147–55.

13 Leichty, E. (1971). 'Demons and Population Control'. *Expedition Magazine*. 13 (2) Penn Museum.

14 Conybeare, F.C. (October 1898). 'The Testament of Solomon'. *The Jewish Quarterly Review*. University of Pennsylvania Press. 11 (1), 1–45.

15 From the Testament of Solomon (translated from the Codex of the Paris Library, after the edition of Fleck, Wissensch, Reise) Conybeare.

16 On the medical aspects of infertility see McLaren, A. (1984). *Reproductive Rituals: The Perception of Fertility in England from the Sixteenth to the Nineteenth Century*. London & New York, NY: Methuen; Evans, J. (2011). "'Gentle Purges Corrected with Hot Spices, Whether They Work or Not, Do Vehemently Provoke Venery"': Menstrual Provocation and Procreation in Early Modern England'. *Social History of Medicine*. Oren-Magidor, D. (2012). "'Make me a Fruitfull Vine"': Dealing with Infertility in Early Modern England'. (PhD dissertation, Brown University)

17 Oren-Magidor, D. (2015). 'From Anne to Hannah: Religious Views of Infertility in Post-Reformation England'. *Journal of Women's History*. 27 (3), 86–108.

18 Sennert, D. (1664). *Practical Physick; The Fourth Book*. Quoted in: Evans, J. (May 2016). "'They Are Called Imperfect Men"': Male Infertility and Sexual Health in Early Modern England'. *Social History of Medicine*. 29, (2), 311–32.

19 Gowing, L. (2003). *Common Bodies: Women, Touch and Power in Seventeenth-Century England*. New Haven and London: Yale University Press, 115.

20 Oliver, J. (1688). *A Present to be Given to Teeming Women*. London. p.3.

21 Sharp, J. (1671). *The Midwives Book, Or, the Whole Art of Midwifry Discovered*. London. p.16.

22 Chaplin, J.E. (2003). *Subject Matter: Technology, the Body, and Science on the Anglo-American Frontier, 1500–1676*. Cambridge, MA: Harvard University Press.

23 Moore, L. (20 August 2012). 'Rep. Todd Akin: The Statement and the Reaction'. *New York Times*.

24 Tønnessen, L. (2015). 'Women's Right to Abortion after Rape in Sudan'. CMI Insight, Norwegian Centre for Humanitarian Studies. Accessed online 29 November 2020.

25 de Boer, M.L., Archetti, C. & Solbraekke, K.N. (2019). 'In/Fertile Monsters: The Emancipatory Significance of Representations of Women on Infertility Reality TV'. *Journal of Medical Humanities.*

26 Chandra, A., Copen, C.E. & Stephen, E.H. (2014). 'Infertility service use in the United States: data from the National Survey of Family Growth, 1982–2010'. *National Health Statistics Reports.* 22, 1–21.

27 Nsiah-Jefferson, L. & Hall, E.J. (1989). 'Reproductive Technology: Perspectives and Implications for Low-Income Women and Women of Color'. In Ratcliff, K.S. et al. (eds.) *Healing Technology: Feminist Perspectives.* Ann Arbor: University of Michigan Press.

28 Inhorn, M.C. (2012). *The New Arab Man: Emergent Masculinities, Technologies, and Islam in the Middle East.* Princeton: Princeton University Press.

29 Greil, A.L., McQuillan, J. et al. (2010). 'The hidden infertile: infertile women without pregnancy intent in the United States'. *Fertility and Sterility.* 93, 2080–3

30 Lo, W., Campo-Engelstein, L. (2018). 'Expanding the Clinical Definition of Infertility to Include Socially Infertile Individuals and Couples'. In: Campo-Engelstein L., Burcher P. (eds) *Reproductive Ethics II.*

31 Fledderjohann, J. & Barnes, L.W. (January 2018). 'Reimagining infertility: a critical examination of fertility norms, geopolitics and survey bias'. *Health Policy and Planning.* 33 (1), 34.

32 On *BBC Culture Show*, September 2011.

33 Connors, K. & Bayley, S. (eds) (2007). *Eye Rhymes: Sylvia Plath's Art of the Visual.* Oxford: Oxford University Press.

34 The Arden Shakespeare Edition. (1998) London: Bloomsbury.

35 Quoted in Alfano, B. 'The Honest Truth: Ferrante's Frantumaglia'. Arcade, Stanford University. https://arcade.stanford.edu/content/honest-truth-ferrantes-frantumaglia#_edn2

36 Raper, V. (15 February 2010). 'Witchcraft tried by 100,000 aspiring mums, survey finds'. BioNews, 545.

37 Ben-Yehuda, N. (1980). 'The European Witch Craze of the 14th to 17th Centuries: A Sociologist's Perspective'. *American Journal of Sociology*. 86 (1), 1–31.

38 Dimmitt, C. & Buitene, J.A.B. (1978). 'Putana: The Child Killer'. *Classical Hindu Mythology: A Reader in the Sanskrit Purānas*. Pennsylvania: Temple University Press.

39 Chesnut, M.B. (1905). *A Diary from Dixie, as Written by Mary Boykin Chesnut, Wife of James Chesnut, Jr., United States Senator From South Carolina, 1859–1861, and Afterward an Aide to Jefferson Davis and a Brigadier-General in the Confederate Army*. Isabella D. Martin and Myrta Lockett Avary (eds). New York: D. Appleton and Co.

40 From the Introduction by Catherine Clinton. *Mary Chesnut's Diary* (2011). London & New York: Penguin.

CHAPTER VII

1 Garay, K. & Jeay, M. (2007). 'Advice Concerning Pregnancy and Health in Late Medieval Europe: Peasant Women's Wisdom in the Distaff Gospels'. *Canadian Bulletin of Medical History / Bulletin Canadien d'Histoire de la Medecine*. 24 (2), 423–43.

2 From the US National Institutes of Health. The Office of NIH History & Stetten Museum, hCG research group.

3 Ettinger, G.H., Smith, G.L.M. & McHenry, E.W. (1931). 'The Diagnosis of Pregnancy with the Aschheim–Zondek Test'. *Canadian Medical Association Journal*. 24, 491–2.

4 Bosman, L.P. (1937). 'Early Diagnosis of Pregnancy'. *British Medical Journal*. 2 (4009), 939.

5   Elkan, E.R. (1938). 'The Xenopus Pregnancy Test'. *British Medical Journal*. 2 (4067), 1253–74.

6   Boston Legacy News. (27 June 2012). 'Brooklyn Gallery Cancels Frog Pregnancy Tests After PETA Outrage'. *Metro US* https://www.metro.us/update-brooklyn-gallery-cancels-frog-pregnancy-tests-after-peta-outrage. Last Accessed 13 June 2020.

7   Olszynko-Gryn, J. (2017). 'The feminist appropriation of pregnancy testing in 1970s Britain'. *Women's History Review*. 28 (6), 869–94.

8   I. Gal, B. Kirman & J. Stern. (7 October 1967). 'Hormonal pregnancy tests and congenital malformation'. *Nature*. 216, 83.

9   Olszynko-Gryn, J., Bjørvik, E. et al. (2018). 'A historical argument for regulatory failure in the case of Primodos and other hormone pregnancy tests'. *Reproductive Biomedicine & Society Online*. 6, 34–44.

10 Romm, C. (2015). 'Before there were home pregnancy tests'. *The Atlantic*.

11 Chapman, S. (2013). 'The Sexual Revolution'. *Southwell Folio*. 9, 32–3.

12 From www.bioamd.com, accessed 18 March 2020.

13 From Boots' website, https://www.boots.com/clearblue-early-detection-visual-pregnancy-test-10221963, Accessed 30 November 2020.

14 Papen, U. (2008). 'Pregnancy Starts with a Literacy Event: Pregnancy and Antenatal Care as Textually Mediated Experiences'. *Ethnography*. 9 (3), 377–402.

15 Gnoth, C. & Johnson, S. (2014). 'Strips of Hope: Accuracy of Home Pregnancy Tests and New Developments'. *Geburtshilfe und Frauenheilkunde*. 74 (7), 661–9.

16 Bell, T. (19 December 2017). 'A New Flushable Pregnancy Test Could Help Women in Abusive Relationships'. Vice. https://www.vice.com/en_us/article/43qdpb/new-flushable-pregnancy-test-helps-women-in-abusive-relationships

17 Olivo, T. (2018). 'UPenn Grads Use Nonwovens to Develop First Flushable Pregnancy Test'. Non Wovens Industry , 15 January 2018. https://www.nonwovens-industry.com/contents/view_online-exclusives/2018-01-15/upenn-grads-use-nonwovens-to-develop-first-flushable-pregnancy-test/ Last Accessed 14 June 2020.

18 Winner, L. (1986). *The Whale and the Reactor.* Chicago: University of Chicago Press.

19 Kennedy, P. (27 July 2012). 'Who made that home pregnancy test?' *The New York Times Magazine.*

20 Layne, L.L. (2009). 'The Home Pregnancy Test: A Feminist Technology?' *Women's Studies Quarterly.* 37 (1 & 2), 61–79.

21 Petersen, E.E., Davis, N.L. et al. (2019). 'Racial/Ethnic Disparities in Pregnancy-Related Deaths. United States, 2007–2016'. *Morbidity & Mortality Weekly Report.* 68, 762–5.

22 As of 15 October 2020.

23 'Grief' by Elizabeth Barratt Browning. https://www.poetryfoundation.org/poems/47646/grief-56d2283e927df

CHAPTER VIII

1 Hayman, R. (1991). *The Death and Life of Sylvia Plath.* New York: Carol Publishing Group.

2 Banerjee, A. (2010). 'Reorienting the ethics of transnational surrogacy as a feminist pragmatist'. *The Pluralist.* 5, 107–27.

3 van den Akker, O.B.A. (2007). 'Psychosocial aspects of surrogate motherhood'. *Human Reproduction Update.* 13 (1), 53–62.

4 Festinger, L. (1957). *A Theory of Cognitive Dissonance.* Stanford, USA: Stanford University Press.

5 Lewis, Sophie. (2019). *Full Surrogacy Now: Feminism Against Family.* London: Verso Books.

6 Dworkin, A. (1983). *Right-wing Women*. New York: Perigee Books.

7 Sandelowski, M. (1993). *With Child in Mind: Studies of the Personal Encounter with Infertility*. Philadelphia: University of Pennsylvania Press, first edition (this book was awarded the Society for Medical Anthropology's 1994 Eileen Basker Memorial Prize).

8 Ragoné, H. (2003). 'The Gift of Life: Surrogate Motherhood, Gamete Donation and Constructions of Altruism'. In Cook, R., Sclater, S.D. & Kaganas, F. (eds.) *Surrogate Motherhood: International Perspectives*. Portland, OR: Hart, 209–226.

9 Nadimpally, S., Banerjee, S. & Venkatachalam, D. (2016). 'Commercial Surrogacy: A Contested Terrain in the Realm of Rights and Justice'. Kuala Lumpur: Asian-Pacific Resource and Research Centre for Women (ARROW).

10 Pande, A. (2010). 'Commercial Surrogacy in India: Manufacturing a Perfect Mother-Worker'. *Signs*. 35 (4), 969–92.

11 Ginsburg, F. & Rapp, R. (1991). 'The Politics of Reproduction'. *Annual Review of Anthropology*. 20, 311–343.

12 Beynon-Jones, S.M. (2013). 'Expecting motherhood? Stratifying reproduction in twenty-first century Scottish abortion practice'. *Sociology*. 47 (3), 509–25.

13 Rapp, R. (2001). 'Gender, Body, Biomedicine: How Some Feminist Concerns Dragged Reproduction to the Center of Social Theory'. *Medical Anthropology Quarterly*. 15(4), 466–77.

14 Pande, A. (2017). 'Gestational Surrogacy in India: New Dynamics of Reproductive Labour', chapter in *Critical Perspectives on Work and Employment in Globalizing India*. Ernesto Noronha and Premilla D'Cruz (eds), Delhi: Springer: 267–82. Pande, A. (2017). 'Cross-Border Reproductive Surrogacy in India', chapter in *The Handbook of Gestational Surrogacy*, International Clinical Practice & Policy Issues, edited by E. Scott Sills, Cambridge University Press.

15 Daneau, L. (1594). *A Fruitfull Commentarie Vpon the Twelue Small Prophets*, Iohn Legate, printer to the Vniversitie of Cambridge [and at London, by J. Orwin] 1594. Quoted in Merriam-Webster Dictionary.

16 Woolf, V. (1930). *Street Haunting*. San Francisco: Westgate Press.

CHAPTER IX

1 Jadva, V., Imrie, S. & Golombok, S. (February 2015). 'Surrogate mothers 10 years on: a longitudinal study of psychological well-being and relationships with the parents and child'. *Human Reproduction*. 30 (2), 373–9.

2 Jadva, V., Murray, C. et al. (October 2003). 'Surrogacy: the experiences of surrogate mothers'. *Human Reproduction*. 18 (10), 2196–204.

3 Williams, Margery. (2017). *The Velveteen Rabbit*. London: Egmont.

4 James, W. (1890). *The Principles of Psychology*. New York: H. Holt & Co.

5 Pappas, S. (4 June 2015). 'Oxytocin: Facts About the "Cuddle Hormone"'. LiveScience.com.

6 Feldman, R., Weller, A. et al. (2007). 'Evidence for a neuroendocrinological foundation of human affiliation: plasma oxytocin levels across pregnancy and the postpartum period predict mother–infant bonding'. *Psychological Science*. 18 (11), 965–70.

7 Neutral Citation Number: [2019] EWHC 2384 (Fam), Case no. FD18F00035, High Court of Justice, Family Division and the Administrative Court, before the Rt Hon Sir Andrew McFarlane. Royal Courts Of Justice, Hearing Date: 2 May 2019. https://www.judiciary.uk/wp-content/uploads/2019/09/TT-and-YY-APPROVED-Substantive-Judgment-McF-25.9.19.pdf

8 MacDonald, T., Noel-Weiss, J. et al. (2016). 'Transmasculine individuals' experiences with lactation, chestfeeding, and gender identity: a qualitative study'. *BMC Pregnancy Childbirth*. 16, 106.

9   Neutral Citation Number: [2019] EWHC 2384 (Fam), Case no:
    Fd18f00035, High Court Of Justice, Family Division And The
    Administrative Court, Royal Courts Of Justice, before the Rt Hon
    Sir Andrew McFarlane. Hearing Date: 2 May 2019. https://www.
    judiciary.uk/wp-content/uploads/2019/09/TT-and-YY-APPROVED-
    Substantive-Judgment-McF-25.9.19.pdf

10 Stroumsa, D. et al. (16 May 2019). 'The Power and Limits of
    Classification – A 32-Year-Old Man with Abdominal Pain'. *New
    England Journal of Medicine.* 380, 1885–8

11 Kim, P., Strathearn, L. & Swain, J. E. (2016). 'The maternal brain and
    its plasticity in humans'. *Hormones and Behavior.* 77, 113–23.

12 Athan, A.M. & Reel, H.L. (2015). 'Maternal psychology: Reflections
    on the 20th anniversary of Deconstructing Developmental Psychology'.
    Feminism & Psychology. 25, 311–25.

13 Shaughnessy, B. (2012). *Our Andromeda.* Copper Canyon Press.

14 Plath, S. (2015). 'Morning Song' from *Collected Poems.* London: Faber.

15 Plato. (2007). *The Republic.* London: Penguin Classics.

16 Bell, A.F.G. (1912). *In Portugal.* London and New York: John Lane.

17 Brennan, G. & Gruhn, L. (2016). *The Pleasure You Suffer: A Saudade
    Anthology.* Chicago: Tortoise Books.

18 Morrison, T. (1987) *Beloved*, Alfred & Knopf.

19 MacNeice, L. (1979). 'Entirely' from *The Collected Poems of Louis
    MacNeice*, ed. E. R. Dodds. London: Faber.

20 Nelson, M. (2015). *The Argonauts.* Greywolf Press.

CODA

1   O'Reilly, A. (2010). 'Outlaw(ing) Motherhood: A Theory and Politic
    of Maternal Empowerment for the Twenty-first Century'. *Hecate.* 36
    (1/2), 17–29.

2 Kristeva, J. (2005). 'Motherhood today'. Retrieved from http://www.kristeva.fr/motherhood.html

3 From 4 September 2020.

4 Kay, J. (1991). *The Adoption Papers*. London: Bloodaxe.

5 Bowlby, R. (2013). *A Child of One's Own: Parental Stories*. Oxford: Oxford University Press.

6 Braidotti, R. (1989). 'On the Female-feminist Subject, or From She-self to She-other', in G. Block and S. James (eds), *Beyond Equality and Difference*. London: Routledge.

7 Rich, A. (1976). *Of Woman Born: Motherhood as Experience and Institution*. Norton.

8 Lewis, Sophie. (2019). *Full Surrogacy Now: Feminism Against Family*. London: Verso Books.

9 Benard, S., Paik, I. & Correll, S.J. (2008). 'Cognitive Bias and the Motherhood Penalty'. *Hastings Law Journal*. 59 (6), 1359–87.

10 Agarwal, P. (2019). 'All Mothers Welcome: Are Our Workplaces Inclusive Enough For Mothers?'. Forbes. https://www.forbes.com/sites/pragyaagarwaleurope/2019/03/30/all-mothers-welcome-are-our-workplaces-inclusive-enough-for-mothers/

11 Nargund, G. (2 April 2020). 'Infertility is a disease. The indefinite delay of treatments like IVF must end'. *The Telegraph*.

12 UNFPA (2020) 'Ensure universal access to sexual and reproductive health and reproductive rights: Measuring SDG Target 5.6', February 2020. Last accessed 08 December 2020.

13 United Nations 'World Fertility and Family Planning Highlights 2020', Department of Economic and Social Affairs Population Division, New York.

14 Paul, M., Essén, B. et al. (2017). 'Negotiating Collective and Individual Agency: A Qualitative Study of Young Women's Reproductive Health in Rural India'. *Qualitative Health Research*. 27 (3), 311–24.

PERMISSION CREDITS